Britain's Railways Under Steam

Britain's Railways Under Steam

J. B. Snell

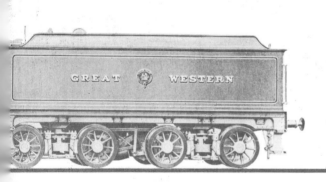

LONDON
IAN ALLAN LTD

First published 1965 by Arthur Barker Ltd.

Second revised edition 1977 published
by Ian Allan Ltd, Shepperton, Surrey.

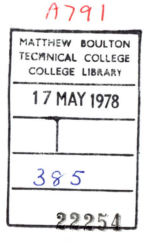
*Filmset by W. S. Cowell Ltd, at the Butter Market, Ipswich
and printed in Great Britain by
Lowe & Brydone Printers Limited, Thetford, Norfolk*

Acknowledgements

The author would like to thank those who have helped him in the preparation of the text of this book. Most notably these include C. R. Clinker, who has checked and made valuable comments on the historical sections, and A. J. Pearson, who has done the same for the chapter on Grouping and Nationalization; while A. E. Durrant and A. C. Sterndale have both made important contributions to the chapter on locomotives. J. W. Blanchard has examined the maps and expunged (we both hope) all the author's errors in drawing them; George Ottley of the British Museum assisted his researches, and the information regarding dividend records was collected by P. W. Parker.

Particular thanks are due to those many photographers who provided pictures; it is a pity that the final selection could only be a small fraction of the total. The pictures that are included are due to the following (number refers to page where photograph appears, an asterisk means that the photograph is from the owner's collection rather than his camera).

J. H. L. Adams	*page*	172
P. M. Alexander		37, 58, 119, 122, 171
Dr Ian C. Allen		166
E. G. Ashton		21, 65
J. W. Blanchard		127
R. J. Blenkinsop		19, 22, 24, 68, 176 (*bottom*), 183 (*bottom*), 187, 193 (*top*)
British Railways		77 (*bottom*), 78 (*bottom*), 182 (*top*), 198, 207
I. S. Carr		105
C. R. L. Coles		29, 124–5, 209
S. C. Crook		14, 33, 106 (2), 137 (*top*), 139, 150, 151, 152, 153, 168, 191
Derek Cross		12, 17, 48 (2), 59, 71 (*bottom*), 74, 77 (*top*), 90, 92, 98, 113, 114, 120–1, 132, 134, 135, 137 (*bottom*), 157 (*top*), 181 (*top*), 202, 206 (*top*)
J. G. Dewing		66, 115 (*bottom*), 146 (*bottom*), 173 (*bottom*), 201, 208, 211, 213 (*top*)
A. E. Durrant		24, 123, 140 158 (*middle*)*
M. W. Earley		43, 164, 165
A. W. Flower		16
Fox Photos Ltd		26, 49, 107
Locomotive Publishing Co.		89, 143
G. H. Malan (British Railways)		67 (*bottom*)
B. E. Morrison		41, 184, 185
Eric Oldham		30
A. W. H. Pearsall		214
I. S. Pearsall		96 (2), 102–3
Ivo Peters		60, 61 (2), 62, 63, 154, 176 (*top*), 181 (*bottom*)
M. Pope		52, 75, 94, 95, 128, 174, 180, 183 (*top*), 205 (*bottom*)
Real Photo Co.		79, 80, 158 (*top*)
P. J. T. Reed		67 (*top*)*
R. C. Riley		35, 38, 39, 40, 44, 45, 78 (*top*), 119, 216
J. Russell-Smith		205 (*top*)
J. B. Snell		13, 51, 54, 55, 56, 115 (*top*), 116, 161, 167, 175, 181 (*middle*), 182 (*bottom*), 212, 215, 217, 218 and all colour EXCEPT 17, 53 (*bottom*), 93 (*top*) and 157 (*top*)
G. C. Stead		42
A. C. Sterndale		10, 20*, 53 (*bottom*), 57, 71 (*top*), 85, 86, 87, 88, 93 (*top*), 108, 117, 126, 149, 178*, 203, 206 (*bottom*), 213 (*bottom*)
J. L. Stevenson		144, 145, 146 (*top*), 170
S. E. Teasdale		194
H. Gordon Tidey (& Real Photo Co.)		28, 34, 64, 73, 76, 89, 97, 99, 133, 141, 173 (*top*), 179, 193 (*bottom*), 210
The Times Publishing Co.		101, 177
A. R. Thompson		100
P. B. Whitehouse		15, 50 (2)*, 158 (*bottom*)*, 171 (*top*)*

Contents

Foreword to the Second Edition

This book was first published in 1965, with the intention of giving an account of the British railway system as it had developed during the age of steam, and as it stood at the end of that era. Apart from a few paragraphs in the last chapter, which then looked forward to see what future existed for steam, and as altered still do but from a new point in time, nothing has been changed; and from time to time the modern reader must bear this in mind.

The most notable way in which things have changed since 1965 is that with a second generation of non-steam motive power we are at last being offered long-distance passenger services decisively better, in speed and in frequency, than ever before. On the other hand, line closures on a substantial scale have continued. They are too many to list here, but they include the Great Central line from near Sheffield to near Aylesbury, part of the Midland's line across the Peaks between Derby and Manchester, the whole of the Waverley Route, the Somerset & Dorset, and almost all ex-London & South Western track west of Oke-hampton. The modern reader should also remember that there was a time, not yet out of mind, when the railways carried over half the nation's freight, were not a burden on the taxpayer, gave respected employment to many more than now, and when any suggestion that these things would ever change would have been received with much greater scepticism than forecasts of regular daily long-distance trains running at speeds of 100 or 125 miles an hour. These were, after all, foreseen by Stephenson and Brunel.

Author's Note

This book has two intentions. One is to provide a pictorial record of British main-line trains during the last 30 or 40 years of steam, giving some idea of the variety that once existed. The other is to describe the development of the railway network over the country as a whole. Plenty of company histories describe parts in detail, but there seems room now, particularly as the reshaping of the network is a matter of some current public interest, for an account which pays more heed to geographical than to ownership boundaries; even though to cover so large a field in one book necessitates very brief treatment. The second section of the book is intended to cover the geographical bones of the first with some small amount of flesh, in considering something of how the railways were operated and turned to public advantage.

The Maps

The maps are primarily intended to show the main lines, with pre-grouping ownerships; branches are indicated, but without detail. Two basic conventions are followed throughout. Firstly, while railways in ordinary single ownership are shown as a broad line, either solid or with some repetitive pattern, e.g.:

jointly-owned railways are always shown as a thin line with cross-hatching, thus:

Secondly, the maps show closures. Any kind of broken line represents a railway that has been closed to all traffic. Partly due to the rate at which abandonments have taken place recently, this information has proved very difficult to obtain in some cases, but it is hoped that errors are confined to the rural freight branches whose mortality has lately been serious. (Since the 1962 Transport Act it has been possible for British Railways, unlike any others in the world, to terminate freight services at will, without any form of government supervision, control, or appeal.)

Generally speaking, the maps show the situation during the early part of 1965, with two important exceptions involving major closures of the kind that we were promised would cease after the 1964 election. The Taunton-Barnstaple line, and the Dumfries-Challoch Junction section of the Portpatrick and Wigtownshire, were both still operating at the time of going to press, but have been shown as abandoned since they seem unlikely to survive until publication date. The same applies in a third case, the original Highland main line from Forres to Aviemore.

The scale does not allow all lines to be shown in certain urban and industrial areas, or all the spurs at various complex junctions; some less important ones are therefore omitted. Separate stations are shown only in the largest cities (London, Birmingham, Liverpool, Manchester, Glasgow, and Edinburgh); this does not mean that only one main station exists in every other case. It is a much safer rule to assume that any town served by two or more pre-grouping companies will have at least two main stations, especially where neither line terminates (e.g. Leeds, Bradford, Nottingham, Sheffield, Rugby, Derby, Peterborough, Gloucester). Only in a few minor cases have two stations since been merged into one (e.g. Salisbury, Oxford, Barnsley). Carlisle, Perth, Doncaster, Preston, Bristol, and Shrewsbury are the major exceptions to this rule, each having had a single jointly-owned or 'Union' station more or less from the start.

Part One
The Main Line Network

Introduction

The Liverpool & Manchester Railway, opened on
15 September 1830, was the first main line in Britain
and the world. All previous railways, whether or not
they used locomotives, had been intended to connect
mines, or factories, or towns, with navigable water or
the sea. They were feeders to a more important method
of transport. The L&M was intended to form in itself
the principal communication between two cities, and
its contribution was to prove that a railway on this new
model was effective and profitable. Thus it gave
impetus to proposals for building a network of lines all
over the country.

It was at this stage in most other European countries that the government intervened with a plan
saying where the main lines should be built; and any
plan like this, however organized, would in the nature
of things be bound to establish a rational basic skeleton
for the future system. In Britain nothing like this ever
happened, except for a half-hearted experiment in the
late 1840s when a committee of the Board of Trade
was set up by Gladstone to adjudicate between rival
proposals; but since the losers usually appealed to
Parliament and got their way this proved fruitless.
Each scheme had, of course, to come before Parliament
for an Act giving it power for compulsory purchase of
land, and at this stage only was there any discussion of
the merits of any particular line. Beyond this the
government declined to intervene, so far as construction was concerned. Current political philosophy
taught that the best government was the least government, and that commerce and industry should be left
alone to act in their own best interests. So the British

(*Left*) Driver's-eye view at Risca, from the cab of a 72XX class
2-8-2T hauling a freight from the Sirhowy valley towards
Newport; a 42XX 2-8-0T crosses his bows with a train from the
Ebbw Vale line (1953)

railway system was left to grow haphazard. Nobody
ever stood up to say 'Let us build a railway from
London to Scotland', for instance, because such a
scheme would have been too big for the money market
to digest. Instead, railways were conceived in sections
and built for the most part with local interests chiefly
in mind; they were joined together as an afterthought,
often inconveniently, and trunk routes developed as a
result of this anarchic process. The effects of this,
particularly on high speed running, are still noticeable.
Furthermore, no company could feel secure in any
area, for if it proved profitable a competitive scheme
would be launched; much money and effort would be
needed to thwart this, with no guarantee of success.
So British railway geography can only be explained in
terms of British railway history.

Competing lines began to appear even before the
main trunk routes were finished, but as a rough
general rule, the earlier any railway, the more useful
and profitable it remains to this day. In the more
populous parts of the country most lines built after the
1860s tended, on the whole, to be more concerned with
abstracting some rival's profitable trade than with
meeting needs of their own. It is no new discovery,
indeed the realization of it was the guiding motive for
most companies during the nineteenth century, that
the only really profitable railway business is in carrying
passengers and freight over long distances in heavily-
loaded trains; consequently, wherever such traffics
existed, each company wanted a line of its own to tap
them. This naturally led to the construction of many
miles of parallel routes, some of which are redundant
now all railways are in national ownership.

On the other hand, it is altogether too easy to
accuse nineteenth-century railway companies of over-
building. Granted, there were a few projects which
showed what, by present day standards, seems a pretty
fatuous optimism; but one must remember that rail-

ways were on a rising market. The country was getting richer, and population and trade were both steadily increasing; even though a line might at first seem unnecessary, it could reasonably be expected to become a moneyspinner in time. There was also a feeling that the companies owed something to the public; that a single-minded pursuit of profit was unwise, and that therefore some facilities should be provided as a public service. George Carr Glyn, the Chairman of the London & Birmingham, put the point as early as 1838. 'The railway companies must consider themselves as holding their privileges in trust for the benefit of the public, as it was for this consideration that they principally obtained possession of them. They have *no* privileges but for the public benefit ... It is highly necessary, therefore, that in their communications with government, and with each other in their arrangements for an interchange of traffic and for the conveyance of passengers, the companies should cherish a feeling of liberality, and a regard for the comfort and accommodation, and just expectations of the public.' This was not a bad moral standard for the railway companies to set themselves. It was not always lived up to; but on the whole they did not fall far short of it.

The railway system, then, grew up as a patchwork. Today two things have changed. Firstly, mechanical power has also been applied to road transport. This has altered the picture much less than is commonly believed (measured by present statistical methods, not two-thirds of the country's freight moved by rail even in 1900); although it has meant that the public is now sometimes better served by road in rural districts. Secondly, all but a few minor railways have been since 1948 under the same ownership. The effects of this are bound in the long run to be very great, although they have been rather slow to appear. The men who are now planning the future British railway system are having to assemble a jigsaw puzzle from a pile of pieces of which a few were always missing, some have been thoughtlessly destroyed, and more belong to different puzzles altogether. They have sometimes seemed to underestimate the complexity of their task.

By coincidence, these changes are taking place at the same time as the steam locomotive is disappearing. It is giving way to two rivals. The diesel, although it also suffers from the disadvantage of having to carry its power plant around with it, is cheaper to operate than steam. More expensive to build, it is or should be also capable of doing more work by spending a greater proportion of its time in traffic. Engineers were working on improvements to steam locomotives which they hoped would enable diesel economy in this respect to be equalled, but it was felt that this was not sufficient. The more successful diesel locomotives have also improved on the train-hauling performance of steam, but certainly by no greater margin than one would expect from twenty years' advance in design.

Electric traction, on the other hand, is fundamentally different from diesel or steam. Power is generated more economically and efficiently at a central point, and can be applied almost without limit by a simpler locomotive. This basic idea is almost as old as railways, but it failed in earlier applications because mechanical power transmission, by rope or vacuum, was impractical. Properly applied, electrification is the ideal answer to the railway traction problem under British conditions.

The days when the steam railway held a near-monopoly of inland long-distance transport are now past, but they are worth remembering. Until quite recently every reasonably populated place in Britain, and not a few deserted ones, could be reached by steam train; and whatever the shortcomings of that system, it worked. Those who have been trying to set up a new transport system designed on political and ideological, or even certain kinds of economic, principles, instead of practical and technical ones, would do well to remember this. But whatever the effect of recent changes, the basic structure of the railway network is still determined by the course which nineteenth-century engineers and businessmen, hoping to make money, laid down.

(*Left*) Between Tring and Berkhamstead; rebuilt 'Royal Scot' 4-6-0 no. 46108 'Seaforth Highlander' on a Manchester-Euston express passes a northbound local hauled by a Class Five 4-6-0 (1959)

Symbol of the Age of Steam; the statue of George Stephenson in Philip Hardwick's magnificent Great Hall, centrepiece of the old Euston (1962)

Deputizing for a failed diesel, 'Duchess' Pacific no. 46250 'City of Lichfield' storms uphill near Penrith with the southbound 'Royal Scot' (1963)

1 London to Lancashire

The First Trunk Line

By 1830, when the Liverpool and Manchester opened, several other railways were under construction in Britain. In 1833 two more were authorized; the Grand Junction, and the London and Birmingham. Together these joined the L&M with London and thus formed the first trunk route.

The Grand Junction was projected to run from Warrington, already the terminus of a short branch from the L&M, for 78 miles through Stafford and Wolverhampton to Birmingham. It was mainly built by George Stephenson's pupil, Joseph Locke, and although it was his first major work it showed some of his characteristic touches. Locke liked to minimize earthworks, had a particular detestation of tunnels, and was much more confident of the ability of locomotives to climb hills than either of the Stephensons. So the GJ had only one very short tunnel, near the original Wolverhampton station, and just south of Crewe had three miles of what was then considered the rather venturesome gradient of 1 in 177. The line was opened throughout in July, 1837. At first it ran north from Birmingham via Bescot, a length planned more with an eye to easy construction than usefulness, which served Wolverhampton very badly; it was replaced for passenger traffic by the better-sited Birmingham, Wolverhampton and Stour Valley route via Dudley Port after 1852.

The London and Birmingham was laid out by Robert Stephenson on very different principles. Except for the cable-worked drop at 1 in 70 into the London terminus at Euston, the ruling gradient (that is, the steepest one long enough to influence train loading) was 1 in 330; to maintain this there were very considerable earthworks and eight tunnels, including one of a mile at Watford and another 1½ miles long at Kilsby. Everything about the line, including tunnel portals, bridges, and viaducts, was vastly solid and substantial, built with a marked sense of the railway's importance, the terminus at Euston in particular. The famous arch, calculated to inspire a proper feeling of reverence in those who entered, cost £35,000; William Cubitt, starting to build King's Cross some ten years later, declared he could complete the whole job for less than double the cost of this ornament. Unhappily for Euston's grandeur, it fairly soon got smothered by increased traffic and pinchpenny enlargements. For more than half a century before its current demolition and rebuilding it was, arch and all, one of the major railway slums of Britain behind the scenes, relieved only by Philip Hardwick's magnificent Great Hall and Shareholders' Meeting Room; pearls in a very crusty oyster.

Rebuilt 'Scot' no. 46156 'The South Wales Borderer' leaving Shugborough Tunnel, on the Trent Valley line near Stafford (1953)

One of the persistent stories about the London and Birmingham is that local opposition stopped it from running through Northampton, and forced it to build the Kilsby Tunnel. The truth of the matter is quite the opposite. Stephenson disliked the idea of taking the railway through Northampton, because it lay in a valley and would involve gradients, while a tunnel through the Kilsby Ridge, some miles to the north, was in any case inescapable. One might have thought that the most bookish historian would have been convinced of this by a journey over the loop from Roade to Rugby via Northampton, finally built in 1881, with three tunnels and a ruling grade of 1 in 200.

The L&B was opened in stages between July 1837 and June 1838; when the last section, from Rugby to Denbigh Hall (just north of Bletchley) was completed, London was linked by rail with Lancashire. But Birmingham was rather a barrier at first. The L&B and GJ stations lay side by side at Curzon Street, linked by crossover connections, and for some years

Doubleheaders on the Trent Valley Line (A + B)
'Jumbo' 2-4-0 no. 5062 piloting 'Claughton' 4-6-0 no. 5967 on a northbound express near Brinklow (1930)

'Jubilee' 4-6-0 no. 45703 'Thunderer' on the 1 in 75 at Shap Wells with a Morecambe-Glasgow excursion (1964)

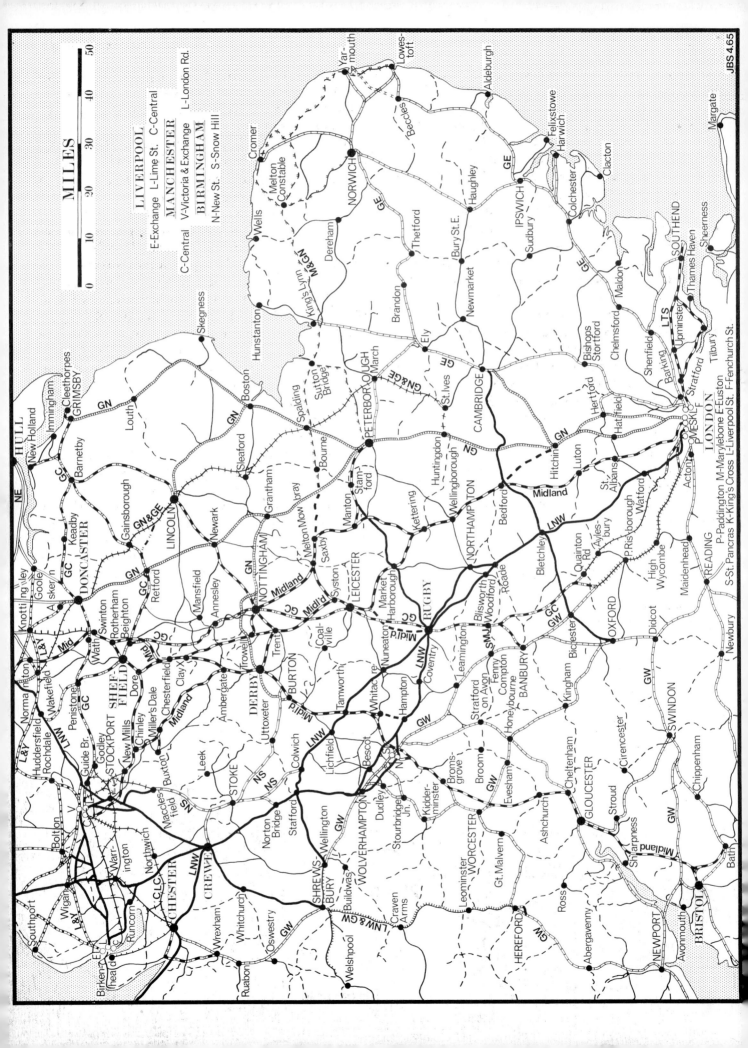

(until both lines were extended through the tunnel into New Street station in 1854) each company's trains, while continuing to depart from their own terminal, arrived at the other; an arrangement which minimized the inconvenience of changing. There was no through passenger service until 1846, as it was some time before companies got used to the idea of trusting their rolling stock on a foreign line.

From 1838 to 1850 the L&B formed the only route from London to the north, and during this time the company's southern outposts, the twin lodges fronting on the Euston Road, were decorated with the carved and gilded names of towns which the railway served. This meant, of course, everywhere north of the Thames. Nowadays they are a rather fraudulent prospectus (for they still stand); it is more than a century since the road to Derby, Hereford, or Peterborough began at Euston, and no wise man would go that way to get to Aberystwyth, Cambridge, or Cork. Still, the lodges are far enough away for their connection with the railway to seem a little tenuous.

Both the L&B and the GJ were financially successful from the first. The Grand Junction Chairman declared shortly after the line was opened that 'the experience of the first two months has been as satisfactory as the most sanguine could desire. Most of the direct public conveyances have been superseded, and many of the collateral ones diverted upon the railway; private travelling alongside it has been annihilated, while traffic on all the routes pointing towards it has

been stimulated to an extraordinary degree.' So it was not long before proposals for parallel lines were put forward, and in the next eight or nine years a rather complicated situation developed.

The Grand Junction was more vulnerable to competition, since it connected at right-angles with the mid-point of the Liverpool & Manchester, forming an indirect route to both cities. So far as Liverpool was concerned, it was protected by the Mersey estuary, which would have to be crossed by a substantial bridge; there was no short cut here until the Edge Hill-Weaver Junction line through Runcorn was opened in 1869. Manchester was a different proposition, and the Manchester & Birmingham Railway was opened in August 1842 from Manchester (London Road) via Stockport to join the GJ at Crewe, cutting the distance between these points from 44 to 31 miles. The GJ was not happy about this; but it finally agreed to co-operate at Crewe to avoid the much worse alternative of a competing line right through to the L&B at Rugby via Stoke-on-Trent, which would freeze it out of the London-Manchester trade altogether.

A quarrel over the M&B gave the Grand Junction some reason to feel suspicious of the London & Birmingham, and two further bones of contention were soon found. One was an independent line, the Trent Valley, completed in December 1847. While its 51 miles from the GJ at Stafford to the L&B at Rugby through Lichfield and Nuneaton were under construction, this concern was eyed with some mistrust.

Four tracks, three trains: a 'Crab' 2-6-0 no. 42889 facing a 'Duchess' and a Stanier 2-6-0 on expresses for Euston and Birmingham at Whitmore, between Crewe and Stafford (1956)

A Birmingham-Paddington express, running via Oxford before the New Line through Bicester was opened near King's Sutton, headed by a Dean 2-4-0 of 1892, no. 3247 (1910)

By avoiding Birmingham and reducing the distance from London by nine miles, it short-circuited some sixty miles of existing track; and if either large company took it over, it would be a nasty poke in the eye for the other. Since the L&B had subscribed nearly a third of the TVR's capital in the first place, the Grand Junction had particular reason to feel apprehensive of this.

The other disagreement was more complicated. The Great Western Railway was proposing an extension of its broad-gauge line north from Oxford to Rugby and Birmingham. Mark Huish, the Secretary of the Grand Junction, saw his chance here to checkmate the L&B. He blandly announced that his directors, 'having ascertained that the broad gauge could be added to their line at very reasonable cost', were proposing to make an arrangement for through working with the GWR. The dagger was driven home by a number of highly moral observations about the virtues of competition and the evils of monopoly, which frightened the London & Birmingham very much.

And so matters came to a head, just as Huish desired. Despite their mutual suspicions, the L&B and GJ were really natural allies, and viewed objectively,

the TV and the M&B were valuable improvements. It was geographically absurd that the four companies should quarrel. In 1846, therefore, they amalgamated to form the London & North Western Railway. Linking the capital with the two most important and populous areas in the country, this company deserved (if only for geographical reasons) the self-bestowed title of 'The Premier Line'. But once comfortably settled at Euston, Huish forgot all his high-minded remarks about monopoly, as we shall see.

Another neighbouring railway was also founded in 1846; the North Staffordshire. It might well have been included in the amalgamation, but it had just survived a parliamentary battle with the GJ and feelings were still too ruffled. The NS filled the gap which had been left when the M&B stopped at Crewe, abandoning Stoke-on-Trent and the Potteries. The disappointed locals resolved to do the job themselves, and planned a whole network of railways in the area, with a main line from Macclesfield to Norton Bridge and Colwich, and another from Crewe through Stoke to Burton-on-Trent. The entire system was completed in 1848–9, and only minor additions were made to it subsequently; more remarkably, the NS succeeded in remaining independent until 1923. But to do this it had to fight. It short-circuited the M&B just as that line had the GJ, by building along the third side of a triangle, and it commanded the shortest route to Manchester of all, via Stoke-on-Trent. Before the amalgamation, the L&B had promised to send its Manchester traffic that way; afterwards, the L&NW refused to. Lawsuits followed, and the NS repeated Huish's own gambit against him when they threatened to build south from Colwich to connect with the Great Western and add broad gauge to their system. Throughout the 1850s hostilities continued, with the NS eking a living meanwhile from local traffic, until eventually the L&NW got bored. The armistice terms gave them running powers over the whole NS system, so that further conquest would have been pointless, and a number of Manchester trains were diverted through Stoke. The little company's independence was rather like that of the ruler of a native state in British India; it was tolerated so long as it kept quiet.

Unrebuilt 'Scot' no. 6159 'The Royal Air Force' on a northbound express in Shugborough Park, on the Trent Valley line (1939)

Broad Gauge to the Mersey

The Great Western, having completed its seven-foot gauge main line to Bristol in 1841, found itself beset by enemies. One of Brunel's justifications for the broad gauge proposal in 1835 had been that the GW would monopolize the West of England, and that any inconvenience due to break of gauge would therefore be confined to frontier points. By 1845 it was apparent that this wasn't going to happen, for the company's home ground was under threat. The standard gauge was pressing down from the north, and had already reached Gloucester; there was also a demand for a line to join the Midlands with the South Coast, cutting straight across broad-gauge territory. If the GWR did not build it, somebody else would. So war had to be carried into the enemy's camp.

In this way the broad gauge invasion of the north began. In 1845 a company supported by the GWR was authorized to build north from Oxford via Banbury to Rugby, and the following year the Birmingham & Oxford Junction was authorized to build north-westward from a junction with the Oxford & Rugby north of Fenny Compton to Birmingham.

Both proposals were fiercely attacked by the L&NW, whose real objection to them of course lay in the fact that they threatened its monopoly. Since this was not a respectable reason for opposition, they fought on the question of gauge, and the expense and inconvenience incurred at places where it was broken. This was a real issue, which had already been experienced at Gloucester, and one which finally proved decisive; but not yet. The Gauge War of 1845/6, which was fought before a Parliamentary Commission inquiring into the technical merits of the question, ended in a draw. The Commissioners admitted they were impressed by the performance of broad-gauge locomotives and stock, but they did not think that this advantage compensated for the inconvenience of break of gauge, and recommended that the broad gauge be abolished. The Government disagreed. The Prime Minister, Sir Robert Peel, said that since Parliament had given authority for it in the first place, any enforced conversion would have to be paid for out of public funds, and this was out of the question; besides (*sotto voce*), if the conversion was as necessary as all that, sooner or later the GWR would have to find the money to carry it out itself. So the extension of the broad gauge to Rugby and Birmingham, and subsequently Wolverhampton, was allowed, with the proviso that standard gauge would have to be added at the company's expense on notice from the Board of Trade.

The O&R was opened from Oxford to Banbury in September 1850; but one result of all the fuss was that the GWR lost interest in going to Rugby, and construction ceased some chains north of the intended junction at Fenny Compton. The abandoned formation can still be seen. The GWR chairman made a plaintive speech deploring the L&NW's attitude, saying there had never been any intention to compete, and that all the GWR wanted was the north-south link; but, like so many Chairmen's Statements, this needed to be taken with a pinch of salt. The Birmingham & Oxford promoters had snubbed Huish when he suggested that they sell their line to the L&NW, saying that a competitive route was what they intended to have. The need for a north-south link via Rugby was forgotten, and traffic moved round circuitous ways until 1900, when something like it was finally provided by the Woodford-Banbury branch of the Great Central London Extension. The Fenny Compton-Rugby line is one of the very few, authorized but never built, whose existence would really have been useful over the years. Today it would carry the GC's traffic more economically and, with connections to all lines at Rugby instead of none, more flexibly.

The GWR reached Birmingham (Snow Hill) in October 1852, at which time standard gauge was added to the whole line north of Oxford. For some years it was little used; the L&NW had prevailed on the Board of Trade to insist on it, mainly to cause their competitors profitless expense. Another piece of wasted construction was at Birmingham, where the L&NW had obtained a legal requirement that the GWR should install a connexion between the two lines. A long curved viaduct, facing from Banbury towards New Street, was therefore built as far as the L&NW boundary in 1853. It has never yet been used, although

the current proposal to close Snow Hill station and concentrate all traffic on New Street may involve its finally being finished. The line was extended to Wolverhampton, again with mixed gauge, in November 1854. Like the closely parallel L&NW Stour Valley line to Wolverhampton via Dudley Port, opened the same year, it runs through a now rather derelict industrial area with some quite sharp grades.

The broad gauge never got any farther north than Wolverhampton, but the GWR did, largely thanks to Huish. There were three railways together reaching from Wolverhampton to Birkenhead, across the river from Liverpool, and Warrington, within striking distance of both Liverpool and Manchester. The Shrewsbury & Birmingham, opened in 1849, ran from Wolverhampton to Shrewsbury, where it met the Shrewsbury & Chester, which had been opened in stages between 1846 and 1848. The Birkenhead Railway completed the chain. The S&C was the most promising of the three, serving coalmines around Wrexham and Ruabon; it also had several longish grades of the order of 1 in 80, and its viaduct across the Dee at Cefn, at one time the tallest in the country, was 148 ft. high.

The two Shrewsbury companies were, however, in an exposed position. The S&B's access to Birmingham had been intended to be over the L&NW's Stour Valley line, while the L&NW was at both Wolverhampton and Chester, and for that matter also at Shrewsbury, having purchased the Shropshire Union line from Stafford to Wellington with its running powers over the S&B. The two companies would have

'King' class 4-6-0 no. 6020 'King Henry IV' sweeping down Hatton Bank at 70 mph with a Wolverhampton-Paddington express (1955)

had to tread very gently to avoid trouble, but instead of this they trampled about gaily cutting fares. A frightful rate war with the L&NW resulted, and for three years the first class fare from Wolverhampton to Shrewsbury, 30 miles, was 1/–, with other rates in proportion. As Huish had foreseen, this cut-throat competition soon brought the Shrewsbury companies to their knees; what he did not foresee was that it also threw them into the arms of the Great Western. In 1851 the GWR agreed to purchase them as soon as it reached Wolverhampton. Huish fought back; the L&NW purchased Shrewsbury shares and, taking advantage of an anomaly in company law which allowed each share to be split into as many as ten parts, each carrying a vote, Huish carved them up and distributed the confetti among clerks and porters at Euston, running special trainloads to pack the Shrewsbury Annual General Meetings. When even this failed to achieve the desired result, he organized Extraordinary meetings himself, using a forged seal doubtless manufactured at Crewe (it was a proud boast of the Works that they filled all the company's needs). It was an extraordinary business, fully told in McDermot's History of the Great Western. But despite everything Huish could do, the amalgamation went through, and in 1854 the GWR reached Chester on the standard gauge in its own right. Wolverhampton remained a break-of-gauge point until October 1861, when the Reading-Paddington line was mixed and a through service to London began; broad gauge trains finally ceased to run north of Oxford in March 1869.

The Birkenhead Railway remained; it was torn between self-interest (as most of its traffic came from the direction of Wrexham) and fear of the L&NW, and for a while there was some rough play at Chester, with booking clerks flung out of ticket offices and so on. The GWR, however, was not to be bullied, and obtained from Parliament the legal right to run over the Birkenhead, which settled that; finally, the railway became joint GW-L&NW property.

The GWR route to the north was always worked competitively with the L&NW, to Chester and Birkenhead (for Liverpool) as well as to Birmingham. The extra distance via Oxford (129 miles to Birmingham as against 112 from Euston) was always a handicap, but not so great as one might think since L&NW trains at this time were pretty sluggish. In 1852 the GWR put on two remarkable trains which did the 129 miles in $2\frac{3}{4}$ hours; Oxford was reached in 70 minutes from Paddington, which is faster than the majority of diesel-hauled trains today, running on a better line at Didcot which avoids the sharp curve through the station. But they did not last.

The Great Western eventually came to have the shorter route, 110 miles to Birmingham compared with 112. From quite early broad-gauge days there had been a meandering rural loop from Maidenhead to Oxford via High Wycombe, Princes Risborough, and Thame. In 1897 the GWR obtained power to construct a new direct line to High Wycombe from Acton, mainly with the idea of drumming up suburban traffic in competition with the Metropolitan, which had a parallel route to Aylesbury and was currently building to Uxbridge. Two years later the Great Central, dissatisfied with its access to London via Aylesbury, came in on the deal, and the line was made a joint one. The old single track over the Chiltern ridge to Princes Risborough was improved and doubled, and a new line built north from Princes Risborough for 15 miles to Grendon Underwood, where it rejoined the GC. This scheme, including the Acton-High Wycombe line, was complete by 1906.

For some time the GWR debated whether or not to convert the railway from Princes Risborough to Oxford to main line standards and open it as a new direct route; it was after all eight miles shorter than via Didcot. However, this was not done, and it remained a rural branch until it lost its passenger service in 1962. Instead, it was decided to build from Ashendon through Bicester to Aynho, south of Banbury, shortening the distance to Birmingham by 19 miles. This was completed in July 1910, the last new main line to be built in Britain. From then on the two routes were on equal terms; the GWR had a slight edge on distance, but worse gradients. To bring the story up to date, the competition survived nationalization by some years, and it was long before some realized anything had happened. A junior member of the staff at Paddington in the mid-1950s was given the task of arranging for a party of visiting foreign railwaymen to travel to Liverpool. He sent them off from Euston, the journey being over an hour faster (not counting the time taken on the Mersey ferry), and was subsequently reprimanded for 'throwing traffic away'. However, the Euston-Birmingham trains were to all intents and purposes taken off in 1959 on account of electrification work. Since then Paddington has carried the load, but when the Euston electrification is completed the position will be reversed and the future of the 'New Line' from Princes Risborough to Aynho is doubtful.

Welwyn Viaduct, with a V2 class 2-6-2 pounding northwards at the head of a fast freight (1957)

A northbound freight on the Derby-Manchester line crossing the viaduct in Monsal Dale, hauled by 4F 0-6-0 no. 44592 (1961)

2 The Midlands and East Anglia

The Formation of the Midland Railway

At the same time as the railway was being built from Lancashire to London, another line was being carried northwards along the other side of the watershed towards Leeds. Three companies were involved in this. The first was the Birmingham & Derby Junction, opened through easy country from a junction with the L&B at Hampton (between Coventry and Birmingham), via Tamworth and Burton-on-Trent to Derby in August 1839. The branch from Whitacre to a new station in Birmingham at Lawley Street (now a freight depot) was not completed until February 1842.

The second company was the North Midland, which ran from Derby to Leeds via Ambergate, Chesterfield, Staveley, Rotherham, and Normanton, and was opened in two stages during 1840. At Normanton it met the York & North Midland, opened simultaneously to that point, which served York and also Hull. The NM had been surveyed by George Stephenson, and although it ran past some fairly rugged country along the edge of the Peak District around Ambergate, he did not have much difficulty in selecting a comparatively easy location; the heaviest gradient was the 1 in 250 through Clay Cross tunnel. But this was at the price of avoiding the most important intermediate city. Sheffield had to be content with a branch line from Rotherham, since Stephenson balked at the gradients and tunnel that would be needed to cross the hills to the south. The direct link from Chesterfield, which finally put Sheffield on the main line, was not opened until 1870, and with its long climbs at 1 in 100 and the 1¼-mile Bradway tunnel at the summit it always remained quite a proposition for steam power. The original route still survives and is used by much of the through freight.

While the Birmingham & Derby and North Midland companies were allied, both having been en-gineered by George Stephenson and mainly financed from Liverpool, the Midland Counties Railway was independent. It also joined Derby with the London & Birmingham, but via Leicester, and with a branch from Trent to Nottingham. For some time it could not decide whether to connect with the L&B as soon as possible, or at some point farther south, after passing through Northampton. The shorter route via Rugby was eventually chosen. The first section, from Derby to Nottingham, was opened in 1839 and Rugby was reached in July 1840.

There were now two rival routes between Derby and the south, and violent competition ensued, with the usual rate wars. Each company loudly proclaimed that theirs was the Shortest Route; but, as so often with this kind of advertising, that depended entirely on where you wanted to go. The B&D had the edge if you were travelling to Birmingham, but the MC clearly had the better road to London. The hostilities went on for some time, until it became clear to all concerned that the only beneficiaries were the public. So in 1844 the three companies amalgamated to form the Midland Railway.

The B&D Whitacre-Hampton line at once lost its importance; a token passenger service of one or two trains a day was kept going until the first world war, although the track was not finally lifted until 1952. Curiously enough, the southern section of the Midland Counties has also now ceased to exist, when the wrong railway between Leicester and Rugby was closed at the end of 1961.

Soon after the amalgamation in September 1847, the Erewash Valley line, from Trent on the Midland Counties to Clay Cross on the North Midland was opened. This avoided Derby and shortened the route to Chesterfield and points north by 7 miles; it also served a number of collieries, and although plagued nowadays by the resulting subsidences, became part

of the Midland's main line to the south.

The man behind the formation of the Midland was George Hudson, the 'Railway King'. When his brief career in the industry began, he had already been Mayor of York; he was a crafty and none too scrupulous financier who knew no more about railway operation than any intelligent layman (which helped his popularity, as the public belief that any outsider knows how to run a railway better than any professional was already firmly held), but he earned and deserved the reputation of being a good administrator. He had certainly got the North Midland out of a bad patch caused by short-sighted economizing in 1842. His reputation as a railway strategist, although it made him briefly master of hastily-built lines from London to Berwick and Carlisle, was perhaps less well deserved, as we shall see.

The Great Northern

Another reason why the Derby companies had amalgamated was to counter the scheme for a direct route from London to York, which would destroy their monopoly. But the way for their rivals lay wide open; at this time there were no railways in eastern England between the Humber and the L&B's long and rambling branch from Blisworth to Peterborough via Northampton, still building and not finished until 1845. To protect this exposed flank, the newly-formed Midland therefore promoted a branch of its own to Peterborough from Syston, north of Leicester, and extended from Nottingham to Lincoln in 1846. But this still left the ground largely empty.

Before 1845 there were in fact two London to York schemes. One was to build north from Cambridge in extension of the Eastern Counties Railway; the other, backed by Edmund Denison of Doncaster, was for an independent line the whole way, 15 miles shorter, and as direct and uncomplicated as possible. Denison's line, as the more ambitious proposal, came under

A splendid line-up of power at King's Cross. Of the three Pacifics, no. 2795 'Call Boy' is preparing to leave with the 'Flying Scotsman', and no. 2598 'Blenheim' with the 10.5 relief. No. 2746 'Fairway', on the left, has just arrived from the shed coupled to two Atlantics; in the suburban platforms on the right two N7 class 0-6-2Ts stand at the head of their trains, and an Ivatt 4-4-0 waits its turn to proceed back to the shed tender-first. The St Pancras clock in the background reads 9.45 a.m. (1936)

Shortly after the grouping, Ivatt 4-4-0 no. 1346 and large Atlantic no. 274 leaving King's Cross with the 5.45 p.m. to Leeds and Harrogate (1924)

heavy fire from all the experts. The 'Railway Times' lashed it particularly. 'Was it because the undertaking was not large enough for public support' it queried sarcastically, 'that Cambridge as a starting point had been dropped, that seat of learned travellers deserted, the large traffic of taking students to and from the colleges removed from the table of estimates, and despised in comparison to proceeding direct to so celebrated and extensive a city as St Neots? ... The addition of 50 more miles of railway, with a new terminus in London through some 100 furlongs of house property, is a further sign of the extraordinary caution exercised by the promoters ... Without doubt it will shortly be announced that York Minster has been scheduled for removal to make way for a proper station at the northern end.' Nevertheless, Denison stuck to his enlightened layman's point of view and prevailed.

In 1845 the Great Northern Railway asked for powers to build its main line from London to York, with a loop from Peterborough via Boston and Lincoln to Doncaster, and various other branches; a total of 327 miles of track. It was the largest railway scheme ever placed before Parliament, and it caused probably the fiercest Parliamentary battle. The promoters spent well over £400,000 on legal expenses; Hudson's companies did not stint themselves either. It was not difficult to prove a case for a new line; the coal trade alone was a weighty argument. The London & Birmingham had thought itself too grand a concern to dirty its trucks with such stuff, and coal was still coming to London by sea. The GNR's estimate that the effect of rail transport would reduce the price in London from 29/- to 21/- a ton therefore had great force, and in fact the line did a very large business in coal when built. Hudson's reasoned arguments could not make

28

much headway against this, so he resorted to other methods. His lawyers had instructions to fight every inch of the way, manufacturing objections as necessary; so they claimed that the published plans of the GN line were inaccurate, even though the errors complained of were merely caused by the paper shrinking after it had been dampened during the printing process. Aspersions were cast on the financial standing of those who had undertaken to buy GNR shares, so that they had to attend an all-night sitting of Parliament to prove their solvency. A bogus committee of GNR shareholders was set up, which issued pamphlets of lamentation and lack of confidence, and the Cambridge route was urged as greatly preferable. In fact not a chance was missed; Hudson had never heard of any Queensberry Rules and fought like a tiger. He had some unexpected help during the fight, when Lord Dalhousie, President of the Board of Trade, declared that his committee were in favour of a line through Cambridge; but since the noble lord made the mistake of breaking the rule 'if your reasons are unsound, don't publish them', his intervention in the end fell rather flat. So Hudson lost, and the GNR got its Act in June 1846.

But Hudson had not contented himself with Parliamentary obstruction. He also planned to make himself master of a rival route to London. The Eastern Counties was now building a line to Peterborough, via Cambridge and Ely, which was opened in December 1846; Hudson had himself made chairman of that company in 1845. Most of the Midland's branch to Peterborough was opened in 1848, but here Hudson met a worthy opponent in Lord Harborough. The uncompleted gap, from Melton Mowbray to Stamford, was where the railway passed through his lordship's estate, and here there had been trouble. The surveyors had originally been ordered off the property; there had been chases, horsewhippings, battles between armies of rented warriors, arrests, courts, fines and imprisonments; Lord Harborough himself had driven his carriage in the best Boadicea manner at gatherings of railway officials. As a result, when the Midland finally came to build the line they found that the distracted surveyors had made an error in the levels, and a diversion was essential. So the whole gruesome process had to be gone through all over again. The railway was not finally finished, complete with Lord Harborough's Curve and a speed restriction, until May 1848. Hudson's rival route to London now existed. But it was a poor thing, meandering all over the map, and Hudson had already lost interest in it. For by this time the GNR was well under way, and he

Ex-GNR J1 class 0-6-0 no. 3007 (of 1908) with a northbound ballast train at Hadley Wood (1938)

A Manchester–St.Pancras express passing Chinley North Junction, on the climb to Peak Forest, behind 4-6-0 no. 44822; a Class Five substituting for the more usual 'Jubilee' (1957)

had to come to terms with it. He was in a quandary. The GNR was a natural ally of his lines north of York, but a natural enemy of the Midland, and so it was a wedge splitting his empire in two. Early in 1849 he resigned from the Eastern Counties and the Midland, and came to an agreement with the GNR that they should abandon their plans to build from Doncaster to York, reaching York instead by running powers from Askern to Knottingley over the Lancashire & York-

shire, and thence by the York & North Midland.

This was Hudson's last throw. By losing the GNR war, he had lost his reputation of infallibility, and he had made too many enemies to survive. Rumours of financial impropriety began to be listened to, and in 1849 things came to a head. The most commonly reported charge against him is that he maintained his position and kept shareholders quiet by paying dividends out of capital; so he did, but this was common practice at the time. The GNR itself did exactly the same until the practice was made illegal. But there were other indiscretions. He had rewarded himself for his services, not perhaps outrageously but certainly generously and in secret; he had traded in railway materials, selling them to his companies not perhaps at unreasonable prices, but in a conspiratorial manner. Justice had not been seen to be done. Each of his companies set up committees of investigation to seek for evidence of mismanagement, and although nothing much was found, they all turned venomously on their fallen idol and sued him for every penny to which they had a legal claim, whether they had a moral one or not. In a few months Hudson was broken and ruined.

Meanwhile the Great Northern was pressing on. The East Lincolnshire loop, running across level country, made best progress, and the first section opened was from Louth to Grimsby, in March 1848. From Grimsby the GNR had running powers over the Manchester, Sheffield & Lincolnshire to New Holland, whence ferries operated to Hull. By the end of 1848 trains were running from Peterborough to Lincoln, via Boston, and from Boston to Grimsby. There was also a short isolated section from Doncaster to Askern, so far used only by the Lancashire & Yorkshire. In return, the L&Y granted running powers north from Askern, and since that company was itself dependent on the Midland to reach Leeds, GNR trains at first reached that city over the metals of their arch competitor. During 1849 the gap between Lincoln and Doncaster was closed, not by the intended line through Gainsborough (which was not completed till 1861), but as a temporary measure from Lincoln to Retford over the MS&L, and thence the GNR main line.

The southern section, from Peterborough to London, was opened on 7 August 1850, at first to a temporary station at Maiden Lane; King's Cross was not ready until October 1852. The line had involved some heavy engineering, as its approach to London was much more difficult than the London & Birmingham's; several tunnels, the impressive viaduct at Welwyn, and a long climb at 1 in 200 up to Potter's Bar were necessary. But the GNR was now in business, and although it was still using the loop line via Boston it could already equal the best time of the Rugby route from London to York. When the main line from Peterborough to Retford via Grantham and over Stoke Summit was completed in August 1852, saving 20 miles, the Midland was no longer in the running so far as train times were concerned.

But the GNR still had to establish itself commercially. The L&NW-Midland combination, led by Huish, were not yet beaten. This time the fight was a diplomatic one, over pooling arrangements and the proportion of total receipts allocated to each company. A five-year agreement to pool traffic from points north of York to London was made between the L&NWR, MR, and GNR in 1851; Denison regarded the GNR's share as very inadequate, but bided his time. As he said, 'no fallacy would be so great as to suppose that the public would travel circuitously if it could go directly; such a theory might do very well for railway makers, but not for the public ... Sooner or later traffic, like water, will find its own level and come to the shortest line.' In 1856 he was able to prove that the GN was doing the bulk of the work while the Midland and L&NW were getting the bulk of the revenue, and after a brief rate war matters were put right. From points south of York to London no agreement could be reached; a fierce rate war was waged during the summer of 1851, much to the benefit of the Great Exhibition, as enormous trainloads of passengers took the opportunity to travel up to London for a few shillings. Finally, Gladstone, who had been called in to arbitrate, made an award dividing total receipts in a manner quite favourable to the GNR. Huish was trying to sweep back the sea. He still persisted, evading the letter of Gladstone's award by forcing passengers to re-book at Rugby and similar dodges; but finally the L&NW, which had by now acquired a most unsavoury reputation for crooked and dishonest dealing, decided it might be more profitable to tread the path of virtue instead. They sacked him in 1858, and peace was restored.

However, all these difficulties had forced the GNR to the conclusion that it needed its own lines to every traffic centre in the Midlands, and slowly and consistently it set about getting them. Its first success was in reaching Nottingham. A minor company, the Ambergate, Nottingham, Boston, and Eastern Junction Railway, had built a line from Nottingham (where it shared the Midland's station) to Grantham and then fallen on hard times before it could get any farther. It would undoubtedly have been taken over by the Midland and London & North Western had not a loyal GNR supporter privately bought a large shareholding and made a fuss; consequently, in 1852 it became an ally of the GN. The Midland was exceedingly angry, and impounded the first Great Northern engine to arrive at Nottingham, but beyond making itself objectionable it could do nothing.

In later years the GNR consolidated itself in the Nottinghamshire coalfields by building branches up the Leen and Erewash valleys, parallel to Midland lines. It also reached Cambridge, and Leeds and Bradford in its own right via Wakefield, in 1866, Derby and Burton-on-Trent in 1878, and finally petered out in the remoter uplands between Halifax and Keighley, over lines now mostly closed, in the early eighties. But its biggest coup was when its trains reached Sheffield and Manchester, as described in the next chapter.

Much of the main line to London was quadrupled in due course, with the notable exception of two lengths in the London area; some relief was available here after the Wood Green-Enfield branch was extended via Hertford to Stevenage (in 1920), forming a loop. But the double track bottleneck over Welwyn Viaduct and through the tunnels to Woolmer Green remains, and the other one through the tunnels at Hadley Wood and Potters Bar was not widened until 1959.

The Manchester, Sheffield and Lincolnshire

This company started life as the Sheffield, Ashton-under-Lyne, and Manchester Railway, and set about connecting the towns of this title in 1838. It was not the first trans-Pennine railway, since the Manchester & Leeds, through the summit tunnel at Littleborough, was already under way and was opened earlier, in 1841. But it was the more ambitious of the two. Charles Vignoles and Joseph Locke, the engineers, laid out a line which included many miles of 1 in 100 or 1 in 120 gradient and several impressive viaducts, notably at Dinting, and whose major work was the 3-mile Woodhead Tunnel, until 1886 the longest in Britain. Remotely situated and difficult to supply, it took 7 years to build; and so although the first section of the line from London Road station, Manchester (shared with the Manchester & Birmingham) to Godley was open at the end of 1841, it was not until December 1845 that trains started to run throughout from Manchester to Sheffield. Before long, the company wanted to go further east; in 1847 it amalgamated with two lines under construction to form the Manchester, Sheffield & Lincolnshire Railway, and during the following two years began to run from Sheffield through Retford to New Holland and Grimsby, via Gainsborough and via Lincoln. As we have seen, the GNR also used the Retford-Lincoln

section. There was also a junction with the original North Midland main line at Beighton. The MS&L later became possessed of a considerable network of lines, mostly paralleled by the Midland, in the coalfields between Penistone, Sheffield, and Doncaster; the South Yorkshire Railway, which had owned most of them, together with a branch to navigable water at Keadby, was a cantankerously independent company finally taken over in 1864. When the Keadby branch was straightened out and extended to Barnetby, the MS&L possessed a third route to Grimsby.

Although it served busy industrial areas around Sheffield and Manchester, prosperity eluded the MS&L. Its mountainous main line was expensive to work, it had a large mileage of poorly paying rural track in Lincolnshire, and it had still to build a second tunnel at Woodhead, the first carrying only a single line. It therefore felt it had to keep on good terms with the neighbours. In 1850 its most powerful neighbours were the London & North Western and the Midland, and so it made a seven-year traffic agreement with them, the principal provision of which was that all parties agreed to be as nasty as possible to the Great Northern. As a result, MS&L trains (and, at New Holland, steamers) mysteriously failed to connect with the GNR. But by 1857 the roars of the paper tiger at Euston had ceased to terrify, at least in Yorkshire. The MS&L realized there was more to be gained by a change of alliance, since it could then become part of a second route from London to Manchester; and after a brief courtship with the GNR it was so. The schedules were rearranged to make GNR connections and break L&NW ones, and suddenly, at the end of 1857, the L&NW found that its trains having trundled leisurely up from Euston were tending to be met at Manchester by grinning passengers who had left King's Cross at the same time. Another frightful rate war resulted, and worse; the L&NW evicted the MS&L booking clerk at London Road, and its officials even arrested passengers presenting tickets issued by the GNR at the barrier (until a lawyer happened to do so). But finally matters settled down with each company matching the other's times. Since they had the longer (203 v. 188 miles) and hillier route via Sheffield, honours definitely lay with the GNR and MS&L.

N1 class 0-6-2T (ex-GNR, 1907) no. 69450 leaving Leeds for Dewsbury (1958)

The Expansion of the Midland Railway

Regardless of the Great Northern, it could not be expected that a company as important as the Midland would be satisfied indefinitely with depending on another for connection with London. Even apart from his pantomime war with Lord Harborough, Hudson recognized this and in 1847 obtained power for a line from Leicester via Bedford to Hitchin, there to connect with an extension of the Eastern Counties, saving the detour by Peterborough. After his fall matters were delayed, but in 1853 fresh powers were obtained and the line was built, opening in May 1857. By now the Midland and Great Northern were on better terms,

and so the GN granted running powers from Hitchin into King's Cross. A through service of Midland trains started in March 1858. The Leicester-Hitchin line was built through rolling country, perhaps rather too cheaply; it had some undesirable curves, notably at Market Harborough where it crossed the L&NW Rugby-Peterborough branch, and its gradients were also something of an embarrassment, particularly the 1 in 120 on either side of Sharnbrook summit, south of Wellingborough. When the tracks were quadrupled here in the eighties, the opportunity was taken to put the freight lines through the ridge in a mile-long tunnel, so that while passenger trains still ground and sweated over the top, coal rode less tumultuously below.

A St. Pancras-Manchester express leaving the Elstree tunnel; Johnson 4-2-2 no. 672 piloting Compound 4-4-0 no. 1042 (1921)

But worse than all this was the congestion south of Hitchin. The GN, having its own trains to worry about, was not inclined to do much to expedite anybody else's. The Midland stood this for as long as it could, but in 1863 took powers to build a line of its own from Bedford to London via St Albans. This was opened for freight in 1867, for suburban passengers to Moorgate in July 1868, and finally to the great new Gothic terminus at St Pancras, just across the road from King's Cross, three months later. South of Bedford, the new construction was more substantial, with a ruling grade of 1 in 176. Just as important, the MR took pains to connect itself thoroughly with existing lines in the London area, in contrast to the GN, which

still suffers from a relative lack of effective transfer connections for freight.

Having emulated the GNR in getting to London, the Midland now proposed to do as much for Manchester. There already existed a branch from Ambergate to Rowsley, opened in 1849, which had recently been extended through the great limestone dales, much to Ruskin's disgust, to Buxton. In February 1867 this line was projected from Miller's Dale over Peak Forest summit and through the $1\frac{3}{4}$-mile Dove Holes tunnel down to New Mills, where it met a branch of the MS&L and thus gained access of a sort to Manchester (London Road). The directors of the MS&L seem to have granted this facility to the

Coal for London: 9F 2-10-0 no. 92009 arriving at Cricklewood with a train from Toton (1955)

In the last months of steam working at King's Cross. V2 2-6-2 no. 60854 and A4 no. 60034 'Lord Faringdon', receiving a final polish outside the shed (1962)

Midland in a fit of absence of mind, since the new route to London was now shorter than the one they had an interest in themselves to King's Cross. But they did very nicely for the Midland. Later on, it reached its own terminus at Manchester (Central) via Stockport (Tiviot Dale) in 1880, by means of running powers over the Cheshire Lines (q.v.), and after 1897 also on its own tracks through Cheadle Heath and the 2¼-mile Disley Tunnel. This brought the mileage from St Pancras to Manchester down to 190, compared with 188 from Euston. However, the Midland had much worse gradients, especially the 1 in 90 on either side of Peak Forest.

A further series of improvements were made to the Midland's main line network subsequently. The 16-mile Swinton & Knottingley, jointly owned with the North Eastern and opened in 1879, shortened the distance to York and avoided the congested area round Cudworth and Normanton; an exchange of running powers between the two companies at the same time brought Midland trains into York and North Eastern trains into Sheffield. In 1880 the route from Kettering via Melton Mowbray to Nottingham was completed, using the part of the old Peterborough branch that had caused such offence to Lord Harborough. This was another expensive piece of construction, with a ¾-mile viaduct at Harringworth and two tunnels each over a mile long. By means of a short connection across to the old Erewash Valley line at Trowell, this put Nottingham onto a main line for the first time.

Now, between Kettering and Clay Cross, and again from Chesterfield to Leeds and York, the Midland didn't have a main line so much as a main ladder; two parallel routes with cross-connections. Fortunately, so far as the already sufficient complication of the story is concerned, the plan for a direct link between Cudworth and Bradford, avoiding Leeds, languished, and although a lot of construction work was done it was never completed.

One more through line was, however, built by the Midland in this area; up the Hope Valley for 20 miles from Chinley to Dore & Totley. Opened in June 1894, it was intended to enable the Midland to compete for business between Manchester and Sheffield. It was an extremely expensive railway, with two major tunnels; the Cowburn, over 2 miles, and the Dore & Totley, over $3\frac{1}{2}$ miles and the second longest in Britain. But it was 45 miles from Manchester to Sheffield this way, 4 miles farther than via Woodhead, and the competition was never very successful.

The Midland was a great railway, and one can argue that it has left a more permanent mark on today's system than any other of the old companies. It was well managed, it avoided sharp practice, and unlike all the other lines which served London, it remained provincial in the best sense of the world. Its centre of gravity was always at Derby, and seen from there the country had quite a different aspect. London-based managements tended to see Britain as divided into wedge-shaped slices; the Midland from its central position sent tentacles into almost every part of England and Wales, and even into Northern Ireland. Its writ ran from Bournemouth to Carlisle, from Swansea to Lowestoft, and from Southend to Stranraer. It was the nearest thing in existence to a national railway system.

East Anglia

The Eastern Counties Railway was responsible for the first main lines in East Anglia; it was an unfortunate concern at first, short of money and, since it served a wholly agricultural area, short of traffic also. It had been authorized in 1836 to build from London via Colchester to Ipswich, Norwich, and Yarmouth; it opened its first section, to Romford, in June 1839,

and reached Colchester by March 1843. There it stopped. It had had a lot of trouble with the clay hills north of Brentwood, had spent more than it bargained for on its Bishopsgate terminus and the approach viaduct, and was disillusioned about the profitability of any further extensions.

More promising seemed to be the line which had been promoted by the Northern & Eastern Railway, leased by the ECR in 1844. This shared the same London terminus, but from Stratford branched north up the Lea Valley and was intended to run through Cambridge to Norwich, and to the north also. (The junction point remained at Stratford until the cut-off from Bethnal Green via Clapton was opened in 1872.) Lincoln and York were thought of as possible terminals, and having ambitions in this direction the

A Colchester-Liverpool Street train climbing past Stanway, behind K3 class 2-6-0 no. 61830 (1951)

ECR and the N&E were both naturally opposed to the Great Northern scheme. But, due to shortage of money, they made no very impressive progress themselves. Matters were not helped by the fact that their muddleheaded engineer, John Braithwaite, had decided on a gauge of five feet, a mistake that had to be put right in 1844. The N&E had reached Bishop's Stortford in 1842 and Hertford in 1843, but it was not until July 1845 that the line was opened through Cambridge and Ely to Brandon, where the Norfolk Railway (purchased in 1848) continued it to Norwich and Yarmouth. The branch from Ely to March and Peterborough was opened in December 1846, and as we have already seen it eventually became part of Hudson's Indirect Northern. Another branch from Ely, to King's Lynn, was opened (by an independent company) in October of the same year.

Around Ely the country is flat and so for the most part these lines were easy to build. But crossing the broad, sluggish drains and rivers tended to be expensive, since substantial bridges were needed and the ground was too soft to support their foundations.

After the Eastern Counties lost interest in the area north of Colchester, another company stepped in. The Eastern Union completed the line from Colchester to Ipswich and northwards to Bury St Edmunds during 1846, and finished the abandoned part of the Eastern Counties scheme by opening from Haughley to Norwich in December 1849. The ECR looked at this interloper with hatred, and arranged its time-tables to prevent any possibility of connections between trains at Colchester. Hostilities were maintained for some years, but the EUR was even less solvent than the ECR and finally agreed to sell its line to the larger company in 1854. The ECR then consolidated its hold on the area by building numerous branches during the late forties and fifties, including the line to Harwich (1854) and from Ipswich to Yarmouth direct (1859), which completed the pattern of main lines in its original territory. In 1862 all the companies operating in the district except one amalgamated to form the Great Eastern Railway.

East Anglia was still pretty thin gruel from the economic point of view, and GE dividends, when they

J15 class 0-6-0 no. 65467 on an Ipswich-Yarmouth local freight at Woodbridge; a GER design dating from 1883 (1957)

A Yarmouth-Ipswich local leaving Woodbridge behind 4-4-0 no. 62546 'Claud Hamilton'. This class, which took its name from this engine, was a GER express design of 1904, and rebuilt during the 1930s. (1956)

were paid, seldom reached as much as 3%. The company therefore still longed to carve itself a slice of the cake which seemed to be divided by all those railways which served coalfields. For nearly thirty years this remained a dream, although several proposals were put forward; eventually, in 1879, an agreement was reached with the Great Northern which gave the Great Eastern what it wanted. As early as 1865 the GNR had been agreeable to selling a half-interest in its line from March to Spalding (opened in 1867) and thence from Spalding to Doncaster via Boston, reasoning that it would be better to have a competitor only owning half a railway than a completely new one; but the GER's poverty had prevented this offer from being taken up. In 1879 a similar plan went through, taking effect from the opening of the new line between Spalding and Lincoln direct (via Sleaford) in 1882. The GER purchased a half share of the GNR line from March to Doncaster, via Spalding, Sleaford, Lincoln, and Gainsborough, while the GNR bought half the GE section between March and Huntingdon,

via St Ives. After further negotiations, the GER obtained running powers over the GNR and North Eastern to York in 1892 and to Sheffield in 1900, and over various colliery branches as well.

One can argue that the Great Eastern got very much more out of the joint line project than the Great Northern, whose behaviour seems quite unnecessarily charitable. There was some truth in Denison's belief that half a competitor was better than a whole one, but the GN shareholders, as they watched GE coal trains starting from Doncaster instead of Peterborough, could be forgiven for murmuring that bites were the reward of those who helped lame dogs over stiles. The GER was most unlikely to have been able to raise the money to build a new line on its own. The GNR obtained only one limited asset; an alternative route as far south as Huntingdon, which at the time had a certain value in relieving congestion even though everything still had to be funnelled over one pair of tracks south of Huntingdon. But the St Ives-Huntingdon section has now been abandoned.

39

A Norwich-Liverpool Street express leaving the Ipswich tunnel, headed by B12/3 4-6-0 no. 61571. These engines were designed for GER expresses in 1911, and rebuilt after 1932 (1957)

The only important independent railway in the Great Eastern's territory was the London, Tilbury, & Southend. This had originally been promoted by the Eastern Counties and London & Blackwall Railways jointly, and was opened from Forest Gate, on the ECR main line, to Tilbury in April 1854. It had one main objective; to reach Gravesend by means of a ferry, and so compete for the traffic which had originally moved from London to Blackwall and thence by steamer down the Thames, which had been usurped by a direct line on the other side of the river. At this time the north bank was still quite undeveloped. The railway was extended to Thames Haven in 1855 and Southend in 1856; in 1858, by means of a new connection from Barking to Burdett Road and thence by running powers, it reached the Blackwall company's London terminus at Fenchurch Street without having to use Eastern Counties metals.

As one might imagine, the LT&S line was originally a shocking moneyloser, but its shareholders were happily protected from the effects of this by having farmed the operation out to a contractor, so it was his money which got lost. In 1875 the contract expired and the company had to start running trains itself; but by now urban expansion was well under way and a busy passenger traffic developed. When Tilbury Docks opened in 1886 freight also improved. After the completion in 1888 of the LT&S's direct route to Southend via Upminster and in 1889 of the GE's branch from Shenfield to Southend, there was strong competition between the two lines, and the Great Eastern came to regret having disposed of its controlling interest during the small company's unprofitable days. Paying dividends of around $2\frac{1}{2}\%$ itself, it now felt unable to buy the LT&S out, as it paid 4%, which was a little humiliating. The LT&S was finally bought up in 1912 by the Midland, rather to everyone's surprise.

Like the LT&S only more so, the Great Eastern did a very considerable passenger business in the London area, especially after the large new terminus at Liverpool Street replaced Bishopsgate in 1874. Frequent trains and some extremely cheap fares were almost embarrassingly successful; Liverpool Street had to be doubled in size in 1894 and eventually it came to have what was probably the world's most intensive steam-worked suburban service. Intelligent operation, and poverty, both helped it also to be one of the last. Electrification did not start until 1949 and was not finished until 1960. On the other side of GER territory, the Great Northern also had a fairly large suburban trade, which once added greatly to congestion at King's Cross. But the busiest lines were electrified and taken over by London Transport after 1940, leaving only a moderate traffic to be steam (or now diesel) worked.

Later Lines in the Midlands

There was a final spurt of main line railway projects in the Midlands during the eighties and nineties. The first was the Great Northern and London & North Western Joint, running from Market Harborough via Melton Mowbray to the Grantham-Nottingham line at Bottesford and Saxondale, with a GN-owned link to the main line at Newark, opened in 1883. This line was useful to the L&NW, as it brought it to part of the

Nottinghamshire coalfields, and also served part of the Leicestershire ironstone area; but any other advantage to the GNR is not quite so easy to see. They built a branch from it at John o' Gaunt to Leicester, with a large and (at any rate in later years) almost useless terminus at Belgrave Road. Grinling, in his admirable History of the Great Northern, is unable to suggest any better reason for this venture than to say that the GNR directors had discovered that there was a traffic in wool from Yorkshire to Leicester and of woollen underwear in the opposite direction, which seems as frivolous a reason for building over fifty miles of railway as any. The joint line is now closed to passengers; Belgrave Road continued to be used by excursion trains to the east coast three or four times a year until 1962.

Much more important was the Midland & Great Northern Joint. This organization was formed in 1893 to take over and develop the old Eastern & Midlands, which ran from Peterborough and Spalding to Yarmouth via Sutton Bridge, South Lynn, and Melton Constable, with branches to Cromer and Norwich. All of it had been built by various small companies between 1866 and 1887, and was of little interest except to the locals. But although there was a bare living to be made out of ordinary agricultural traffic all over East Anglia, the Norfolk coast offered a bonus in the shape of a growing holiday business. The Great Eastern had started to cash in on this by extending its old Fakenham branch to Wells, and by the Norwich-Cromer line, completed in 1877; the Eastern &

Gresley 'Sandringham' class 3-cylinder 4-6-0 no. 61643 'Champion Lodge' leaves Doncaster on a stopping train to March (1954)

Midland & Great Northern 4-4-0 no. 11 at the head of a return
excursion from Yarmouth to Leicester, struggling up the 1 in
100 out of Melton Constable with 12 packed coaches (1932)

Midlands line offered the Midland and Great Northern companies the chance to claim a share very
cheaply. So they jointly purchased it. They then extended it to Lowestoft in 1898 by the Norfolk &
Suffolk Joint Railway (in which the GER, who already
possessed a parallel route, was persuaded to share by
some miracle of diplomacy), and the Midland and the
M&GN each built half the connection from Spalding
to Saxby. The Midland now ran quite a successful
service from Leicester and beyond to Yarmouth via
Spalding; the GN did not have so much luck with its
indirect services to London via Peterborough.

But although the M&GN was smartly worked, it
never really paid, and after 1914 began to lose alarm-
ing amounts of money. All the places it reached worth
serving were also served by the GER, and a parallel
through route existed via March, Ely, and Norwich.
Bar a few short sections retained for local freight, and
the N&S line from Yarmouth to Lowestoft (retained
in preference to the GE route via Beccles), the M&GN

was abandoned in February 1959.

The most important of these late lines by a large
margin was the Great Central London Extension, a
railway which owes its existence to the drive and per-
tinacity (or, alternatively, pig-headedness) of one man.
Sir Edward Watkin had been Chairman of the Manchester, Sheffield, & Lincolnshire since 1864, and even
before that had played a part in arranging for the
Great Northern to reach Manchester. But like others
before him, he felt that no railway could prosper while
it remained provincial, and dreamed of a route to
London. By 1872, when he also became Chairman of
the Metropolitan, he was on the way to achieving it.
In addition, he was planning to extend through
London to connect with the South Eastern (of which
he was Chairman as well) and so to France by means
of the Channel Tunnel (of which he was, again,
Chairman). He told of this design in a letter to the
Chairman of the Midland in 1872. But it took him a
long time, and it was not until the early nineties that
his scheme finally got under way.

The first step was for the MS&L to build a branch
from Beighton to Annesley, whence Nottingham was
reached over the GNR. This was opened in 1893, but
while it was under construction Watkin attempted to
enlist GN support for his London Extension scheme.
He argued that traffic was increasing, and that while
no doubt it would be possible to accommodate it by
continuing the process of four-tracking, it was better
to build through fresh country than to 'keep on
plastering the old lines'. The Great Northern weren't
interested, so Watkin went ahead on his own, and after
an unsuccessful attempt in 1891 obtained his Act in
1893. He was opposed by the L&NW and the GNR,
both arguing that there was no need for a new main
line; and also by the enraged inhabitants of St John's
Wood, who in the language of their grandfathers protested against the intrusion of a railway which would
carry not only passengers, but 'coal, manure, fish, and
other abominations' as well through (or rather under)
their tasteful streets. But his supporters included coal-
owners from Sheffield and Nottinghamshire who welcomed the idea of further railway competition, and he
finally carried the day.

Starting from Annesley, the London Extension ran
through Nottingham, Leicester, and Rugby to Quain-
ton Road, and then by running powers over the
Metropolitan line opened in 1892 through Aylesbury
to a new terminus at Marylebone. There was also a
branch from Woodford to Banbury, connecting with

Ex-Great Central B7 class 4-6-0 no. 5469 on a southbound excursion train near Seer Green, on the GW&GC Joint line (1938)

the Great Western, which eventually proved the most valuable part of the whole scheme as it enabled freight from the Midlands to the South-west to avoid the congested and longer route via Birmingham. A defect was that the new line sailed right across the L&NW at Rugby with no connections at all. It was an expensive railway to build, particularly passing through Nottingham and Leicester, and it had a $1\frac{3}{4}$-mile tunnel at Catesby, north of Woodford; but it was well laid out for high speed running and had a maximum gradient of 1 in 176. On the Metropolitan section south of Aylesbury, which crossed the Chilterns with long climbs at 1 in 105 and had a nasty curve at Rickmansworth, it was a different story.

Having risen from its provincial status, the MS&L changed its name to the Great Central in 1897. Wags, who had referred to the old company as the 'Money Sunk & Lost', soon got into the habit of calling the new the 'Gone Completely', and with justice. While ordinary shareholders were paid a few per cent by the MS&L, they never got a penny from the GC. The line was opened to freight in 1898, and to passengers in March 1899, although the full service did not start for some months until work finished at Nottingham (Victoria). At the same time, although this entailed a

fairly substantial deceleration, the GNR diverted some of its London-Manchester trains from their old route through Retford to run via Nottingham and the GC. The final step was to supplement the unsatisfactory route into London via Aylesbury with the GW&GC Joint route via High Wycombe, opened in 1906.

By now Watkin was an old man; he had retired in 1894, but he lived to see the London Extension completed. It was, so far as the services it offered were concerned, a success, and the Banbury branch filled a substantial need. Yet, taken as a whole, we can now see that the scheme was a mistake. It certainly never paid; the MS&L would have done far better for its proprietors to forget about the bright lights and stop at Annesley. Nor was there really justification for another route to London. The GC main line was worked hard and competitively for sixty years; even after nationalization, when it might be supposed that such things would have been stopped, a rash of posters appeared in London at one time saying 'Marylebone for Manchester!' But the line is now definitely in the shadows, and although a token passenger service is still maintained at the time of writing it cannot be long before much of the London extension is abandoned, and rightly.

However, this does not mean that Watkin was un-reasonable; we are not gifted with foresight, and certainly no wise man in 1893 would have foretold the course of history over the following half-century. Nor were some of those who opposed him any more clear-sighted. Watkin had good reason to be indignant when immediately after Parliament had rejected his 1891 Bill, it approved the Lancashire, Derbyshire, & East Coast Railway. 'As mad a scheme as ever was presented' Watkin fumed, and he was right. The LD&EC was indeed the last lunatic flowering of British railway promotion.

It was intended to build from Warrington and Macclesfield to Buxton, with a branch from Manchester joining the main line there. Onwards to Chesterfield, there was to be some awesome mountaineering, including a viaduct over Monsal Dale nearly 300 ft. high; beyond Chesterfield the line struck across easier country, with some coal, to Lincoln and thence to the celebrated and extensive metropolis of Sutton-on-Sea. The Great Eastern, thirsting after coal, had a finger in it, but in 1907 the already moribund company was bought out by the GCR. Only the Lincoln to Chesterfield section was completed (in 1897), with a long jerry-built tunnel and some high jerry-built viaducts, and much of that has now been closed. Its only worthwhile function was and still is to serve some collieries.

(*Right*) The 'Britannia' Pacifics scored their biggest success in East Anglia, where their arrival coincided with improved schedules. No. 70040 'Clive of India' topping the grade from Liverpool Street at Bethnal Green with a Norwich express (1957)

Great Eastern suburban: N7 class 0-6-2T no. 69671 leaving Bethnal Green with a Liverpool Street-Chingford train (1957)

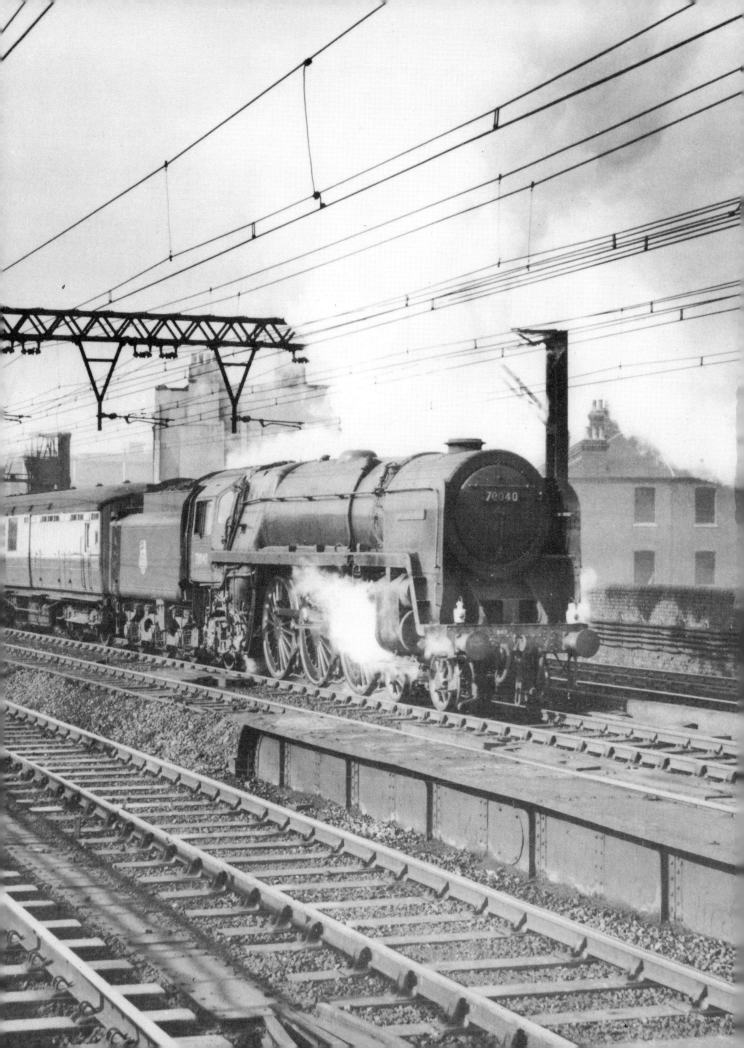

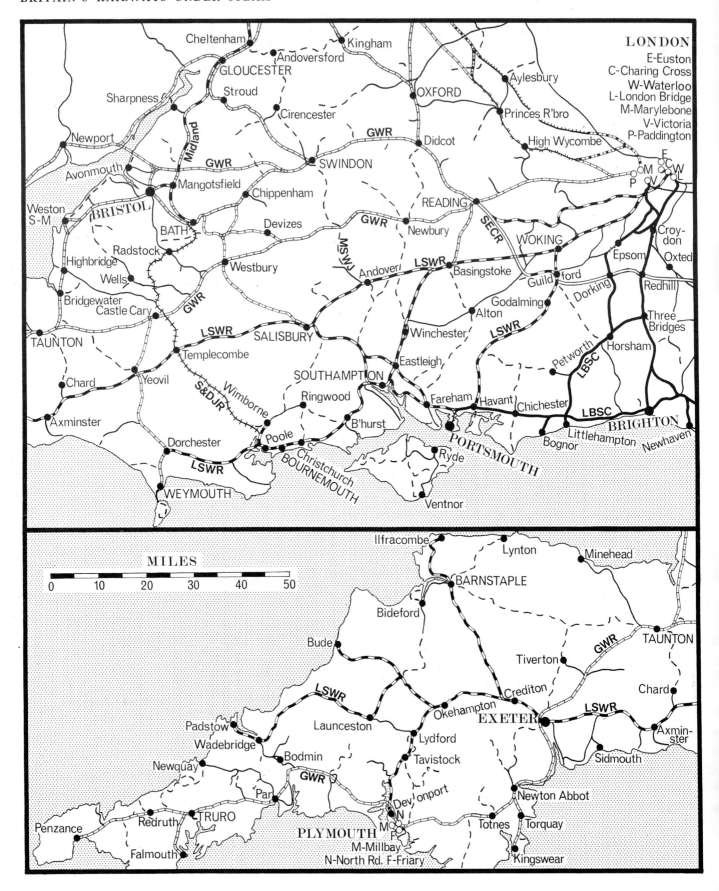

LONDON
E-Euston
C-Charing Cross
W-Waterloo
L-London Bridge
M-Marylebone
V-Victoria
P-Paddington

MILES
0 10 20 30 40 50

3 The West and South-East

London to Bristol and Exeter

Bristol in the 1830s was still the greatest port in the country; it did not lose ground to Liverpool or to London itself until steamships had ousted sail. A railway from London to Bristol was therefore more than just a way to the West Country or even to Ireland; it was the first step on the road to the New World. After he had been appointed Engineer to the London & Bristol Railway Committee in 1833, Isambard Kingdom Brunel therefore had some reason for saying that he was now carrying out 'the finest work in England'. In the same way, the project's original title was soon felt to be too local and limited, and it was dropped in favour of the simpler and grander Great Western Railway.

Brunel rejected the idea of carrying the line through Trowbridge and Hungerford, following the Bath Road and the Kennet and Avon canal, and chose a more northerly route through the Vale of White Horse since it offered better gradients and fewer constructional difficulties. It was, however, less direct and it meant abandoning the plan of sharing the track of the proposed London & Southampton for the first 45 miles. Instead it was intended to use the London & Birmingham for the five miles from Kensal Green to Euston, and the GWR was authorized by Parliament to follow this route in 1835. But it proved impossible to come to a satisfactory agreement with the L&B company, since they would only offer a tenancy terminable at five years' notice; so it was decided in 1837 to divert the line from Kensal Green into an independent terminus at Paddington.

There was, however, more to these changes than met the eye. Brunel's ideas of future railway speeds and traffic were even grander than Robert Stephenson's. He laid out a magnificent main line up the Thames Valley, with gentle curves, bold earthworks, and a maximum gradient of 1 in 660 (and very little of that). Gradually the idea grew in his mind that the GWR deserved something more ambitious than a railway on the Stephenson model, and should be built to a broader gauge. Having meanwhile ensured that the GWR Act, unlike most others, failed to define this point, in September 1835 he put his case for a gauge of seven feet in a letter to the Board. He specifically denied that he wanted the additional width to allow for larger vehicles, and although the loading gauge he established was appreciably larger than standard (11 ft wide and 14 ft 9 in high, compared with 9 ft 8 in and 13 ft 6 in respectively) it was not as large as it could easily have been and even so full advantage was never taken of it. Instead, Brunel based his argument on higher speeds through increased stability and a reduction of friction by using larger wheels running outside the body with a slower-turning axle. (Few, if any, vehicles were built to this odd specification, nor was it ever proved that it would, in fact, reduce friction.) Brunel admitted that difficulty would arise at places where broad met standard gauge, but declared it was unlikely that this would happen to any great extent, since the GWR was isolated and served a well-defined area of its own. In any case the inconvenience of trans-shipping freight could be minimized by the use of containers and transporter trucks. But the main emphasis was placed on fast running on the particularly level and easy road to Bristol. Brunel's case was accepted by the Board and the shareholders, against considerable expert advice, and the broad gauge was adopted.

The railway was opened in stages between June 1838 and June 1841. From London up the Thames Valley and to Swindon it remains one of the very best laid out main lines in the world. But beyond Swindon there was a surprising change; 1½ and later nearly 3 miles down at 1 in 100, quite unlike the London &

Bathampton
No. 5933 'Kingsway Hall' waits in the loop with a freight, as 'Castle' no. 5076 'Gladiator' overtakes with a Bristol-Portsmouth train (1958)

A Portsmouth-Bristol express coming off the WS&W line, with 2-6-0 no. 6320 piloting no. 5947 'St. Benet's Hall'; a 2251 class 0-6-0 shunts in the background (1958)

Birmingham, and to make things worse the second incline was through the 1¾-mile Box Tunnel, when built the longest in Britain. Brunel originally contemplated cable haulage on these sections, but decided against it. From Box to Bristol the line was again easily graded, but with a number of curves which restricted fast running and several short tunnels through the narrow part of the Avon Valley beyond Bath. By what is generally described as an amazing coincidence, the sun shines right through Box Tunnel annually at dawn on Brunel's birthday.

Even before the railway from London to Bristol was finished, plans were made to continue it to Exeter. The first section of the Bristol & Exeter, to Bridgwater, was opened in June 1841, and the line was completed in May 1844. Until 1849, when the local company took over, the GWR worked it, and the 194 miles from London to Exeter was at that time the longest section of railway in Britain under one management. As far as Taunton, across the North Somerset plains and marshes, the B&E was as straight and level as most of the GWR; south of Taunton came the climb to Whiteball tunnel, with 3 miles between 1 in 90 and 1 in 80, and a descent thence to Exeter, part of which was at 1 in 115.

More heavily graded still was the Cheltenham & Great Western Union Railway, from Swindon to Cheltenham via Gloucester, completed in May 1845. This line was authorized by Parliament in preference to one backed by the London & Birmingham from Tring via Aylesbury, Oxford, and Witney to Cheltenham. The L&B scheme would have reduced the distance from London to Cheltenham to 99 miles, compared with 121 by the line built. E. T. MacDermot, who was after all writing the GWR Official History, said that the L&B scheme would have involved worse gradients; from the lie of the land this seems highly unlikely. The only advantage of the C&GWU scheme, apart from serving the Stroud Valley, was that despite its wandering round through Gloucester it involved less new construction, and this was decisive. It was a considerable victory for Paddington over the Euston interests when the C&GWU was authorized in 1836; it opened the gateway to South Wales for the GWR. However, it was and remains a most unsuitable railway for high speed running west of Kemble; much of the mile-long Sapperton tunnel descends at 1 in 90, and from the western portal the line falls into the Stroud Valley with a ruling grade of 1 in 60 and continuous sharp reverse curves.

The only other important branch from the GWR at this time was from Didcot to Oxford (10 miles), opened in 1844 and as we have already seen later the springboard for the broad-gauge invasion of the Midlands. Still in the Thames Valley, it was at least reasonably straight and level, once it was round the bend at Didcot. For already by the mid-forties, one of the flaws in Brunel's argument had become apparent. The superlative main line on which the whole case had been based remained the only one of its kind in the West of England. The farther the broad gauge penetrated, the wilder and more unsuitable for it the country became.

The West Midlands

The first trespasser in broad gauge territory was the Birmingham & Gloucester Railway, a line of some individuality authorized in 1836. Its object was to connect Birmingham with the seaport newly established at Gloucester at the head of the ship canal from Berkeley. Due to opposition from the burghers of Worcester, the line had to bypass the town through Spetchley, but its most remarkable feature was farther north. Here the railway met the not very formidable obstacle of the Lickey Hills by charging at them like a bull at a gate, shooting straight up the slope with two miles of 1 in 38. The company's engineer, Captain Moorsom, took a Nelsonian view of this aberration in an otherwise well-graded line by declaring that it was no steeper than several locomotive-worked inclines he had seen in America, and if necessary he would import American engines to work it. (He did.) What his blind eye had failed to observe, however, was that even in the 1830s an American engineer would have avoided the problem altogether with a few gentle

Winter morning in West London: no. 5933 'Kingsway Hall' pauses at Hayes while a 'Castle' pounds through with a down express (1935)

curves, allowing the hill to be climbed diagonally at any convenient gradient.

For 120 years the railways have made an absurd fuss about the Lickey, with shedfuls of banking engines and reams of special precautions. Whatever excuse there was for this when trains were worked by single-wheelers had vanished by later days. Finally one used to see a 'Patriot' or 'Jubilee' 4-6-0, having stopped in the yards at the foot of the hill, coming chuffing languidly upgrade with perhaps 12 coaches, doing no more work than decency demanded (if indeed as much), while two or three sweating and panting 0-6-0's struggled at the back. By avoiding the unnecessary stop at Bromsgrove and charging the grade at even 30 mph a modern steam engine, as long as the regulator was opened, could easily have got up unaided. Many main-line crews regarded the Lickey as a welcome break, an opportunity to get the fire into shape; it was exceptional to see an express engine hauling its share of the train. At least dieselization has stopped this nonsense. With freights, of course, it was a different matter; but even then it was often instructive to look at loose-coupled stock going by and see just how many couplings the train engine was managing to keep tight. Still, it all made for a very fine smoky afternoon's entertainment by the lineside for five or six generations of small boys.

The Birmingham & Gloucester was completed in December 1840. There was a statutory obligation to add broad gauge rails between Cheltenham and Gloucester (as there was for 8 miles beyond to the point where the C&GWU diverged at Standish), but these were not needed until that railway was eventually finished in 1845. The first Birmingham terminus was a temporary one at Camp Hill, and the line was extended a few months later into the London & Birmingham station at Curzon Street. Most trains moved to New Street with the L&B in 1854, but the present connection from King's Norton to the west end of the station, avoiding the need for reversal before continuing north-east, was not opened until 1885.

The first contact between broad and standard gauges took place at Gloucester when the Bristol & Gloucester line was opened in July 1844. The GWR had looked coldly on the Birmingham & Gloucester; it pointed straight at the holy city of Bristol, where visitors were not welcome. The only way to keep it out seemed to be to build a broad-gauge branch to meet it. But here, and not for the last time, GWR parsimony

and sloth led to serious defeat. The parsimony led to inadequate arrangements for transfer of freight between the gauges at Gloucester; Brunel's ideas of containers and transporter trucks were rejected in favour of manhandling by a disorganized army of porters, and the resulting chaos (carefully stage-managed on a famous occasion before a Parliamentary committee) led for the first time to public hostility to the broad gauge. John Ellis, Chairman of the Midland Railway and also a millowner who imported wool through Bristol, was one of those injured. Parsimony and sloth combined led the GWR to take so long and offer such poor terms to the two Gloucester companies, which it was proposing to buy out, that Ellis, acting on his own responsibility as soon as he heard of the negotiations, made a better offer and snatched both from under the GWR's nose in 1846. So the very thing that company had most feared happened; the Midland reached Bristol. The GWR still had statutory running rights from Bristol to Gloucester, so the broad gauge had to be maintained, but the Midland added narrow in 1854 and the prospect of broad gauge engines grunting up the Lickey was finally scotched. One wonders what kind of job they would have made of it.

Another wayward child of the GWR in the same area was the Oxford, Worcester & Wolverhampton, which was authorized in 1845 to build this 90-mile length on the broad gauge, with narrow added north of Worcester. The OW&W had been promoted, and given a guarantee, by the GWR, but money ran out, work came to a standstill, and a quarrel began. The OW&W considered the GWR's later promotion of the Oxford-Banbury-Birmingham line was competitive and a breach of faith. When the trouble started a majority of shares had been bought up cheaply by a scheming solicitor, John Parson, who saw the chance to fish in troubled waters with profit to himself. The London & North Western was to reach Oxford from Bletchley in 1851, and Parson hoped to force the two large companies to bid against each other for the OW&W. To some extent he succeeded; the original Worcester-London service was worked to Euston via Bletchley, and although legally bound to add broad gauge throughout its length, the OW&W purposely botched and failed to complete the job, and so despite GWR protests it was never used in service. Not that Parson's standard-gauge equipment was so much better. On the other hand, it was not until 1863 that the OW&W became attractive enough for the GWR to propose amalgamation; the L&NW had soon lost

The Midland's largest locomotive by far was the unique 4-cylinder 0-10-0, LMS no. 2290 (BR 58100), which spent its entire life banking trains up the Lickey. Here she shoves a freight out of Bromsgrove (1953)

interest. By then Parson was no longer in control, and the Old Worse & Worse, having absorbed several local lines, had become the West Midland Railway.

The first part of the OW&W to be completed, in October 1850, was from a junction with the Birmingham & Gloucester at Abbotts Wood into Worcester. This was later extended north through Droitwich to join with the B&G main line again at Stoke Works, south of Bromsgrove, forming a loop which was and still is used by Midland trains serving Worcester. The railway reached Wolvercot Junction, just north of Oxford on the GWR, in June 1853, and was linked with the Oxford branch of the L&NW by a spur from Yarnton nearby, opened some months later. Wolverhampton (Low Level) was reached in December 1853, a year before the direct line from Oxford via Birmingham was finished. The branch from Stourbridge Junction to Smethwick, linking the OW&W with Birmingham (Snow Hill) was not added until 1867.

From Oxford to Moreton-in-Marsh the OW&W followed the River Evenlode closely enough to avoid any very heavy construction, and is quite easily graded; from the east the Cotswolds presented no problem. But past Campden the line had to descend into the Vale of Evesham, with a ¾-mile tunnel and 4½ miles of 1 in 100 down to Honeybourne. From there via Worcester and Kidderminster to Stourbridge Junction there are only minor ups and downs, but beyond lay the same hills that Captain Moorsom had disregarded at the Lickey. These involved several miles of 1 in 75 on the original main line to Wolverhampton, while the Birmingham branch climbs past Old Hill at 1 in 50.

As might be imagined from its wandering course on the map, the OW&W as a whole never became a main line; the section north of Worcester proved to have only a local importance, and finally lost its passenger service between Stourbridge Junction and Wolverhampton in 1962. More important altogether was the line from Worcester to Hereford, in which the Midland (and at first the L&NW also) had an interest, because it was a step towards South Wales. This was not an easy line to build, since the Malvern Hills were in the way and a 1¼-mile tunnel was needed through their ancient sandstone at Colwall, another of ¾-mile and a substantial viaduct at Ledbury, and a ruling grade of 1 in 80 each way. It was finally completed in September 1861; the Midland retained running rights after the GWR took over in 1863. Both tunnels still remain

'Jubilee' 4-6-0 no. 45564 'New South Wales' leaving Gloucester with a Bristol-Derby express (1963)

Sparkling clean after overhaul, 28XX class 2-8-0 no. 3812 in Sonning Cutting with a coal train from South Wales (1962)
(*Below*) Heavy 2-8-0 no. 4704 at Acton with a relief Paddington-West of England express. The 47s, Churchward's last design, appeared in 1919; they were intended for fast freight, but were also capable of passenger work, and led active lives until late in dieselization. That only nine of these excellent engines were built is an indication of the post-Churchward stagnation at Swindon (1960)

single-line bottlenecks; the Colwall one was duplicated during the 1880s but in 1926 the original bore became unsafe and had to be abandoned.

So much for the original network of main lines in the West Midlands. There were, however, three later additions, two of which can be called main lines only by some courteous stretching of the definition. The first was the East & West Junction, later the Stratford-on-Avon & Midland Junction, which started as a branch from Fenny Compton (on the GWR Birmingham line) to Stratford in 1873. It burgeoned at each end until by 1881 it linked Broom, on a rural Midland loop off the Birmingham-Bristol line, with Ravenstone Wood, a signalbox in the wilds on another Midland branch, from Bedford to Northampton. The importance of this was that it formed the southernmost link between the London and Bristol tentacles of the Midland, and thereby enabled that company, and later the LMS, to compete after a fashion with the GWR, at times to the extent of two freights a day each way. Trainloads of bananas, for instance, which the LMS got hold of through its joint interest in Avonmouth Docks, were apt to find themselves trundling towards the hungry millions of London by way of Binton, Kineton and Towcester on the SMJ. The company also solicited traffic from the L&NW by a connection at Blisworth, and nearly reached its moment of glory when the Great Central London Extension connected with it at Woodford. The GC dreamed of getting to Birmingham that way, and actually put on a short-lived express from Marylebone to Stratford. Recent years have not been kind to the SMJ; its rather skeletal passenger service vanished in

1952 and most of it has since been closed altogether. The Fenny Compton-Stratford section may, or may not have a future hauling iron ore from the mines near Banbury; a lot of money was spent on a new junction layout at Fenny Compton in 1959, designed for this traffic.

The second wandering rural railway with ambitious ideas was the Banbury & Cheltenham Direct, promoted by an independent company but always worked by the GWR. This line, by extending two branches which ran from the OW&W at Kingham to Chipping Norton and Bourton-on-the-Water, ran along the tops of the Cotswolds for 41 miles from Cheltenham to King's Sutton, just south of Banbury, and was completed in 1887. It had some mountainous grades, starting with an immense climb from Cheltenham to Notgrove at 1 in 62 and worse; like the SMJ, it was smiled on by the Great Central, which after 1906 sent over it a restaurant car express from Newcastle to Cardiff and Barry which survived until 1939. It also had some cut-price viaducts, the condition of which served as the excuse for abandoning passenger service at the eastern end of the line in 1951. A child who had purchased the first ticket from King's Sutton on the opening day turned up as an old man on closing day to buy the last. The service west of Kingham lasted a decade longer; it was, after all, the shortest route from London to Cheltenham (109 miles v. 121 via Swindon) and not by any means always the slowest. But it went in 1962, and now most of the B&CD has ceased to exist.

The last new railway in the area revenged the GWR at last on the Midland for getting to Bristol. There were already two branches serving Stratford-on-

(*Left*) 'Castle' 4-6-0 no. 7007 'Great Western' (one of the last batch built after nationalization) at Wolvercot Siding, Oxford, with a Paddington to Worcester and Hereford express (1952)

Hereford, 1954

will continue is of course another question; we cannot go on being so frightened of that little local difficulty.

Lines in Wessex

The London & South Western Railway was an older-established concern than the GWR by a small margin; the company was incorporated a year earlier, and its first section of track, from the original London terminus at Nine Elms to Woking, was opened in May 1838, two weeks before the GWR began to run from Paddington to Taplow. The line was originally called the London & Southampton, and the change of title took place in 1839, when it had been decided to serve Portsmouth as well. Southampton was only just beginning to be a seaport, but the potentialities of the place were obvious. Steamers to Le Havre and St Malo commenced soon after the railway was completed in May 1840.

Joseph Locke, fresh from building the Grand Junction, was the engineer, and he laid out the line with a magnificence to equal Stephenson or Brunel; the long cutting near Pirbright certainly rivals the GWR's better-known excavation through the same ridge at Sonning, while the long and lofty embankments exceed any on the Bristol road. On the other hand, there were no viaducts of importance, while simple geography and the need to cross a major watershed meant that steeper gradients were unavoidable. Even so, Locke managed the climb out of the Thames Valley to Basingstoke with nothing as steep as 1 in 300, and from there through the chalk downs, over the summit at Litchfield, and down through Winchester to Eastleigh the ruling gradient was only 1 in 250, although this was more or less continuous. On this section Locke was unable to avoid tunnels as completely as he liked, and there are four very short ones. The line ended at the present Southampton Terminus station, 77 miles from Nine Elms; the branch from Eastleigh through Fareham to Gosport (opposite Portsmouth) was opened in November 1841, and the extension from Nine Elms to a better-sited London terminus at Waterloo in July 1848. In addition, an early start was made on local branches in what became London suburbia. Hampton Court, Windsor, Richmond, and Hounslow were all reached by 1850, and L&SW trains were running to Reading from 1856.

The L&SW was a standard gauge line, and mainly because of a more competent fleet of locomotives it soon came to outshine the London & Birmingham in

Avon, apart from the SMJ; from Hatton on the Birmingham line and from Honeybourne on the OW&W, and in 1906 a somewhat cheaply-built 21-mile double line was opened extending the second one along the foot of the Cotswolds from Honeybourne to Cheltenham. The GWR now possessed a route of its own from Birmingham to Bristol, which was improved when the direct line from Birmingham to Stratford via Henley-in-Arden was opened in July 1908. Announcing that this new route to Bristol was only 10 miles longer than the Midland's (99 miles v. 89), the GWR then established a service of expresses over it. These continued until 1962. The passenger service south of Honeybourne is now to all intents and purposes non-existent, but the line still carries considerable through freight, taking this route to avoid the Lickey. How long this

speed and comfort. It was in fact the premier standard-gauge railway until outclassed by the Great Northern a decade later. Since it also pointed towards the West of England, land which the GWR had already marked out as its own broad-gauge kingdom, there was plenty of tinder about to start the long-lived feud between the two companies.

The disputed lands lay between Southampton and Exeter, and the first shots in the war were fired in 1844. The L&SW proposed a two-pronged attack, with a line from Basingstoke to Salisbury and Yeovil, and another (put forward by an independent company) from Southampton to Dorchester. The GWR countered with the Berks & Hants line from Reading to Hungerford, with the eventual idea of extending it somehow to Taunton or Exeter, and the Wilts, Somerset, & Weymouth, which was to hold the fort for the broad gauge with a star-shaped system between the Bristol main line and the south coast. The broad gauge won a partial victory in this first battle, since both its lines were approved while the Basingstoke-Yeovil

scheme was disallowed; but the Southampton & Dorchester went ahead, and was opened by the L&SW in June 1847. Quite cheaply built through rolling country (having been promoted by a gentleman named Castleman, its many curves caused it to be rudely known as Castleman's Corkscrew), it did not follow the course of the present main line through Bournemouth because that city did not exist. Instead it ran farther inland, through Wimborne.

Bournemouth's railway history, in fact, is a little involved. A branch from Ringwood to Christchurch was opened in 1862, and extended to Bournemouth (the present Central station) in 1870; in 1872 it was extended again to Bournemouth West. The same year another branch was opened, from Broadstone to Poole, which was in turn extended to Bournemouth West in 1874. Bournemouth was now on a loop, but a very lightly-built and unimportant one with a ruling grade of 1 in 60. The direct line from Brockenhurst to Christchurch via Sway was not opened until 1888, and the final diversion of the Weymouth main line was not

(*Right*) The five Urie H16 class 4-6-2Ts of 1921 were built by the L&SWR for freight transfer work in the London area, and performed this until diesels took over. No. 30519 leaves the GC yard at Neasden (1957)

A Blisworth-Stratford-on-Avon freight toiling up the grade towards Woodford on the SMJ, behind a 4F 0-6-0 (1952)

The Drummond T9 4-4-0s, built by the L&SWR after 1899, were extremely successful and long-lived engines, with a notable turn of speed. No. 30282 enters Southampton Central with a Portsmouth-Andover train (1951)

carried out until the Holes Bay Curve between Poole and Hamworthy Junction was opened in June 1893. From then on the importance of the Ringwood line steadily declined until it was abandoned in 1964; the original branch to Christchurch went during the 1930s.

Meanwhile the GWR had settled down to consolidate its gains. The Berks & Hants line was duly opened from Reading to Hungerford in 1847, and the branch from Reading to Basingstoke the following year; but things did not go well with the Wilts, Somerset, & Weymouth. The only length this company ever managed to finish was the easy bit down the Avon Valley from Thingley Junction (near Chippenham) to Westbury, in 1848. Then the money ran out and work stopped; the GWR had to buy the WS&W out before anything more was done, and even then construction was slow. The larger company was having financial trouble itself, and the WS&W lines, quite costly to build and serving a wholly rural area, promised to be unprofitable. The strongest motive for pressing on was to keep the standard gauge out of the area, but not quite enough was done to manage this. The connection from Trowbridge to Bathampton and the lines from Westbury to Salisbury and Yeovil were finished in 1856 (the GWR had already been beaten to the latter town by the Bristol & Exeter, which had opened a branch from Taunton), and Weymouth was finally reached in January 1857. This last section in particular was built as cheaply as possible, climbing from Yeovil to Evershot and again out of Weymouth at 1 in 50. Between Dorchester and Weymouth standard gauge had to be added to accommodate the L&SW; in return for this the GWR insisted that broad gauge rails be laid for an equal distance towards Southampton, ending at a point halfway across the Dorset heaths.

But if the GWR had any idea that the broad gauge could get to Southampton through the back door, it was far too late. Opinion had swung round against them, partly over the gauge question and partly due to the sloth with which they had been moving. When it came to consider how to fill the remaining gap west of Yeovil and Weymouth, Parliament knocked the GWR scheme on the head. Military objections provided another reason for doing this. Were Britain to be invaded, the army did not wish to have to face the extra complication of breaks of gauge along the south coast. So the field was left open after all to the L&SW.

Salisbury had been reached back-handedly in 1845 by a branch from Eastleigh; something better than this was needed with a line to Exeter in prospect. So the direct line from Basingstoke through Andover and across a corner of Salisbury Plain was exhumed and opened by stages in 1854–7. Between Salisbury and Yeovil work had been started by an independent company, which was leased, and L&SW trains reached Exeter in July 1860. The extension from Queen Street (now Central) station down the hill at 1 in 37 to the broad gauge encampment at St Davids, without the city walls, took place two years later. The line west of Salisbury, running through some quite hilly country, was fairly heavily graded, with ups and downs more or less continuously at 1 in 80 or 100; on the other hand, curves were easy, high speed running was possible, and

as a result these gradients were not as restrictive as they might have been. With a route from London 172 miles long, compared with the 194 miles of the GWR line through Bristol, the L&SW had a decisive advantage.

However, there later came a time when the GWR, having got rid of the broad gauge, shook off its torpor and decided that it could no longer endure the reproach of being called the Great Way Round. We have already seen how it shortened its line to Birmingham; now the plans for a direct route to Exeter were taken out of the archives, dusted off, and put into effect. The Berks & Hants line, which had been extended from Hungerford to Devizes in 1862, was woken up and doubled, and in 1900 a cut-off was opened from Patney to Westbury. This reduced the distance between Paddington and Weymouth from 163 miles via Chippenham to 154 via Newbury, which compared better, though still not well, with the 143 from Waterloo. But much more important was the opening of the cut-off from Castle Cary on the Weymouth line to Langport and Taunton in July 1906. The distance from Paddington to Exeter now came

The S15 4-6-0s of 1920 were intended for L&SWR main-line freights, but also performed a great deal of passenger work, particularly at summer weekends. No. 30833, one of the 1927 series, at Worting Junction (Basingstoke) with a down West of England freight. (1960)

down to 174 miles, only 2 more than from Waterloo, and things were on a level footing. The GWR route west of Newbury was physically very like the Salisbury & Exeter line, with panting climbs and hell-for-leather descents, but it was if anything somewhat easier, and fast running was helped by the fact that, unlike the L&SW route, it did not pass through any places worth stopping at. So on balance, although the Salisbury road always rivalled the best the GWR could do with its fastest trains, the latter had the edge in overall average speeds because fewer trains made stops.

As we have seen, the L&SW's second original destination, Portsmouth, was at first served by a station across the water at Gosport. This did not last very long, as in September 1848 the town itself was reached by a branch from Fareham to Cosham and thence over a line owned jointly with the London, Brighton, & South Coast. Portsmouth now had two railways to London, but both were pretty long-winded affairs. The LB&SC wandered round for 95 miles

through Brighton and along the coast; the L&SW route via Eastleigh set off in the wrong direction and took 96 miles to get to Waterloo. But the two companies, having pooled the traffic, were happy; after all, they charged by mileage.

Nevertheless, there was a clear case for a Portsmouth Direct Railway. Curiously enough, this was built by a contractor as a speculation, and lay idle for a year after it was completed in 1858. It ran from Godalming, since 1849 the terminus of an L&SW branch from Woking, to Havant on the LB&SC. The snag, apart from spoiling the racket, was that between Havant and Cosham trains would have to run over the LB&SC, which was of course hostile. And so was fought the Battle of Havant, when the L&SW finally took the new line over and tried to run a train, only to find an LB&SC engine in the way and an army of gangers in possession of the junction. However, matters were eventually patched up, the railway was opened in January 1859, and the distance to London came down

The Somerset & Dorset 2-8-0s (above and opposite top)
These engines, although of Midland design and construction (1914) were larger than any in ordinary service on the Midland itself. No. 53806, one of the 1925 batch with large boilers, on a Bath-Templecombe freight near Binegar, banked up the 1 in 50 by a 'Jinty' 0-6-0T (1954)

(*Above*) No. 53810, rebuilt with smaller boiler, climbing to Combe Down tunnel with a Radstock-Bath freight (1954)

(*Left*) 'West Country' Pacific no. 34107 'Blandford' coming across the Midford viaduct with a southbound Somerset & Dorset express (1958)

to 74 miles. The Direct Portsmouth was another railway built on the roller-coaster principle, with a lot of 1 in 80; the unfortunate thing was that in many cases there was no opportunity to get rolling downhill before a climb began. So the line remained an uncommonly tough proposition, especially considering its heavy traffic, for steam traction. It was electrified in 1937.

The L&SW was originally completely cut off from the rest of the country by the belt of broad-gauge territory to the north, and it remains to chronicle the lines which pierced this barrier. First was the GWR's own Reading-Basingstoke branch of 1848, shortly afterwards coupled with that company's line from Oxford to Birmingham. This route had little practical value as a north-south link until the gauge was mixed between Oxford and Basingstoke in 1856 (standard gauge rails were already in position, but little used, from Oxford to Birmingham). The gauge barrier also destroyed the value of the Bristol-Salisbury-Southampton route, where through running was not possible until the WS&W lines were all converted in 1874.

These gauge difficulties gave an additional impetus to the Somerset & Dorset Railway. This started as two local companies, the Somerset Central and the Dorset Central, which owned a broad gauge line from Highbridge on the Bristol & Exeter to Glastonbury and a standard-gauge line from Wimborne on the L&SW to Blandford respectively. With a rather out-of-date belief in the necessary virtues of a coast-to-coast railway, the two companies combined and completed a standard-gauge connecting line via Templecombe and Evercreech in 1863. They also pestered the L&SW into building the Broadstone-Poole-Bournemouth branch, but they soon found that they were not going to get rich simply by joining the Bristol Channel with the English Channel. Since the B&E line to Bristol remained exclusively broad gauge until 1875, their northern terminus was left in mid-air; to remedy this a new line was needed, and they decided to build over the Mendips from Evercreech to Bath, there meeting a branch of the Midland. This was an expensive piece of railway, with a mile-long tunnel under Combe Down, some sizeable viaducts, and long 1 in 50 grades; it was completed in July 1874, and it left the S&D company financially breathless. They had to sell out, and in 1875 they approached the GWR.

But Paddington, as usual, took its time. It considered the matter from this angle and from that, and after sniffing at the S&D with some distaste decided that it was only interested in the northern half; the rest could go to the L&SW for all they cared. When informed of this charitable donation, however, Waterloo tipped off Derby; the Midland octopus was only too willing to extend a tentacle to Bournemouth, and within a matter of days the thing had been done. The S&D was purchased jointly by the L&SW and the Midland, and the GWR was left to complain about it. It had been given a bad fright, and in order to forestall a possible similar Midland coup it hastily made overtures to the Bristol & Exeter. These were more successful, and the B&E was absorbed in 1876.

The Midland connection was the making of the Somerset & Dorset. The railway was overhauled, doubled for most of its length, and turned into an extension of the Derby-Bristol main line. The section over the Mendips was always something of a headache, but right up to 1962 trains ran that way between the Midlands and Bournemouth, swelling into a positive procession at summer weekends. Unfortunately, the gradients, the largely seasonal nature of the traffic, and operational stagnation made the S&D increas-

Salisbury & Exeter line expresses Rebuilt 'Merchant Navy' no. 35011 'General Steam Navigation' on an up West of England train, bending vertically over the summit at Buckhorn Weston, near Templecombe (1959)

'Battle of Britain' no. 34059 'Sir Archibald Sinclair' heads out of Seaton Junction towards Waterloo, while a westbound local waits in the other platform (1964)

63

ingly unprofitable to work, and in that year the through services were all diverted either to the Oxford-Basingstoke or Westbury-Salisbury routes. The object of this was to allow the line to be closed; but this has not proved possible, so far at any rate. The S&D still therefore survives with all the expensive trappings and accessories of nineteenth-century main-line status, an absurdly slow and ill-timed service of local trains, and the knife at its throat. It must be losing a frightful sum. One thinks of the parallel case of the Midland & Great Northern Joint line with some foreboding, yet the analogy is not exact, for no alternative routes are so satisfactory. The S&D's great tragedy, a legacy from the days of the gauge barrier, was that it went to Bath and not Bristol; its usefulness would have been immeasurably increased had it served the more important place. The idea of correcting the mistake, possibly by building a spur to the recently closed but still intact GWR Cheddar Valley branch at Shepton Mallet, still seems worth considering.

45XX 2-6-2T no. 4553 leaving Torquay for Kingswear with a local from Newton Abbot (1925)

Another north-south line was the Didcot, Newbury & Southampton. This was promoted by a local company, but the GWR saw another opportunity to get to Southampton and took it up. It was opened from Didcot to Newbury in 1882 and to Winchester in 1885, but there it stuck; GWR trains had running powers over the L&SW to Southampton for local traffic only. In fact, although the line was slightly shorter between Didcot and Winchester than the Reading-Basingstoke route, its much steeper grades more than outweighed this advantage and it never achieved any importance. Most of it was doubled for wartime traffic in 1943, but the remaining freight trains ceased in 1964 and the line is now closed. It had very little justification as a local route, and even less as a through one.

The last of these cross-country lines was the Midland & South Western Junction, which was completed from Andover Junction on the L&SW main line, through Swindon to Cirencester by 1883. There the money ran out, and it was not until 1891 that it reached through the Cotswolds to Andoversford on the Banbury & Cheltenham Direct, and so gained the Midland at Cheltenham. It was a steeply-graded rural single line, but after it was taken in hand by Sam Fay very smartly worked, and in effect it formed another Midland tentacle, reaching Southampton over the L&SW branch from Andover to Romsey. So well-run was the M&SWJ indeed, and so much the worst of a poor bunch was the GWR Paddington-Cheltenham service, that at one time it was faster to travel from Waterloo via Andover, even though it was 14 miles farther. But the motive for this energy was removed in 1923 when the line was taken over by the GWR. Through trade was diverted via Westbury and Salisbury, and the local pickings were too thin to keep things going. All but two sections retained for freight traffic were abandoned in 1961.

West of Exeter

In 1844 the South Devon Railway was authorized to extend the broad gauge from Exeter to Plymouth, and in 1846 the Cornwall and West Cornwall Railways obtained sanction to continue it westwards to Falmouth and Penzance respectively. But what with one thing and another, construction took rather longer.

The South Devon was quickest off the mark. The line was opened in stages, starting with Exeter to Teignmouth in May 1846, and reaching Laira, on the eastern outskirts of Plymouth, in May 1848. The last

The 'Streamlined' 'King'; no. 6014 'King Henry VII' (considering the bulbosity of her paunch, they should have treated Henry VIII instead) nears Dainton summit with a down express (1938)

couple of miles over Mutley hill and through the town to the terminus at Millbay took almost another year; meanwhile the branch from Newton Abbot to Torquay was opened in December 1848. But in this particular case, there turned out to be more to opening the railway than just building it, for the SDR was the scene of Brunel's most extraordinary error of judgment, the atmospheric system.

In this a large pipe was laid between the rails, and air was pumped out of it by engines stationed every few miles along the track. In principle, trains were then drawn by a piston running along the pipe and attached to a small truck; this involved a continuous airtight valve along the top of the pipe. The point of the idea, apart from abolishing smoke and smuts, was that locomotives could give way to more economical stationary engines. Also, since the complete train weighed less, gradients ceased to be so important, for the power source would not have to be hauled uphill as well as the payload. Several engineers, including Brunel, saw these advantages at once and determined to give the idea a trial. Old George Stephenson remained sceptical, and observed rather acutely, 'Believe me, it's only the stationary engine and rope all over again. The hempen rope failed, and I don't believe the rope of air will do any better.'

The South Devon was particularly tempted by the atmospheric system because on its line heavy gradients were inescapable. But having decided to adopt it,

Brunel altered his original survey and made economies by steepening them even more. As a result the line was carried over the ridge at Dainton, and over the shoulders of Dartmoor to Rattery and Hemerdon, with a ruling grade of 1 in 42 and an absolute maximum of 1 in 36. Sharp curves prevented these banks from being charged at any speed, and they could all have been greatly eased if the line had been intended for locomotive working, Hemerdon in particular by a simple detour to the south.

And in the event far more money than was saved on construction was spent on the atmospherics, which never actually operated except on the level section along the coast between Exeter and Newton Abbot; and there only from September 1847 till June 1848, when the entire installation was abandoned. It was installed, but not used, over Dainton to Totnes, where incidentally a larger diameter pipe would have necessitated the equivalent of an engine change at Newton. Apart from awkwardness in stations, where the pipe was incompatible with points and crossings, the continuous valve could not be kept airtight and before long the flexible leather seal gave way. In places it was eaten by rats, and chemical action where it was riveted to the iron of the pipe caused it to decompose. As a result of this expensive catastrophe, the SDR as an independent company never had the money to improve its main line, even though the expense of locomotive working on such steep gradients gave it a sub-

An up express on the 1 in 36 section of Hemerdon Bank; no. 7801 'Anthony Manor' piloting a 'Castle' (1949)

stantial motive. It was finally taken over by the GWR in 1876, who never improved it either beyond eventually doubling the track. Dieselization in recent years has taken some of the sting of the atmospheric heritage away, but it remains a most unsuitable railway for its traffic.

The history of the Cornwall Railway was very little happier. Shortage of money delayed construction for ten years, but progress was made after the undertaking was leased to the GWR and the other broad gauge companies jointly in 1855. The line was opened from Plymouth to Truro in 1859 and Falmouth in 1863. Running as it did through hilly country parallel with the deeply-indented coastline, it had a saw-toothed gradient profile with ups and downs as steep as 1 in 60, 8 short tunnels and 42 viaducts of assorted sizes, up to 150 feet high and 450 feet long. To save money these were all originally made of timber, which was never common in British practice. Brunel warned that they might be cheap to build but they would be expensive to maintain, and it was so, particularly as his design did not allow sufficient lateral strength to resist side-forces on curves. One particular viaduct on an S-bend kept tending to become Z-shaped, to the alarm of the engineers' department. All were replaced by masonry structures between 1875 and 1934.

Much the most impressive piece of engineering on the line, however, was the Royal Albert Bridge, at Saltash, carrying the rails across the Tamar and into Cornwall. This was, until the parallel road suspension bridge of 1961, the only crossing of the river anywhere near the coast. Brunel's design, with its two main spans 455 feet long giving a clear space of 100 feet above high water, was an unusual one; the track was suspended from two arched tubes. There were some points in common with Brunel's earlier viaduct over the Wye at Chepstow, but the use of tubes was pioneered by Robert Stephenson's Britannia Bridge of 1850 over the Menai Strait. Unfortunately neither of Brunel's bridges were so solid as this. The Chepstow spans were recently rebuilt on conventional lines; the Saltash spans are slightly springy and will not last for ever.

The West Cornwall Railway was a different proposition again. In part it dated from 1838, when it was opened as a standard-gauge locomotive-worked mineral line from Hayle to Redruth; it was completed from Truro to Penzance in 1852, still quite isolated from the rest of the railway system. In a way it remained so even after the Cornwall Railway reached Truro, until 1866, when it was taken over (like the Cornwall) by a joint committee of the broad gauge companies and a third rail added. (Oddly enough, the West Cornwall company remained in legal existence until 1948.) Like everything else west of Newton Abbot, the line was heavily graded. In fact, none of the railway beyond Plymouth could really lay claim to main line status until it was doubled and the train services much improved around the turn of the century. By then, ironically enough, the old Cornish basic in-

66

On the Broad Gauge
(*Above*) Watchet Harbour, Bristol &
Exeter Railway; 4-4-0T no. 74 on
the turntable (c. 1870)

During the last week of broad gauge
working, 'Tornado' roars through
Uphill Cutting with the Paddington-
Plymouth 'Jubilee'. This particular
engine had a very short career; it
was built new (basically to Gooch's
1847 design) in 1888, and not being
convertible to standard gauge had to
be scrapped after 3½ years (1892)

67

dustries of mining and fishing were in decline, and there was little enough to replace them except tourists.

As early as 1866 the GWR Chairman, Sir Daniel Gooch, had declared that the gradual extinction of the broad gauge was company policy, and Devon and Cornwall were its last strongholds. Mixed gauge was completed from London to Bristol in April 1875 and to Exeter in March 1876; no solely broad gauge branches of any importance then remained east of Exeter, and the third rail was retained only for the benefit of traffic going beyond. In 1878 there were ten broad gauge workings scheduled from Paddington every day; two freights, seven passenger trains, and the one Windsor local normally used by Sir Daniel on his daily journey to the office. One reason why broad gauge lingered on in the west was that until 1889 the Cornwall Railway remained legally independent, and its directors made difficulties about the proposal to replace the timber viaducts with masonry ones wide enough only for double standard track; the disagreement inhibited any action. But after the GWR took over that year, no new non-convertible broad gauge rolling stock was built; the final execution of the broad gauge in May 1892, when the whole line from Exeter to Penzance was converted during a long week-end, was triggered off by quadrupling through Twyford and Reading, where the extra width could not be spared.

It took twenty years for the GWR to penetrate Cornwall, but the L&SW took even longer. As part of the gauge skirmish in 1845 they had proposed a Cornwall & Devon Central line, and with this in mind quietly bought up the little Exeter & Crediton and the remote and ancient Bodmin & Wadebridge railways. The E&C had started in 1851 as a broad gauge branch of the Bristol & Exeter, the L&SW being no nearer than Salisbury; the B&W had been running since 1834. Meanwhile, the broad gauge North Devon

Railway was opened down the Taw Valley from Crediton to Barnstaple in 1854; but the management of the GWR and its allies being what it was the L&SW, after its arrival at Exeter (St. David's) in 1862 had no difficulty in seducing this company as well when it claimed the E&C; and so standard gauge reached Barnstaple in 1863. The extension from Barnstaple to Ilfracombe was opened in 1874; unlike the rest of the line from Exeter, this had ferocious gradients, climbing at 1 in 40 to a summit at Mortehoe and then dropping at 1 in 36 for over two miles into Ilfracombe, in spite of which the station was still perched on the hillside several hundred feet above the town.

The L&SW's more important objective was, of course, Plymouth, and this was reached by stages. Starting at Yeoford, on the Barnstaple line, and passing Okehampton and the north slope of Dartmoor, the track was completed to Lydford in 1874. Standard gauge was added to the South Devon's Launceston branch beyond Lydford two years later, and so the L&SW reached Plymouth at first via Laira. In 1890 their access was much improved by the opening of the better-graded and double-tracked line from Lydford through Bere Alston to Plymouth (North Road). This was built by the Plymouth, Devonport & South Western Junction company. In 1891, after the opening of the new terminal at Friary, competition began in earnest. The L&SW line from Exeter to Plymouth was then 58 miles long, compared with 52 by the GWR; but the easier gradients via Okehampton (maximum 1 in 77) were some compensation. The L&SW ran through much wilder country; the GWR had its dramatic bit along the foot of the cliffs between Dawlish and Teignmouth, but was in farmland most of the way, while the L&SW after crossing the spindly iron Meldon Viaduct really got up onto the moor at Bridestowe and had another scenic section winding along the hillside above the Tamar nearer Plymouth.

The Plymouth-Paddington 'Mayflower' express running along the cliffs near Teignmouth, headed by no. 6028 'King George VI' (1958)

Both companies shared the same stations at Exeter (St Davids) and Plymouth (North Road), and in each case their trains for London left in opposite directions.

Farther west, the L&SW reached Launceston in 1886, Wadebridge in 1895 (so linking at last with its forgotten outpost), Bude in 1898 and Padstow in 1899. But North Cornwall never had the same traffic potential as the south, and beyond Okehampton all these lines are of local importance only.

South-East England

The first (or, to be accurate, the first public, steam-powered, and permanent) railway in London was the London & Greenwich, a 3½-mile affair built on a continuous viaduct, and opened from Spa Road (near London Bridge) to Deptford on 8 February 1836. (London Bridge itself was reached the following December, but the last half-mile into Greenwich took nearly another three years.) In June 1839 the London & Croydon Railway was opened from the L&G at Corbets Lane for 9 miles south to what is now West Croydon; it was for the most part laid along the bed of a canal, which explains not only the 3 miles of 1 in

100 up to Forest Hill, replacing a number of locks, but also perhaps the fact that the first station at Norwood Junction was named Jolly Sailor.

Beyond Croydon two companies were active. The South Eastern Railway was authorized to build from the L&C at Norwood to Dover through Oxted, Edenbridge, Tonbridge, and Ashford, while the London & Brighton proposed to run south from Norwood via Redhill, Three Bridges, and Haywards Heath. Glumly contemplating the expense of two closely parallel lines across the North Downs, both boards decided it would be wiser to come to an agreement. The South Eastern was therefore altered to start from Redhill, using the L&B through the Merstham Gap, and as its contribution to the expense of this section the SER purchased the Coulsdon-Redhill length in 1842. Both companies then allowed each other's trains free passage. This unusually simple system of joint ownership only applied from Norwood to Redhill; after the Brighton company bought up the Croydon line in 1846 the South Eastern had to continue to pay tolls between Norwood and Corbets Lane on the old basis. Fair play here was more or less guaranteed by the fact that the South Eastern had in 1845 purchased the

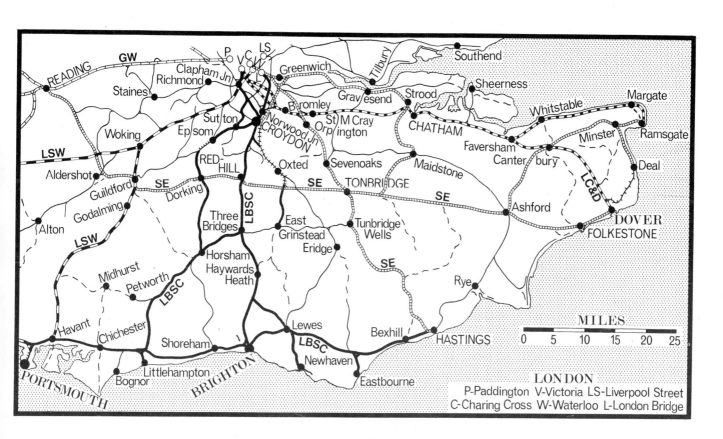

London & Greenwich, on which the Brighton for a long time (until it built parallel tracks) depended to reach London Bridge. It was all a bit complicated.

The London & Brighton was completed in September 1841. It was a much better-built affair than the Croydon line it depended on, and in fact was the best laid-out main line in the South-East. It had a maximum gradient of 1 in 264, an impressive viaduct over the Ouse Valley south of Balcombe, and several substantial tunnels through the downs, notably at Merstham (1 mile) and Clayton (1¼ miles). Business was at first rather slack; the lovely but deserted Sussex countryside offered so little traffic (the 1843 timetable listed only 7 trains a day) that it seemed reasonable to suppose that no other railway from London to the South Coast would ever be needed. The company therefore resolved to serve the seaside towns by building east and west from Brighton, and in 1846 it changed its name to the London, Brighton, & South Coast. But traffic soon grew (by 1852 there were 12 trains each way daily, the best doing the journey non-stop in 70 minutes: today's electrics, considered fast by some, take 60) and in spite of the construction of parallel routes the main line eventually had to be quadrupled as far as the Balcombe Tunnel. Part of this work was the 'Quarry Line', opened in 1900 through a 1¼-mile tunnel parallel to the old route south of Coulsdon and avoiding the complications of Redhill station. Further widening was avoided by electrification, completed to Brighton in 1933.

The Coast Lines, since they were not expected to handle the same business and in any case faced fewer obstacles, were less expensive to build. The section west of Brighton to Shoreham was actually the first part of the LB&SC to open, in May 1840; it reached Chichester in June 1846 and Portsmouth in June 1847. As we have seen, just over a year later the L&SW arrived in Portsmouth from the other direction and bought a half interest in the last few miles from the junction at Cosham. The short extension, also jointly owned, from Portsmouth & Southsea to Portsmouth Harbour was not opened until 1876, and the now important branches to Littlehampton and Bognor were completed in 1863 and 1864 respectively.

East of Brighton, the railway cut inland at first, crossing the valley above the town on another major viaduct, and later getting involved in a 3-mile descent at 1 in 88 from Falmer down to Lewes. For most of the rest of the way it followed the coastal plain, like the Portsmouth branch. It reached Hastings in June 1846,

and the short cut from the main line at Keymer Junction to Lewes, together with the branch from Lewes to Newhaven, opened the following year. The Newhaven-Dieppe ferry service commenced at the same time. Eastbourne, now such a considerable place, was not felt to be worth serving until 1871, when the branch from Polegate was opened.

The LB&SC continued contentedly with its T-shaped system for some years, gently filling in a few gaps by building branch lines. But it was given a rude shock when the Portsmouth Direct railway opened in 1859, and decided that it needed short cuts as well. There was already a branch running westwards from Three Bridges, which had reached Horsham in 1848 and Petworth in 1859; a new link was put in to join this at Pulborough with the coast line at Ford in 1863, saving ten miles compared with going round through Brighton, and the LB&SC was back in the London-Portsmouth business. It still had some disadvantage in distance, but a competitive express service was maintained until after 1923. Then the bulk of the traffic was concentrated on the Waterloo route, although a reasonably fast service is still maintained for the sake of intermediate towns.

Trains from London Bridge to Portsmouth later had a choice of two routes, via Three Bridges or via Dorking, between Norwood and Horsham; both were the same length. The original Croydon line, having been extended from West Croydon to Epsom in 1847 and to Leatherhead (over track jointly owned with the L&SW) in 1859, was continued to Horsham in 1867. It was not built with any very heavy flow of traffic in mind, and had some steep gradients, notably the start southbound from Dorking on 1 in 80. But by means of the connection from Streatham to Sutton, it was more directly served from Victoria than the older line, and so eventually it became the more important.

Building a short cut across the eastern arm of the T was an equally involved business. Branches had been completed from Three Bridges and Lewes to Groombridge (where they joined) and Tunbridge Wells by 1868, while another, the single-track 'Cuckoo Line' from Eridge to Hailsham, gave access to Eastbourne in 1880. But there was no direct link with London until 1884, when the Croydon-Oxted-Edenbridge line, originally proposed by the South Eastern in 1836, was finally built as a joint SER-LB&SCR venture; and 1888, when the connection from Hurst Green (near Oxted) to Groombridge was opened. Although this railway as built had steeper gradients and lighter

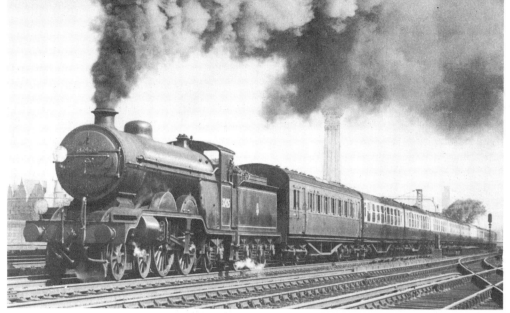

Pride of the LB&SC's express passenger fleet were the eleven Marsh Atlantics of 1904-11, more or less direct copies of the Great Northern engines, and the last of their type in service in Britain. No. 32425 'Trevose Head' crosses the Grosvenor Bridge with a relief boat train from Victoria to Newhaven (1951)

The K class 2-6-0s of 1913 were the LB&SC's principal freight engines; nearing the end of her days, no. 32347 enters Oxted with a weedkiller train (1960)

works than the original specification, the 1¼-mile tunnel north of Oxted remained unavoidable. It provided a roundabout way of getting to Brighton, still used by regular through trains, but oddly enough no advantage has ever normally been taken of the fact that it was the most direct route from London to Eastbourne; the distance by Oxted and the Cuckoo line was six miles shorter than through Lewes.

The other arm of the Oxted line, the sole property of the LB&SC, ran from Edenbridge to East Grinstead; it was later extended via Horsted Keynes to Haywards Heath, where it met again with the main line. This was a useful diversionary loop in preelectrification days; returning Brighton excursions could be shunted out of the way at Haywards Heath and forgotten until in the generous fullness of time

they rolled up shrieking at the South Croydon signals. But no great amount of local traffic developed and the line was closed south of East Grinstead in 1955. It was closed again, legally this time, three years later.

While all this construction was going on out in the country, the LB&SC was also establishing a suburban network in South London. The most important part of this had been the building of a second main line entry and another major terminus, Victoria. The West End of London & Crystal Palace Railway had been opened from Norwood Junction, via Crystal Palace (Low Level) and Clapham Junction to Battersea, on the south side of the river, in 1858; the Victoria Station & Pimlico extended this across the bridge and down the hill into the new terminus in 1860. The London, Chatham & Dover Railway also

BR Standard Class 5 4-6-0 no. 73082 leaving Micheldever with a London-Southampton parcels train (1962)

(*Right*) LB&SC B2X 4-4-0 no. 321 'John Rennie' smoking out Bognor as she departs with the 8.8 a.m. to London Bridge (1919)

had an interest in both these companies, while even the Great Western had a share in the VS&P. Perhaps it had been going through a phase of feeling lonely out in the slummy wilds of Paddington; certainly it wanted a foothold in this new station a stone's throw from Buckingham Palace. And so the odd sight was seen of broad gauge trains wandering round over the West London line past Kensington and Clapham Junction into Victoria. They never did very well. But the LB&SC and the LC&D, in whose natural territory the new line lay, prospered mightily, and Victoria in due course became London's largest terminus (but not its most beautiful).

The LB&SC built several other connections with the Victoria line, notably the cut-off from the WEL&CP at Balham to Croydon via Thornton Heath in 1862, completing what is now the Brighton main line. But it was rather a patchwork job, as anybody who has seen the television test film 'London to Brighton in Four Minutes' will realize. All the way through the suburbs, whenever a Victoria-Brighton train comes to a junction, it seems to take the more sharply curved route, and most particularly so at Balham. The exit on the Portsmouth line via Dorking, turning off just south of Balham at Streatham, is even worse, as trains have to slow down to 20 mph at Mitcham Junction to curve in and out of the single-track branch following the old Surrey Iron Railway of 1803. However, when these lines were built nobody really expected that Victoria would supplant London Bridge as the principal terminus; this came about because of the westwards shift of London's commercial centre of gravity.

We have already seen how the South Eastern came to share the Brighton line as far as Redhill. The first section of the SER main line proper was opened from Redhill to Tonbridge in May 1842; it reached Folkestone in June 1843 and Dover in February 1844. For the most part it ran through very easy flat country,

and once round the curve at Redhill was very nearly straight for 45 miles to Ashford. Beyond, there was quite a lot of the ruling gradient of 1 in 250, climbing to a summit near Sandling and then down through Folkestone, over the 100-foot high Foord Viaduct, and along the flanks of the chalk cliffs to Dover. On this spectacular last stretch there were three tunnels, two of them lengthy; over a mile long at Abbotts Cliff and ¾ mile at Shakespeare Cliff. Ferry services from Dover to France were older than the railway, of course; they will eventually be replaced by the Channel Tunnel, on which work was stopped in 1883 by some more than usually bone-headed militarists, and which nobody has yet been enlightened enough actually to restart. The branch down to Folkestone Harbour was opened for freight at the same time as the main line, but since it descended at 1 in 37 for a mile passenger trains kept well clear of it until 1849. From then until electrification in 1961 it formed a kind of miniature Lickey, with numerous small tank engines of one sort or another pushing and pulling at the heavy boat trains, to the consternation of those inhabiting the trim houses on either side of the tracks.

Branches followed, some of which later became important. Paddock Wood to Maidstone was opened in 1844; Maidstone had been on the main line of an earlier Dover railway proposal, but was shunned by the South Eastern since it lay in a valley which would have to be crossed by fierce gradients. (This line was finally built by the London, Chatham & Dover in 1884.) A longer branch from Ashford reached Ramsgate and Margate through Canterbury in 1846, throwing off a spur from Minster to Deal; and Ashford and Hastings were linked along the coast in 1851. Tonbridge to Tunbridge Wells was opened in 1845, and pushed through to Hastings by 1852; this section was steeply graded, with a lot of 1 in 100 and considerably worse than that on the first part of the climb out of Tonbridge. Much more damaging than this, though,

N class no. 31407, an SE&C design of 1917, passing Abbotscliff with a Margate-Maidstone local (1959)

was the fact that in an effort to economize the tunnels on this line were built to a sub-standard loading gauge, so specially narrow locomotives and rolling stock have always been needed to work it. In remote sidings all over Europe one may therefore come across vans and wagons lettered 'Not to Work Between Tonbridge and West St. Leonards via Battle'. What the average Italian or Czech railwayman thinks of this is perhaps best not enquired into. It seems extraordinary that in this day and age, with all the potentialities of automatic and remote-controlled signalling, that the nuisance has not been abolished simply by singling the short stretches of line concerned.

Two other lines completed the South Eastern system. The Reading, Guildford & Reigate, opened between 1847 and 1849 and purchased in 1852, which depended on running powers over the L&SW for its central section through Guildford, was a fairly bucolic concern, with a lot of 1 in 100 grade over the downlands west of Redhill. Its main importance was that it prolonged the SER main line around London towards

the north and west, forming a useful cross-country link (although again one that could not function properly until the GWR added standard gauge to its lines beyond Reading). The other was the North Kent line, which had its nucleus in the unsuccessful Thames & Medway canal, from Gravesend to Strood. This concern saw the writing on the wall and converted its $2\frac{1}{4}$-mile tunnel at Strood (which had a short open cutting midway to allow barges to pass in daylight) into a railway in 1845. The SER purchased it two years later, and reached it at Gravesend from London in 1849 by a line running via Blackheath, Woolwich, and Dartford. (This had to go through a mile-long tunnel round the back of Greenwich, since trains were forbidden to come closer lest they disturb the delicate instruments at the Royal Observatory; but the astronomers having moved elsewhere, the direct line was opened in 1878.) The loop was completed by a link from Strood to Maidstone in 1856, connecting with the branch from Paddock Wood.

So matters rested for some years; the South

Certain SE&CR 4-4-0s continued in main line service until electrification. D1 class no. 31739, built in 1901 and rebuilt in 1921, with a Dover-bound local in Folkestone Warren (1960)

Eastern had Kent to itself. But it was a poor and un-enterprising company; its reputation has always suffered from the fact that it deposited Charles Dickens in the river at Staplehurst in 1865, but it was none too fragrant earlier. It took its customers a long way out of their way through Redhill, charged accordingly, and frequently added insult to this injury. People longed to give it a shaking.

Eventually somebody succeeded. The East Kent Railway had been formed to build a branch from the South Eastern at Strood to Faversham, opened in 1858. But the company thought that it was capable of greater things, and proposed to extend in both directions; it therefore changed its name to the London, Chatham & Dover in 1859. It reached east beyond Faversham to Canterbury and Herne Bay in 1860, Dover in 1861 (through the 1¼-mile Lydden tunnel near Shepherds Well), and Margate and Ramsgate Harbour in 1863.

Westwards, getting to London was more complicated. We have seen how the line was built between Norwood and Victoria, and noted that the LC&D shared in this project with the LB&SC. By means of three other subsidiary companies the LC&D got from Rochester via St Mary Cray, Bromley, and Beckenham Junction to the WEL&CP at Norwood in October 1860. This gave it the competitive route to London it wanted, but not a very good one since its stake in the line west of Norwood was small. So another, and wholly-owned, railway was built from Beckenham Junction via Herne Hill to Battersea and Victoria through the 1¼-mile Penge tunnel, and opened in July 1863; the branch from Herne Hill through Blackfriars to Holborn Viaduct, and through Snow Hill to the Metropolitan Railway and its northern connections followed shortly after. (The alternative route from Shortlands to Brixton via the Catford Loop dates from 1892; one motive for building this is stated to be that J.S. Forbes, the Chairman of the LC&D during its construction, believed that the Penge tunnel would eventually collapse.)

The LC&D had now, with the friendly help of the

A Charing Cross-Tonbridge local between Orpington and Chelsfield, amply powered by ex-SER F class 4-4-0 no. 172 and a C class 0-6-0 (1927)

LB&SC, the makings of yet another South London suburban network. Its main line was a pretty lightly-built affair, with a saw-toothed profile and a ruling gradient of 1 in 100, but it caused considerable distress to the South Eastern, who set about a programme of improvements in order to compete with it. There were two main plans to this end. The most important was the direct route from Lewisham to Tonbridge via Sevenoaks, a major piece of construction which shortened the main line by 13 miles when it was opened in April, 1868. It cut straight through the Downs with a ruling gradient of 1 in 120, a 1½-mile

tunnel at Polhill and another of 2 miles south of Sevenoaks, and except for the curve at Tonbridge where it joined the old main line it was well suited for fast running. The other new venture was a counter to the LC&D's multitude of London terminals; a short but extraordinarily expensive extension from London Bridge to Waterloo, Cannon Street, and perhaps the best-sited of all London stations at Charing Cross, opened in January 1864. The SER did not have to bear quite the whole burden of this line, as the L&SW until 1919 ran a number of local trains through Waterloo to Cannon Street by means of a rather

The London-bound 'Golden Arrow' on the 1 in 37 climb from Folkestone Harbour, powered by three ex-GWR 57XX 0-6-0Ts. These engines were imported to work the line during the interval between the expiry of the old SE&C tanks and electrification (1960)

Most Continental and Irish ferries have long been owned by the railways. The Calais steamer leaving Dover (Admiralty Pier, before the Marine station was built) around 1900

77

'Schools' class 4-4-0 no. 30920 'Rugby' leaves Cannon Street with the 5.5 p.m. to Hastings (1958)

A view from the roof of Waterloo station, looking towards Charing Cross, in 1946. A brand new 'West Country' Pacific, still unnamed, is approaching with a train for the Kent Coast

'King Arthur' 4-6-0 no. 764 'Sir Gawain' heading a down Continental express on the spur between the LC&D and SER main lines at Bickley. This engine, one of the 1925 batch built for the South Eastern section, with 8-wheeled tenders, is in its original state without smoke deflectors (1926)

awkward single line connection, swept away when the station was rebuilt.

There was a time when town planners and other aesthetes were offended by Charing Cross, declaring it to be illogical that any southern railway should terminate north of the river. It was proposed to abolish it altogether in the 1944 London Plan. Fortunately, the enormous practical advantage (however illogical) of trains crossing bridges was later realized. If only a few northern lines had ended on the south side of the river, the South Bank would not so long have remained such a slum.

The SER and the LC&DR having duly dug in, battle commenced; there was a long period of desperate competition. It was a war which neither company was rich enough to win; they spent so much on building competitive branches and running competitive trains that there was nothing left to provide the plain honest good service which the public really wanted, and which various pundits still assure us

results infallibly from competition. Finally the LC&D was on the brink of bankruptcy, and there was an armistice; from 1899 the two concerns were worked as one under the name 'South Eastern & Chatham Railway', although there was no legal amalgamation. Some of the competitive mileage was closed; more eventually became profitable as population increased. And some years later there was one of the all too rare copybook examples of how to rationalize competing facilities.

This occurred in the Margate and Ramsgate area, with a scheme carried out by the Southern Railway in 1926. Previously each town had had two separate railways; Ramsgate had two terminals, one serving the original SER line from Ashford together with the shuttle-worked branch to Margate Sands, the other the LC&D line from Faversham. At Margate the LC&D had a through station and the SER a terminus; and there were two parallel lines between the towns. In 1926 a new connection was opened at Ramsgate,

79

LB&SC Stroudley 'Gladstone' class 0-4-2 no. 198 leaving Victoria; these engines, originating in 1882, lasted on main-line passenger duties until electrification in the 1930s (c. 1925)

(*Opposite above*) Ex-L&SWR S15 class 4-6-0 no. 30502, one of the original series of 1920, at Litchfield (Hants) on a Southampton freight

(*Opposite below*) The South Eastern & Chatham 'N' class 2-6-0s of 1917 were a very successful mixed-traffic design. No. 31401 leaves Moreton Cutting yard, Didcot, with a freight for Southampton (1964)

both old stations and the SER shuttle abandoned, and a new loop replaced two separate stub-ends, giving both a great economy and an improvement in public utility. The moral of this is that the surgeon's knife was not the only instrument used; to get the best results one must be prepared to spend something too.

A word about London suburban services. Unlike the railways north of the Thames (except the GN, GE, and LT&S), which on the whole did as little as possible to encourage them, the southern companies really went after suburban passengers. They had, after all, very little choice; they could not enter the jammy long-haul business because the sea was in the way. The London & Greenwich was nothing if not a suburban line, even when it was built; the Croydon company's experiments with atmospheric traction in 1845–7 were intended purely to handle local travellers, and the LC&D's London Extension depended on them. Except for the L&SW, whose lines were mainly in easy country, all these South London railways were in hilly districts, built on the cheap and very difficult to work, with steep climbs, sharp curves, and frequent stations and flat junctions. The companies did their best with steam, but by the turn of the century it

wasn't good enough, as a rising tide of complaints and (more to the point) desertions to the new electric trams emphasized. Looking at a picture of a typical LB&SC or SE&C suburban train of the period, a short rake of four- or six-wheeled bouncers hauled by a tiny tank engine, one can see why not. Electrification was the only answer; it was started by the Brighton company (using high-voltage AC and overhead) in 1909, and by the L&SW (with DC 3rd rail) in 1915. After 1923 the Southern Railway rather short-sightedly, as we now see, standardized on the L&SW system and had almost completed the work by 1939.

The exception was the Oxted group of lines, still not converted yet. There is an interesting example of the effects of this at Warlingham, south of Croydon. Here steam (and now diesel) trains wander off up a pleasant green valley towards East Grinstead, regarded only by cows and the occasional stockbroker's cottage. A stone's throw away the electrified Caterham branch is followed into the next valley by continuous lines of houses. The facts that the Oxted line is not electrified, and that it serves the least-developed part of London's southern approaches, are not unrelated; the second is the consequence of the first.

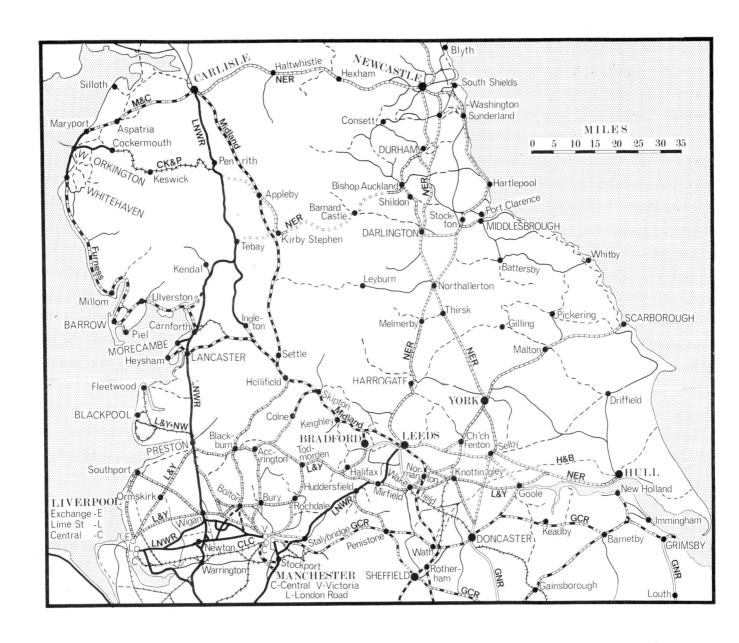

4 The North and North-East

Lancashire and South Yorkshire

Since the Liverpool & Manchester was (by a short head) the first mainline railway in the world, it was necessarily also the first main-line railway in Lancashire. But it was still some way from being a modern railway. At first it was partly dependent on cable haulage through the tunnels to the station and the docks at Liverpool, and on the two 1 in 91 inclines leading up to the summit level at Rainhill, although it was not long before locomotives proved able to tackle these unaided. It also originally suffered from the fact that the distance between the tracks on its double line was only 4 ft 8½ in, the same as the gauge. This caused dangerously tight clearances between trains, and contributed to the famous accident on the opening day when the statesman William Huskisson was killed. The distance was not increased to the present none too generous British standard of six feet until the 1850s.

The L&M remained independent for only fifteen years; it was absorbed, together with several of its connecting lines, by the Grand Junction in 1845, and so passed in 1846 to the London & North Western. Its original success had been due to the fact that passenger traffic was very much greater than forecast; this was fortunate, as freight took some years to build up to the estimates. Until branches and feeders had been built in sufficient numbers the established canal system, tapping remoter areas, remained more convenient. But it was not long before the L&M acquired its branches. One of them, the Bolton & Leigh, was in fact two years older, having been opened to freight in 1828. It was extended by the Kenyon & Leigh Junction company to meet the L&M at Kenyon Junction in 1831. By 1832 other companies had built branches to St Helens, Warrington, and Wigan.

The first railway to form a major extension of the

L&M was the Manchester & Leeds. George Stephenson surveyed the route for this in 1830; it was a very indirect line, striking at first north from Manchester via Rochdale to the 1¾-mile Summit Tunnel at Littleborough; then from Todmorden westwards down the Calder Valley through Sowerby Bridge and Mirfield to Wakefield. Leeds lay north of this town, but to avoid the last spur of the hills the line swung round to the west to pass through Normanton. Since the North Midland Railway was about to build the final 11 miles from here to Leeds, the M&L ended, with statutory running powers on to its destination. The 51 miles from Manchester to Normanton were completed in March 1841. In compensation for its lack of direction, the line was, considering the nature of the country, well graded, with a maximum of 1 in 150 eastbound and 1 in 180 westbound.

The original Manchester terminus of the M&L was at Oldham Road; in 1844 it was extended down the 1 in 54 Miles Platting incline, briefly worked by a stationary engine, to a new station at Hunt's Bank called Victoria, where it met a new spur of the Liverpool & Manchester end-on. A third partner at Victoria station was the Manchester, Bolton & Bury, which had been running from another isolated terminus at Salford since 1838. The successors of the L&M seemed a little half-hearted about the place, for later on they built another station, Exchange, just short of the boundary, and linked it to Victoria by a long platform. The result of all this was the curious layout of the present Victoria-and-Exchange station, which has a junction in the middle and three sets of terminal platforms facing in three different directions.

Since a series of amalgamations and planned extensions had made its original title inapposite, the Manchester & Leeds in 1847 changed its name to the Lancashire & Yorkshire Railway. In 1848 it opened a 28-mile line from Wakefield via Pontefract to the

Two LNER workhorses Gresley 'V2' class 2-6-2 no. 60828 on a southbound Great Central freight passing Staverton Road (1965)

and Peppercorn 'K1' class 2-6-0 no. 62021 crossing the viaduct at Alnmouth with a coal train (1964)

Humber port of Goole, linking Manchester with the east coast. There was also a branch from the new line to the Midland at Methley, and another from Knottingley to Askern, where by means of an end-on connection with the Great Northern, L&Y trains could reach Doncaster. Another important branch, opened in July 1844, was from Sowerby Bridge to Halifax, originally up a gradient of 1 in 45 but later diverted and eased to the present 1 in 118. This line pointed directly towards Leeds, and although the hills stood in the way it was seen to offer a chance of shortening the route very considerably with a ruling gradient no worse than 1 in 100. It was therefore extended to Low Moor in July 1848, and Bradford shortly afterwards; the line from Bowling Junction (near Low Moor) to Leeds was finally built by another company, the Leeds, Bradford, & Halifax, and opened in August 1855. The L&Y had running powers over this length, which continued even after the LB&H was taken over by the Great Northern ten years later. Leeds was only 49 miles from Manchester this way, instead of 62 via Normanton.

Another strategic branch, opened in 1850, was from Huddersfield to Penistone, where it met the Manchester, Sheffield & Lincolnshire and so linked with the GNR route to London. This branch was reached

from the Calder Valley main line near Mirfield by means of running powers over the London & North Western.

The L&NW had reached the area by purchasing (before they opened in 1849) the Leeds, Dewsbury & Manchester, and Huddersfield & Manchester companies. Together these ran from Stalybridge (linked to Manchester by an MS&L branch only at first), through the 3-mile Standedge tunnel to Huddersfield and Dewsbury; and then through the 2-mile Morley tunnel to Leeds. For some 3 miles west of Heaton Lodge Junction, through Mirfield, L&NW trains had running powers over the L&Y Calder Valley main line. This was the shortest route of all from Manchester to Leeds, 43 miles compared with the L&Y's minimum of 49; on the other hand, the gradients were somewhat steeper, reaching 1 in 105. When it took the scheme over, the L&NW added a connection from Heaton Norris (just north of Stockport on the Crewe-Manchester line), to Stalybridge, to give a better link with the south and avoid Manchester; this was also opened in 1849. Having reached Leeds, the L&NW was for once satisfied and only dabbled in plans for further extension into the north-east; the only other line it actually built in the area was a second route between Huddersfield and Leeds via Cleckheaton in

Ex-LNWR 7F 0-8-0 no. 49234, of the 1912 series, on a Yorkshire-bound freight leaving Newton Heath (Manchester) on the L&Y main line via Todmorden. This class remained in service until 1964 (1950)

1900. But although this made it possible to avoid using any other company's tracks it never achieved any great importance and no longer carries passengers.

The L&NW's interests in Lancashire were based on the Liverpool & Manchester and the north-south main line which bisected it, together with the various chords and hypotenuses which joined them. It also possessed a second route from Liverpool to Manchester, wandering round through Warrington and Widnes, but this was chiefly useful for local freight. The company's only other major interest was Bolton, where it had its own terminus at Great Moor Street, serving the old branch to Kenyon Junction and a later competitive line to Manchester through Eccles. Both were closed during the 1950s, part of the former being retained for freight.

The Lancashire & Yorkshire soon felt that there was room for another railway between Liverpool and Manchester, and set about providing it. The Manchester, Bolton & Bury, which as we have seen shared Victoria station, was taken over in 1846, and in 1848 was extended to Liverpool via Wigan. At the same time another line was built east of Bolton through Bury to join the original Manchester & Leeds at Castleton, south of Rochdale, providing a short cut from Liverpool to South Yorkshire. The L&Y route from Liverpool (Exchange) to Manchester (Victoria) was 40 miles long, which compared ill with the L&M's 31 miles; but by 1864 it had been shortened to 37 miles with the building of the Wigan avoiding line and the Salford-Hindley chord, avoiding Bolton via Walkden. By dint of hard running the L&Y managed

to equal the L&NW's time between the two cities.

Southport was another L&Y objective; it was a pleasant coastal town where company directors and owners, and similar captains of industry liked to live, and there was money to be made out of hauling them first class between bed and boardroom. The Liverpool, Crosby & Southport, opened in 1850, was taken over in 1855, and access to Manchester was provided by a branch from Wigan opened in 1848. The LC&S line was electrified very early, in 1904, and is still busy; the recent proposal to close it was not very deeply considered, unless perhaps as some form of polite blackmail on the local authorities.

The complications of the Lancashire & Yorkshire system in north-east Lancashire look quite fearsome on the map, but they can be sorted into three lines radiating northwards from Manchester and one running eastwards from Preston. First of all was the route from Manchester to Preston, via Bolton; this was completed in 1843 by the Bolton & Preston company. Next was the Blackburn, Darwen & Bolton, opened in 1848 and taken over in 1857, by which time it had changed its name to the Bolton, Blackburn, Clitheroe and West Yorkshire. This was a difficult railway, with a considerable climb (at 1 in 73) to the summit at Entwhistle and a tunnel $1\frac{1}{4}$ miles long. By 1880 it had been extended north of Blackburn for 23 miles via Clitheroe to Hellifield, where it joined the Midland and so became part of a rival route from Manchester to Scotland. This later section was not quite so heavily graded, but passed through much less populous

Ex-Lancashire & Yorkshire 0-8-0 no. 52906 (built in 1916) leaving Newton Heath shortly before its withdrawal in 1950. This was probably the last train worked on the L&Y main line by one of these engines.

Although purely L&Y in outline, the Hughes 'Dreadnought' 4-cylinder 4-6-os were actually built for the L&NW and LMS after the amalgamation. Here the last survivor leaves Manchester (Victoria) for Blackpool (1950)

country and finally lost its passenger trains in 1961.

The third north-south line, from Clifton Junction on the Manchester & Bolton to Accrington via Bury, was started by two concerns which amalgamated (with others as well) during construction to form the East Lancashire Railway. This company was also responsible for the line running inland from Preston via Blackburn, Accrington, and Burnley to Colne, and from Rose Grove (just west of Burnley) to the old L&Y main line at Todmorden. All these railways were built between 1846 and 1849. They all ran through hilly country and none could be described as easy, but far the most difficult was the Bury-Accrington section, which included gradients as steep as 1 in 38 on the climb to Baxenden. On the other hand, the rest of the East Lancashire, from Preston to Liverpool (Exchange)

via Ormskirk, was practically flat. The ELR was amalgamated with the L&Y in 1859.

One is normally quite safe in describing a railway as a line, not an area, but the L&Y was an exception to this rule. It formed a positive network, most of which had to be treated as main lines. It served a densely populated district, with many towns which needed to be linked equally with the two great centres of commerce, Liverpool and Manchester. It was therefore a singularly difficult operating and administrative problem, and for a long time it seemed quite to defeat its management. Economists were called in to give advice, and their advice was followed; as a result its slow, antiquated, unpunctual and dilapidated trains became a byword and a reproach. However, around 1880 the company pulled itself together, realized it was

87

The Lancashire & Yorkshire built 2-4-2 tanks for express passenger work; some were even fitted with scoops for picking up water. So no. 50646, built in 1890, had come down in the world to be standing in Horwich station with the push-and-pull for Blackrod (1949)

a special case, ceased to pay undue attention to its accountants, and became really rather a smartly-worked concern, despite the difficulties. It was always on close terms with the London & North Western, and in 1872 an unsuccessful attempt was made by the two companies to amalgamate. When the political climate changed after 1918 this scheme was at once pressed forward and the merger took place in 1922, without waiting for the enforced combination that would have come about in any case the following year.

The third railway in Lancashire was the Cheshire Lines (which did also serve Cheshire, but not so noticeably). These had their origin in the early 1860s, when the Manchester, Sheffield & Lincolnshire and the Great Northern were jointly interested in building some feeders and connections to the Sheffield main line. These ran to Stockport and the area south of Manchester, and by 1863 had reached as far west as Northwich. In 1867 the Midland arrived in Man-

chester, using a section of this joint line, and agreed to join the party. And so the Cheshire Lines Committee was set up by the three companies. The chief moving spirit, however, was our old friend Sir Edward Watkin, the chairman of the MS&L.

The original purpose of the Northwich line had been achieved when it reached Helsby, and so by running powers Birkenhead, in 1869, and Chester in 1874. But Watkin had grander ideas than that. His first priority was a third route from Manchester to Liverpool, which he achieved by stages. The CLC got to Liverpool (Central) in 1874, but trains still had to go all the way round through Stockport to reach Manchester, and then rolled into London Road station from the east. This was not good enough. What was needed was a new station in Manchester facing west, and so Manchester (Central) was opened in 1877. Watkin was now in business, and with a bang; he startled his rivals by running an hourly express service at cheap fares between the cities, taking 45 minutes, and at once got the lion's share of the passengers. After the Warrington avoiding line was opened in 1883, the distance was reduced to 34 miles and the time to 40 minutes (today's diesels are back to 45); the route was still 3 miles longer than the old L&M, but worked so much more keenly that this was more than compensated for. Yet Watkin complained that his associates had not allowed him to work the CLC with as much 'steam and go' as he wished; he had set his heart on a 30-minute headway.

Had Watkin been satisfied with this all would have been well, but unfortunately he never did learn when to stop. He built a line round the back of Liverpool to a new station at Huskisson in 1880, which was useful enough for freight but a hopeless proposition for passengers. To try and change this, it was extended from Aintree to Southport in 1884; this section never paid, and was abandoned during the 1950s. By now the GNR and the MR were getting restive, and refused to have anything to do with branches from Glazebrook to Wigan and St. Helen's; so these were built by the MS&L on its own. Watkin also hoped to extend the CLC beyond Wigan to Blackpool, and made repeated efforts to do so between 1883 and 1895, without any success except in spending £300,000 for land. However, the CLC itself survived profitably enough under independent management until 1947.

North to Carlisle

The West Coast Main Line is carried across central Lancashire by a series of short lines built by a number of local companies, none of whom had any idea of forming part of a trunk route from London to Scotland. Altogether, there were at first six end to end junctions, five of them Engineer's Afterthoughts not laid out with high speeds in mind. Coming north, the Grand Junction line proper ended at Warrington, and was continued over the older Warrington & Newton of 1831. At Earlestown this ended, and trains bound for the north swung sharp right onto the Liverpool & Manchester for just over a mile through Newton-le-Willows to Parkside, where they turned hard left onto the Wigan Branch Railway, opened in 1832. At Wigan, with another bump and grind, they were onto the line planned as the Preston & Wigan, but which before completion in 1838 was amalgamated with the Wigan Branch and the Bolton & Preston to form the North Union Railway. Thinking he wasn't building anything very important, the engineer didn't bother much about gradients, and there is an avoidable summit at Coppull Hall. At Preston, after another savage reverse curve with a speed restriction, the Lancaster & Preston Junction line commenced. This was opened in 1840, and was built competently enough except that it was never imagined that anybody would ever want

A Manchester-Blackpool excursion south of Preston, hauled by L&Y F9 class 0-6-0 no. 1113. The stock looks pretty austere, particularly the six-wheeled bumper in front, but the customers seem happy (1920)

to continue northwards, and so the line terminated on the south side of Lancaster at a level high above the River Lune. Hence, nowadays, at Lancaster No. 1 signalbox, slow, left wheel, and grind down a mile of 1 in 98 to Lancaster (Castle) and the beginning of the Lancaster & Carlisle. This, at least, was conceived and built as a main line.

Things eventually got sorted out a bit. The Grand Junction took over the Warrington & Newton at once, and the Liverpool & Manchester in 1845, itself becoming part of the London & North Western the following year. The North Union was leased by the L&NW and the L&Y in 1846, and divided between them in 1889, the length from Preston to Euxton Junction (where the Crewe and Manchester lines diverged) becoming joint property. The Lancaster & Carlisle leased the Lancaster & Preston Junction in 1849, and was itself leased by the L&NW ten years later. Both were absorbed finally in 1879. Several improvements were carried out over the years, notably in cutting out the Z-bend through Newton-le-Willows by the 2½-mile Winwick Jn-Golborne Jn link in 1864; but to this day the whole length remains an untidy bit of railway, usually traversed with a sloth which the surroundings hardly justify. It remains only to record that Liverpool was given a direct link with the north via Ormskirk in 1849 (a line which later became part of the L&Y), and that Manchester had the benefit of two such northern outlets; the L&Y's half of the North Union via Bolton, and the L&NW's own route via Tyldesley and Wigan, opened in 1848.

One reason for the belief that a railway beyond Lancaster was unlikely was the existence of the Preston & Wyre, opened in 1840 from Preston to Fleetwood, where a new port was established. From here steamers sailed for Glasgow (or rather Ardrossan and a Glasgow train), and for Barrow, Ireland, and the Isle of Man. The two first services were short-lived, the Glasgow boat running only until the railway was completed in 1848; the Isle of Man route functioned intermittently until 1961. On the other hand, the Preston & Wyre line itself is still kept immensely busy serving Blackpool, at first the target of an afterthought branch of 1846 (to what is now the North station), then also reached (at South and until 1964 Central) by a cir-

cuitous extension of the Lytham branch along the coast in 1863 and finally by the 8-mile direct line from Kirkham & Wesham in 1903. The Preston & Wyre company was leased by the L&NW and L&Y jointly in 1849.

When the idea of building a railway between Lancaster and Carlisle was first mooted, there was considerable argument where it should go. The mountains of the Lake District were thought an impassable barrier (for technical reasons, not because of the aged Wordsworth fuming and writing anti-railway sonnets at Windermere). George Stephenson proposed an embankment across Morecambe Bay and a line round the coast in 1836; from time to time this project is brightly thought up again with every appearance of originality by somebody else. It has already reappeared twice in the 1960s, latterly in conjunction with a water supply for Manchester. Doubtless it will get built one day, and one hopes a railway will run along it as well as the inevitable autobahn.

Stephenson's line got to the prospectus stage, but opinion was put off by the Morecambe Bay crossing and also by the fact that it would be a very great way round, over 25 miles longer than a direct line. Joseph Locke, taking up the idea of an inland route, produced a survey through Kendal which got involved in some frightening tunnelling, dropped it, and finally came up with a 69-mile line which, by climbing the hillside above Kendal, slipped over the ridge at Grayrigg into the Lune Gorge and thence passed over Shap Fell at a summit level of 914 feet. This involved a ruling gradient of 1 in 75 for four miles on the south side of Shap, and not much easier than 1 in 100 elsewhere, but a minimum of earthwork and no tunnelling whatever. Locke pointed out that if necessary the Shap incline could be avoided by a tunnel some two miles long, but this was never built (although powers were in fact obtained for it at one time and some preparatory work carried out). Considering the nature of the country, the Lancaster & Carlisle must have been one of the cheapest main lines in Britain. It was opened from Lancaster to Kendal (on the Windermere branch) in September 1846, and completed from Oxenholme to Carlisle three months later.

Partly due to the reluctance of investors after the collapse of the Railway Mania, but more because they could not imagine any profits being earned in running trains across the deserted fells of Westmorland, the Lancaster & Carlisle company had great difficulty in raising money, and eventually half the capital was

Freights on Shap (i)

A Hughes 'Crab' 2-6-0 of 1926; no. 42711 nearing Shap Summit with a northbound freight (1963)

subscribed for by railways farther south. But it became extremely profitable, because it was that thing which the Americans call a 'bridge route'. Rich streams of traffic flowed up and down, generated by sources beyond its terminals so that everything travelled the whole length of the line for the greatest possible fee and lowest possible handling cost. It is a positive advantage for a railway of this kind to have few intermediate towns or industries, since it can then avoid spending time and money shunting about in sidings. Let others do the work, is its motto. When the L&NW leased the L&C in 1859, it had to pay handsomely for the privilege; dividends paid to L&C shareholders were always to be greater by a rate of $4\frac{1}{2}\%$ than whatever was paid on the corresponding L&NW shares.

Lancashire was now linked with Scotland through Carlisle; it remained for a similar connection to be provided from Yorkshire. George Hudson, still in control of the Midland, had his eye on this question. The Leeds & Bradford Railway, with its easily-graded U-shaped route via Shipley staying comfortably in the valley, had been opened in July 1846, and its branch from Shipley to Skipton followed two years later. The North Western Railway, known, to avoid confusion with the concern at Euston, as the Little North Western, had built on from Skipton via Hellifield and Settle to Lancaster and Morecambe, together with a branch from Clapham to Ingleton; these lines were complete by June 1850. The link with Carlisle was provided by an L&NW branch from Ingleton to Low Gill, near Tebay.

Both these small companies fell to the Midland, the Leeds & Bradford almost at once. Hudson was its chairman as well as the Midland's and arranged matters so. But with a typically Hudsonian lack of finesse he presided at the L&B meeting held to ratify the lease, and was heavily attacked for having the impudence to justify a bargain which he had made with himself (wearing a different hat). He got his way, of course; but the row did him no good. The North Western lasted longer, until 1871; in a bold but futile attempt to remain independent it formed an alliance with the Great Northern, which had by now reached Leeds, and went unsuccessfully to Parliament asking for running powers over the MR and L&NWR from Leeds to Carlisle.

The Midland made quite a good thing out of the line to Morecambe. People from Leeds and Bradford liked to go to the coast, more accessible there than at

Freights on Shap (ii)
On the 1 in 75 at Scout Green: 'Austerity' 2-8-0 no. 90317, banked by a 2-6-4T (1963)

Red 'Princess'; no. 46207 'Princess Arthur of Connaught' heading the northbound Midday Scot (Euston-Glasgow) through Kilburn (1961)

Green 'Princess'; no. 46201 'Princess Elizabeth', in her last month of service, at Beattock Summit with the morning Euston-Perth express (1962)

Freights on Shap (iii)
Arriving at the summit: 4MT 2-6-4T no. 42198 and Class Five no. 45386 (1963)

Blackpool; the rich to reside and commute, the poor to paddle on bank holidays. There were also steamers from Morecambe to Belfast, which service was greatly expanded and improved when the MR built the new harbour at Heysham and the line to serve it in 1904. The route to the north via Low Gill was rather a different matter. After the Midland reached London independently of the L&NW in 1858, relations between the two companies cooled, and MR traffic over Shap tended to meet with delays and obstructions. For some time the Midland contemplated building its own route to Carlisle; unwillingly, because over such mountainous country it would be very expensive. In fact, with a little more generosity, the L&NW could have prevented the Settle & Carlisle line from being made at all. In 1865 the two companies nearly came to an agreement for joint ownership of the route between Ingleton and Carlisle, which would have met the Midland's objections; the stumbling block was the L&NW's insistence on the right to control all the charges, which would of course have crippled competition. In 1866, therefore, the MR finally obtained an Act for the new line. Two years later, before work started, it got cold feet and tried to abandon it; this was prevented by the Lancashire & Yorkshire and North British companies, who had been pressing on with new connecting lines. So the Settle & Carlisle went ahead, and was fully opened in May 1876.

Physically, this railway makes as great a contrast with the parallel Lancaster & Carlisle line as can be imagined. It is certainly the most impressive piece of main-line construction through mountain country in Britain, with nineteen viaducts, nearly 3½ miles of tunnels, no curves restricted to less than 70 mph, some 30 miles of nearly continuous 1 in 100 grade, and eleven miles continuously above the thousand-foot contour. A fascinating railway to travel over, but expensive to maintain and, unlike Shap, prone to prolonged blockage by snow in severe winters. As a competitive route, its future now is dim, although parts of it will be needed to give access to various quarries.

West Cumberland and the Lake District

The first public railway west of the Lancaster & Carlisle main line was the Maryport & Carlisle, surveyed across easy country by George Stephenson and opened in stages as the money came in between 1840 and 1845. It was a small company without territorial ambitions, which therefore maintained its indepen-

A Manchester-Glasgow train at Shap Summit, headed by rebuilt 'Patriot' 4-6-0 no. 45545 'Planet' (1963)

dence until 1923; it was content to grow rich on coal (from some pits near Aspatria) and iron ore. The Cumberland iron trade was at its peak in the 1870s and 1880s, but declined thereafter, clearly going downhill by 1918; the railway's prosperity followed a similar course. Having once been in the goldmine class, it dwindled to the mediocre after 1914.

The M&C had a monopoly in its district which was only challenged once; by the Solway Junction, opened in 1869. Starting from Kirtlebridge and Annan, where it connected with the Caledonian and Glasgow & South Western main lines, it crossed the Solway Firth on a viaduct over a mile long, and ended at Brayton on the M&C. The selling point of this railway was the fact that it avoided Carlisle, but this was in practice no advantage, and the venture was always unprofitable. The Caledonian took over in 1895, and found it so too. The Solway Viaduct was rather a jerry-built affair, and frost split the cast iron piers from time to time, stopping traffic. The line closed finally in February 1933.

The second railway in Cumberland was the Furness, which opened its isolated system from Barrow-in-Furness to Kirkby, Dalton, and Piel Pier (whence steamers sailed to Fleetwood) in 1846. It was at first

'Jubilee' 4-6-0 no. 45659 'Drake' near Mallerstang, on the last stage of the climb to Ais Gill, with the Edinburgh-St. Pancras 'Waverley' (1954)

(*Right*) The 4-6-4 tank, popular in some countries, had only a brief run in Britain. LMS no. 11101, built for the Furness Railway in 1920, coasts into Barrow (1923)

Ribblehead Viaduct, at the top of the climb from Settle, with an unrebuilt 'Patriot' crossing at the head of a northbound freight (1954)

predominantly a mineral railway, serving the beginnings of the iron industry, and was extended north to Broughton in 1848 and west to Ulverston in 1854. Farther north, the Whitehaven & Furness Junction Railway originally intended to build a viaduct across the Duddon estuary at Millom, but to save money the line was 'temporarily' diverted round the head of the bay to start from Foxfield, south of Broughton. It was opened from there to Whitehaven (Bransty) in 1850. The Duddon crossing, like the Morecambe Bay scheme, remained in the pigeonhole, being extracted from time to time, currently by motorway enthusiasts. The 1¼-mile tunnel under Whitehaven from Bransty to Corkickle station was completed in 1852, and the W&FJ company remained quietly independent until taken over by the Furness in 1866. The westward connection between Ulverston and the main line at Carnforth, which had two lengthy viaducts across the Kent

and Leven estuaries, was opened by the Ulverstone & Lancaster company in 1857 and purchased by the Furness in 1862. That company's last major extension was the line jointly owned with the Midland from Carnforth to Wennington, connecting to the Bradford and Leeds areas, opened in 1867.

Like the Maryport, the Furness stayed independent until 1923. Normally, these small prosperous companies serving a tight little industrialized area made a juicy mouthful for some hungry giant; but in this case there were two hungry giants in the neighbourhood, the L&NW and the Midland, each so jealous of the other that neither could move.

The main industrial centre of the West Cumberland and North Lancashire area is now Barrow, but during the nineteenth century it was the area around Workington and Whitehaven. This was first served by the Whitehaven Junction Railway, completed between

Maryport and Whitehaven (Corkickle) along the coast in 1846–7. A network of competitive lines, as in most mining districts, then developed in the hinterland, starting with the Cockermouth & Workington in 1847, the Whitehaven, Cleator & Egremont in 1855, and the Cleator & Workington Junction in 1877. Much of this mileage vanished after the 1920s with the decline of local industry. More important was the Cockermouth, Keswick & Penrith, opened throughout in January 1865, a very scenic and steeply-graded line through the heart of the Lake District. Nominally independent, it had been promoted jointly by the L&NW and Stockton & Darlington Railways, principally as an extension of the latter's new line over Stainmore, with an eye to the heavy two-way traffic in coke and iron ore which had begun between Cumberland and Durham. Tourists and local traffic were an afterthought.

Having reached Cockermouth, the L&NW decided to do a little foraging in the district on its own account, and so acquired the line to Workington and the Whitehaven Junction company. In 1879 it also bought the Whitehaven, Cleator & Egremont jointly with the Furness. The local competitive situation was then complex, since both the Furness and the L&NW-CK&P already had their own systems of feeder lines. After 1923, when the whole issue was taken over by the LMS, things were rationalized, and the remaining through freight (except the little that still went over Stainmore) was diverted from the heavily-graded CK&P line to the coastal routes. No corresponding economies were made in operating the railway between Workington and Penrith, however, and to this day the CK&P, like the Somerset & Dorset, retains the whole jangling apparatus of Mid-Victorian main-line signalling and accessories, including some quite unnecessary stretches of double line, to handle a desultory service of railcars, and as a result runs at a frightful loss. Needless to say, the recommended answer to this has been to shut the line down completely.

The North-East

Railways were already quite common in North-east England at the beginning of the eighteenth century, carrying coal from mine to water. The trade in sea-borne coal, particularly to London, was ancient even then. The builders of these early lines had no legal authority, but paid wayleave rents to the landowners; it was in an attempt to reduce these that the 'Grand Allies', three families of coalowners, combined forces in 1726 to build the 5-mile Tanfield Waggonway, linking three of their collieries with the River Tyne. This was the first length of substantial railway construction in the world; it included a 100-ft high

embankment at Beckley Burn, and the famous Causey Arch nearby with a clear span of 102 feet. Parts of this line were in use until recently, although not the arch, which although it still stands, and is a protected monument, has carried no rails for 150 years.

By 1820 there were 225 miles of railway in the Northumberland and Durham coalfields, but they did not form a system. They were disconnected short lines criss-crossing the map, all privately owned and used for private purposes. This did not change until well into the locomotive era. The first public railway in the district was the Stockton & Darlington, authorized in 1821 to serve the South Durham coalfield. Because of its hilliness, this had been neglected by canals, had no navigable rivers, and suffered accordingly; for lack of transport, South Durham coal could not compete in price more than a few miles from the pithead.

Starting near Bishop Auckland, the railway crossed the hills to Shildon by means of two rope-worked

The LMS 4F 0-6-0, Derby's Big Goods, was a 1924 modification of a standard Midland design; 580 were built, and for years they were a mainstay of freight services. No. 44484 passes Derwent Junction (Workington) tender-first with a northbound freight, while Class Five no. 45226 arrives with a load of coke (1964)

Ex-North Eastern R class 4-4-0 no. 2021 leaving York with a Newcastle to Leeds express. These engines, which appeared in 1899, lasted until diesel railcars arrived in the mid 1950s (1924)

inclines (replaced by a tunnel in 1854), and then ran to the port of Stockton-on-Tees, taking a great loop southwards in order to pass through or near the towns of Darlington and Yarm. To avoid obstruction by their northern rivals, the promoters had announced that the purpose of the railway was simply to bring coal cheaply to these three towns, and that they had no intention of shipping it from Stockton to compete in the very profitable London market. Not quite believing this, the northern interests had a clause inserted in the S&D Act prohibiting the company from charging more than $\frac{1}{2}d$ per ton-mile on coal destined for loading on shipboard, believing that this low rate would be impossibly unprofitable.

The line was resurveyed in 1821 by George Stephenson, and ceremonially opened on 27 September, 1825. The original intention had been to build a railway open for all to use on payment, like a turnpike road; the company would confine itself to collecting tolls and maintaining the track. This arrangement natur-ally implied the use of horses. However, Stephenson persuaded the directors to use locomotives, and so also to work trains themselves. At first steam power was used only for a proportion of the coal traffic; every-thing else, including the passenger business, was worked by independent operators using horses, and this mixed system continued for a number of years. It led, of course, to difficulties, partly because the horses often bolted when faced with a fiery monster, and partly because the line was single track and arguments about who had the right of way sometimes led to blows. But locomotives did not wholly replace horses until 1856.

The S&D after a few years became very prosperous. There were some troubles at first with the engines, but already by 1827 the cost of shifting a ton of coal from colliery to quayside, 25 miles, was 10d with steam and 1s 0$\frac{1}{2}d$ with horse power. Since both these figures in-cluded the heavy cost of working the inclines, the economic advantage of steam was even greater than

V2 2-6-2 no. 60856 passing King Edward Bridge Junction, Gateshead, with a southbound parcels train (1962)

first appears, and it certainly allowed the company quite a comfortable profit margin above the 'prohibitively low' maximum charge for 'export' coal. So the trade boomed, and quickly outgrew the limited facilities at Stockton. In 1830 the company therefore opened a 4-mile branch to a new harbour at Middlesbrough, and founded a new town there, the first in Britain to be created by a railway.

But the S&D had a weak point; its great southwards loop through Darlington. As soon as it became clear that there was money in the game, a rival company, the Clarence Railway, was promoted to build a direct line from the S&D at Simpasture to Stockton and a new dock at Port Clarence, on the north side of the Tees opposite Middlesbrough. This line was opened in 1833. Naturally, it had to face strong S&D hostility, and as soon as it was completed the older company played its ace. It declared that, so far as it was concerned, any coal handed over to the Clarence at Simpasture was not transferred to ship (whatever the Clarence did with it), and would be charged at the maximum legal toll of 4d a ton-mile. This meant that it was still cheaper to send export coal over the S&D's longer route. Thus checkmated in the first railway rate

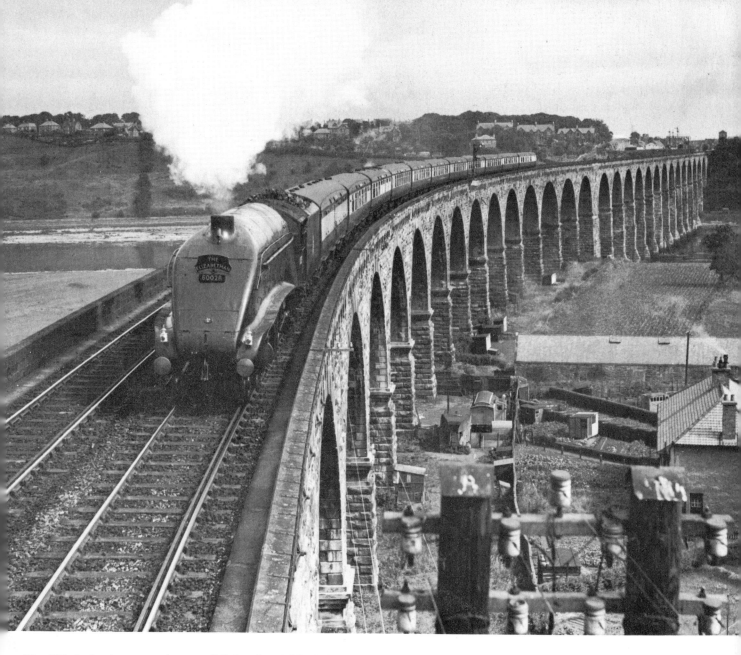

The 'Elizabethan', non-stop between Edinburgh and King's Cross, heads south across the Royal Border Bridge behind A4 no. 60028 'Walter K. Whigham' (whose original name was the more euphonious 'Sea Eagle') (1953)

war, the Clarence had to depend on what crumbs of traffic it could glean locally. It sent a branch northwards from Stillington in the direction of Durham, but soon met similar countermeasures from other railways serving Hartlepool. It built another branch to serve a colliery at Chilton, opened in May 1836 just as the colliery closed down; the only traffic it carried was second-hand machinery from the dismantling sale. All in all the Clarence was an unhappy concern, and in its 11 years of independent existence was taken over twice by the government on account of its failure to repay loans. After it was purchased by the S&D,

matters changed, and especially after it had been linked with Middlesbrough it began to short-circuit the older line to some purpose. Much of it was electrified in 1915 under the successful but regrettably short-lived Middlesbrough (Newport)-Shildon scheme, the first main-line freight electrification in Britain. In very recent times, though, the line from Stillington to Simpasture has been demolished and traffic once again flows via Darlington.

Two other noteworthy railways were built in the north-east in the early 1830s. The first to open, in 1834, was the 20-mile Leeds & Selby. Curiously enough,

An eastbound freight on the Stainmore line crossing the Belah viaduct, with an NER J25 0-6-0 at the head and an LMS 2MT 2-6-0 at the tail (1952)

George Stephenson had advised the use of stationary engines and rope haulage on this line, while James Walker, its engineer, who had given similar advice to the Liverpool & Manchester against Stephenson, decided to use locomotives; he did so on the grounds that the L&S was a less important line and the smaller quantity of traffic would not keep the winding engines sufficiently busy. It was originally intended to carry the railway on to Hull, but this was dropped to save money. Instead, steamers connected with the trains. But since the Humber was tidal and the timetable was not, the ships were always running aground and the service was less than satisfactory. Sometimes the vessels could be floated off a mudbank by the passengers marching abreast from port to starboard and back, obedient to the captain shouting from the bridge, but sometimes they could not. After a while people had enough of this, and the Hull & Selby Railway was opened in 1840.

Farther north, the 63-mile Newcastle & Carlisle was a more important concern, and, at the time it was authorized, the biggest railway scheme in Britain. However, construction was slow, and it was not completed until 1838. Engineering works were quite heavy, particularly at the western end, with a viaduct over 100 feet high and some 4 miles climbing from Carlisle towards Brampton at 1 in 107. The company remained independent until 1862; it had certain peculiarities, including a preference for running on the right, but was well-equipped and had a peaceful history.

In the late 1830s railway-builders in the north-east turned their thoughts from short lines built for local purposes to establishing a through north-south route. The York & North Midland Railway was authorized in 1836, and opened from York via Church Fenton to a junction with the Leeds & Selby at Milford in 1839. The extension from Milford to Normanton and the North Midland line coming up from Derby was opened in July 1840, simultaneously with the NM itself, and so London and York were linked by way of Rugby (or Hampton!), Derby, and Chesterfield. The Great North of England, also authorized in 1836, was still building, but was opened from York to Darlington in March 1841, using part of the Croft branch of the S&D for the last few miles. The secondary line from York to Scarborough was completed in 1845.

Between Normanton and Darlington neither the Y&NM nor the GNoE faced much constructional difficulty; in fact the stretch across the plain north of York has always been one of the great railway race-

tracks of Britain. But beyond Darlington was another matter. Not only was the country more broken, but there was already a complex of colliery and local lines. These almost reached to Newcastle already; admittedly they wandered, taking 56 miles instead of the 34 by road, and there were breaks at Stockton (between the S&D and the Clarence stations) and across the river between Sunderland and Monkwearmouth. And admittedly the weary passenger was eventually washed up not at Newcastle but on the wrong side of the Tyne at Gateshead. But money was short and this would have to do for the time being. George Hudson's motive for pressing on when the time came had more to do with his fight for the East Coast Route to Scotland than any solicitude for the increased convenience of the burghers of Newcastle.

The Newcastle & Darlington Junction company therefore got its Act in 1842. There had been considerable argument about which route it should take; the Stockton & Darlington, among others, had suggested that it should use as much as possible of existing lines, and although Hudson listened with one ear to this, he upset the S&D badly by insisting on building a new line parallel to theirs north of Darlington. In fact, the major new construction was from Darlington to Rainton, near Durham; from there the previously unprofitable Durham Junction was used to Washington, whence Gateshead was reached by a new bridge over the Wear, the Stanhope & Tyne to Brockley Whins and then the Brandling Junction Railway. This route was opened in 1844, and in 1850 was somewhat shortened by a new cutoff from Washington to Pelaw. It was still rather indirect, but was at least practical, and is still used at times by through trains. The direct route from Gateshead to Durham along the Team Valley was not opened until 1868, and did not become the main line until the Durham-Ferryhill connection was completed in 1872.

North of Newcastle, the East Coast Route was continued from Newcastle to Tweedmouth in 1847, but there were still two gaps where the great bridges over the Tyne and the Tweed were building. The Royal Border Bridge, between Tweedmouth and Berwick, one of the best-known large viaducts in Britain, was completed in August 1850, but since trains had been using a temporary wooden trestle since October 1848, it was the High Level Bridge over the Tyne at Newcastle, bringing the railway across from Gateshead in September 1849, that was the last link in the line to Scotland. Both bridges were built by Robert Stephen-

The Victoria Bridge, on the original Darlington-Newcastle main
line near Washington; a B1 4-6-0 crossing with a northbound
freight (1964)

North Eastern Freights
(*Top*) The Q6 class 0-8-0s of 1913 are among the last pre-grouping locomotives to survive in any strength. No. 63344 coasts through Bishop Auckland with a train from the Stockton & Darlington line (1963)

(*Bottom*) A coal train on the Blyth & Tyne: ex-NER J27 class 0-6-0 (of 1906) no. 65792 passes Winning on its way to Blyth (1963)

son, and attracted a great deal of interest; they have very little in common except their height, both being some 120 feet above the water. The Royal Border Bridge is tall, slender, built of brick, and with a sweeping curve at the south end; the High Level Bridge is more massive altogether, built of ironwork on brick piers, and carries three lines of railway on an upper deck and a main road on a lower deck.

The whole length of this part of the east coast main line had been in the hands of the York, Newcastle & Berwick company since 1847, but its monopoly did not last very long. In 1849 one of Hudson's chickens came home to roost. Originally, the passenger from Leeds to the north had to start his journey by riding eastwards on the Leeds & Selby to Milford. Soon after the completion of the Y&NM, Hudson introduced a rationalization scheme, buying up the L&S, closing the Leeds end of it, and despatching northbound trains southwards via Normanton. This neatly eliminated the overlapping facilities, and to add injury to insult, an additional fare was imposed for the extra distance. Leeds people refused to put up with this, even from a fellow-Yorkshireman, and so promoted the Leeds & Thirsk Railway, which opened its line via Harrogate and Melmerby in 1849. It was not an easy railway, with a ruling gradient of 1 in 94, and included the 2¼-mile Bramhope Tunnel, but it saved more than 8 miles even on the route via Milford, let alone the one via Normanton which Hudson was using. The L&T was therefore viewed with great disapproval by the established operators, and the York, Newcastle & Berwick refused to co-operate at Thirsk, charging as much for freight handed over there as it did for the longer haul to York. The small company therefore girded its loins again, changed its name to the Leeds Northern, and set out to build a line of its own. Its extension from Melmerby via Northallerton to Stockton (using the old S&D Yarm branch for the last couple of miles) was opened in May 1852, and thereafter its trains reached Newcastle along the coast. The inevitable rate war followed, during which the return

fare from Newcastle to Leeds came down to 2/-; it was succeeded by the almost equally inevitable amalgamation. In July 1854 the York, Newcastle & Berwick, the York & North Midland, and the Leeds Northern companies combined to form the North Eastern Railway. This was at the time the largest railway company in Britain, with 720 miles of track.

There remained the Stockton & Darlington, still independent, although it had been having its ups and downs. During the 1840s it extended westwards up the Wear Valley and onto the moors in search of coal and limestone, and eastwards from Middlesbrough to Redcar. Through the early forties the S&D dividends ranged around 15%, and £100 shares usually sold for about £300. But most of the extensions had been built by subsidiary companies under guarantee, and consequently rentals still had to be paid even after 1847, when trade declined and profits were insufficient to cover them. In 1851 a S&D share could be purchased

One of the heaviest snow ploughs used in Britain being prepared at Darlington, propelled by a J24 class 0-6-0. These engines, the largest allowed over the WD&LUR viaducts, were not infrequently overwhelmed by snowdrifts in the bleak lands around Stainmore Summit (1936)

Evening in the Lune Gorge; looking ahead from the footplate of 'Jubilee' no. 45671 'Conqueror' as she charges towards Shap at 70 mph with the afternoon Manchester-Glasgow express (1950)

for £30. But the company was rescued just as suddenly by the discovery of iron ore in the Cleveland hills, south of Middlesbrough. With ironstone at one end of its line, the Consett ironworks at the other, and coal-mines and limestone quarries en route, the S&D became an economist's dream railway, and dividends soared again. After a while it was found that for best results, Cleveland ore needed to be mixed with haematite from West Cumberland and Lancashire; this led the S&D to promote a new main line, the South Durham & Lancashire Union Railway, completed from West Auckland through Barnard Castle and over Stainmore to Kirkby Stephen and Tebay in 1861. Beyond Tebay the SD&LU had running powers over

the L&NW and the Furness to Barrow, at first via Carnforth but after 1876 using the Arnside-Hincaster Junction spur built by the Furness for this traffic. The Eden Valley Railway, another S&D promotion, was opened in 1862 from Kirkby Stephen to Penrith; here there was a connection with the Cockermouth, Keswick, & Penrith which led to the West Cumberland mines and industries.

The line over Stainmore was one of the wildest in England. Stainmore summit itself was 1,378 ft up on the fells, and there were miles of 1 in 60 grade on either side. Snow sometimes blocked the track for weeks. There were no tunnels, but several spectacular viaducts. Of these, Belah in particular, quite near the summit, was perhaps the most impressive. It was a slender, towering structure of trembling cast iron constructed on the best house-of-cards principles; crossing it one was apt to remember uneasily that its builder was Sir Thomas Bouch, and that it was his last masterwork but one, succeeded only by the first Tay Bridge. In later years the Stainmore line fell on hard times with the decline of industry in Cumberland, and it had been a chronic moneyloser long before it was finally abandoned in 1961. What freight was left was re-routed via Carlisle, as it had been a century before.

The Stockton & Darlington was finally amalgamated with the North Eastern in 1863; the following year the independent lines around Hartlepool were acquired, and the NER had a monopoly of a large and important area; a situation at that time unique in Britain. The company provided an interesting early proof of the fallacy of the theory still sometimes put forward that competition is the only stimulus of efficiency in transport. For it was a good railway, and its monopoly was an enlightened one. In his speech at the 1866 annual meeting, the Chairman, H. S. Thompson, said 'The directors frame their policy on this assumption: that they hold the district so long, and only so long, as the majority of thinking men in the district believe that they are as well served by the North Eastern as they could be served by other companies'. In 1871 a Parliamentary committee of inquiry, reporting on railway amalgamations, remarked that the NER was a striking illustration of its benefits. 'It is composed of 37 lines, several of which formerly competed with each other, and before their amalgamation they had, generally, high rates and fares and low dividends. The system is now the most complete monopoly in the United Kingdom, and it has the lowest fares and highest dividends of any large English railway. The general feeling in the district it serves appears favourable to the company.'

Meanwhile, a number of improvements were being made to the main line; we have already mentioned those around Durham. The swing bridge over the Humber at Goole, part of a shortened route from Hull to the south via Doncaster, was completed in 1869, as was the cutoff from Micklefield to Church Fenton, which reduced the distance from Leeds to York in

amends for Hudson's earlier lengthening of it. The direct line from York via Selby to the GNR at Shaftholme Junction, just north of Doncaster, shortened the east coast route in 1871 by 3 miles compared with the original line through Askern and Church Fenton. In 1877 the present station replaced the original terminus at York, which had become quite inadequate. (It still survives as a storage yard.)

Its monopoly position did not enable the NER to avoid building unremunerative branches. Apart from the motive of providing a social service (which it could well afford), it was also necessary to block competitive schemes. Thus, for example, the Gilling-Helmsley-Pickering line was built to counter an L&NW-backed proposal for a railway from York through Bilsdale to Stockton and West Hartlepool; the Wensleydale branch, from Leyburn to Hawes, was intended to discourage a line up Ribblesdale and along the top of the Pennines to Consett and Newcastle. But there was no protection against wholly unreasonable schemes, like the Hull & Barnsley. This unnecessary railway had its origin in the fixed belief of Hull Corporation that the North Eastern was starving their docks in favour of the Hartlepools. They admitted that between 1870 and 1878 their trade had expanded 36%, compared with only 9% at Hartlepool, but they still felt badly treated. So the Hull & Barnsley got its Act in 1880, despite NER counsel's demonstration that the line couldn't possibly pay even if the NER made it a gift of all possible traffic. Its 53 route miles were completed in 1885; construction through the hills north of Hull, which the NER avoided by a more direct and perfectly level course beside the river, was extremely expensive, with heavy gradients and a 1½-mile tunnel. It was also costly to work. A Receiver was appointed almost at once, but the company was kept going for years by Hull Corporation's animosity to the NER and their refusal to countenance any end to the competition. Finally, in 1899, an unofficial truce was patched up, and from then to 1914, during the most prosperous years the coal trade ever had, the H&B finally paid a few modest dividends. But for the last forty years of its life the line was again an incubus. With the exception of some useful short spurs at each end it was abandoned, very properly but years too late, in 1959.

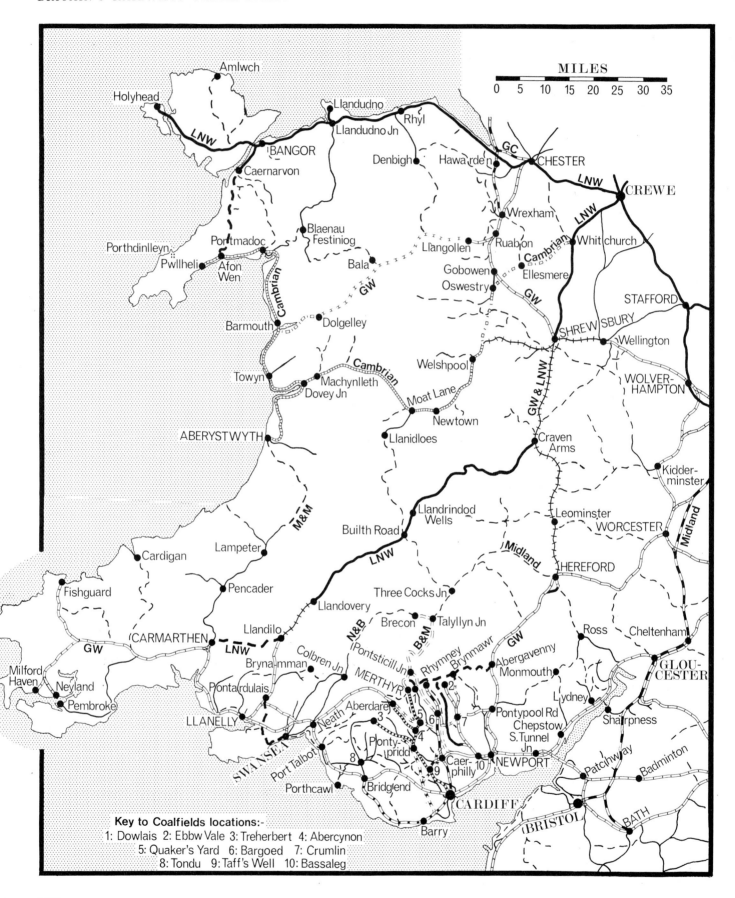

MILES

0 5 10 15 20 25 30 35

Amlwch

Holyhead

LNW

BANGOR

Caernarvon

Llandudno

Llandudno Jn

Rhyl

Denbigh

Hawarden

GC

CHESTER

LNW

CREWE

Wrexham

LNW

Whitchurch

Porthdinlleyn

Portmadoc

Blaenau Festiniog

Llangollen

Ruabon

Cambrian

Pwllheli

Afon Wen

Bala

Gobowen

Ellesmere

STAFFORD

GW

Oswestry

GW

SHREWSBURY

Barmouth

Dolgelley

Cambrian

Welshpool

Wellington

Towyn

Machynlleth

Dovey Jn

Moat Lane

Newtown

GW & LNW

WOLVER-HAMPTON

ABERYSTWYTH

Llanidloes

Craven Arms

Kidder-minster

M&M

Llandrindod Wells

Leominster

WORCESTER

Cardigan

Lampeter

Builth Road

LNW

Midland

HEREFORD

Midland

Fishguard

Pencader

Three Cocks Jn

Ross

Cheltenham

Llandovery

N&B

Brecon

Talyllyn Jn

B&M

GW

CARMARTHEN

Llandilo

LNW

Colbren Jn

Rhymney

Brynmawr

Abergavenny

GLOU-CESTER

Milford Haven

Neyland

Pembroke

Brynamman

Pontsticill Jn

Monmouth

Lydney

Sharpness

Pontardulais

MERTHYR

1

Pontypool Rd

Chepstow

LLANELLY

Neath

Aberdare

3

5

6

7

S. Tunnel

Swansea

Port Talbot

Plonty-pridd

4

Caer-philly

2

NEWPORT

Patchway

Badminton

Porthcawl

8

Bridgend

9

10

Barry

CARDIFF

BRISTOL

BATH

Key to Coalfields locations:-
1: Dowlais 2: Ebbw Vale 3: Treherbert 4: Abercynon
5: Quaker's Yard 6: Bargoed 7: Crumlin
8: Tondu 9: Taff's Well 10: Bassaleg

5 Wales

North and Central Wales

Good communications between London and Dublin were of considerable political importance while Britain and Ireland were united, and for this reason shortly after the Act of Union Telford was given the task of building and improving the Holyhead Road, the present A5. From Holyhead the sea crossing was less than half as long as from Liverpool, and not subject to the hazards of a rocky coastline and the Mersey shoals. Politics also meant that a railway to Holyhead was a very early proposal, and one of the few in which the government took an interest. Brunel, seeing a chance to extend GWR territory, surveyed a broad-gauge line in 1837 from Didcot to Porthdinlleyn (a sandy bay on the north coast of the Lleyn peninsula) via Oxford, Evesham, Worcester, Ludlow, Newtown, Dinas Mawddwy, Dolgelley, Barmouth and Port-madoc. This would certainly have been spectacular, carving across the Welsh mountains as if they weren't there. Most of the course it followed beyond Worcester was, in fact, never used by any railway, and the idea of a Gooch single clambering up over the Mawddwy Pass and down from the Cross Foxes Inn across the screes of Cader Idris to Dolgelley, through some of the roughest hairpin-bend, mountain-goat country in the Principality, is an awesome one. Unfortunately for romance, the Royal Commission turned down Brunel's route in 1844, favouring the relatively pedestrian standard-gauge line along the coast surveyed by Robert Stephenson.

Not that the Chester & Holyhead was in any absolute sense dull. As far as Abergele, 35 miles, it kept out of trouble by following the coastal plain, but between there and Colwyn Bay it did some cliffhanging which served as a curtainraiser to what followed. Beyond Llandudno Junction it had to bridge the Conway and tunnel through the walls of Conway Castle, and was then faced with the two great rocky cliffs at Penmaenbach and Penmaenmawr, obstacles which had forced Telford to divert his road through the heart of Snowdonia. Having tunnelled its way through these barriers and under the two hills at Bangor, the railway finally had to bridge the Menai Strait, allowing a clear 100 feet for ships to pass below, before reaching the comparatively easy last lap across Anglesey and Holy Island. Stephenson's answer to the Conway and Menai Bridges was to carry each track inside a rectangular wrought-iron tube. Only one 490-ft span was needed to cross the Conway, but at the Menai two 460-ft main spans and their approaches meant that the two tubes had to be 1,511 feet long. Huge, four-square, and substantial as the pyramids, guarded at each end by four rather prim stone lions, the Britannia Bridge is still one of the most impressive products of early Victorian engineering, in odd contrast to Telford's spidery suspension bridge a mile to the north.

Chester had already been reached by rail from Crewe and from Birkenhead in 1840; the connection with Manchester via Warrington was built ten years later. The Chester & Holyhead was opened to Bangor in May 1848, and across Anglesey from Llanfair to Holyhead three months later; the link across the Menai was not ready until March 1850. Having been properly connected with everything else at Chester, the railway was finished. Its only two important branches were from Bangor to Caernarvon (1852) and Llandudno Junction to Llandudno (1858). The company was absorbed by the London & North Western in 1856.

Although the Chester & Holyhead is the only railway of major importance in North Wales, there are others with claims to main line status, most notably the Cambrian. This was formed in 1864 by the amalgamation of four local companies. The earliest of these was the Llanidloes & Newtown, whose originally

British Railways still operate the 2-ft gauge Vale of Rheidol line, from Aberystwyth to Devil's Bridge. 2-6-2T no. 8 'Llywelyn' a youngster of 1925, on the horseshoe curve at Erwtomau (1964)

The 2-ft gauge Festiniog Railway's Double Fairlie no. 11 'Earl of Merioneth', built in 1885, near Penrhyndeudraeth (1961)

The narrow gauge is not extinct in Wales; it survives still to handle tourists. On the 2-ft 3-in. gauge Talyllyn Railway, 0-4-2T no. 3 'Sir Haydn', built in 1878, on a train for Towyn at Dolgoch (1955)

isolated 13-mile line connecting with the canal at Newtown was opened in 1859. The canal was, however, superseded in 1861 by the Oswestry & Newtown Railway, which connected the N&L with the national system at Oswestry. The Oswestry, Ellesmere, & Whitchurch prolonged this line towards Manchester in 1864, joining the L&NW Crewe-Shrewsbury section at Whitchurch. In the other direction, the Newtown & Machynlleth was opened from a junction with the N&L at Moat Lane to Machynlleth in 1863.

Of these four railways, only the Newtown & Machynlleth offered much difficulty in construction; the others kept peacefully to the plains and valleys. But the N&M had to go over the watershed at Talerddig, and then dived downhill for 10 miles into the Dovey Valley with a ruling gradient of 1 in 52.

Beyond Machynlleth, the Aberystwyth & Welsh Coast Railway, taken over in 1865, was originally responsible. It completed the line to Aberystwyth without incident in 1864, but the Welsh Coast part gave some trouble. The original plan had been to build a bridge across the Dovey estuary at Aberdovey, but no suitable foundations could be obtained and the idea had to be dropped. As a result of this hitch, the section from Aberdovey northwards was isolated when it first opened in November 1863, and remained so until the diversion, following the mountainous north shore of the estuary, was finished in August 1867. The extension from Barmouth Junction through Barmouth and Portmadoc to Pwllheli was opened two months later.

The Dovey Junction-Pwllheli line is interesting in several ways. It meanders round a scenic coastline, climbing across the Friog cliffs through the only avalanche shelter in Britain, and it retains to this day a great number of timber bridges. Much the largest of these is at Barmouth, nearly $\frac{3}{4}$-mile long across the Mawddach estuary, complete with an opening span which has hardly moved in living memory.

The Cambrian never grew rich, but it remained respectable. Understandably perhaps, it liked to pretend that the Shrewsbury-Welshpool line (a joint GWR-L&NW venture opened in 1862, cutting across the hills to give the most direct connection between Mid-Wales and the rest of the country) was not there; insisting that its own route to Whitchurch, looping carefully to the north of Shrewsbury, was the main line, it sent everything it possibly could that way – a fairly harmless piece of self-deception which no doubt helped the company to stay solvent. When the GWR

Class Five 4-6-0 no. 44865 leaves Conway station with a Crewe-Bangor train (1960)

BR Standard Class 4 4-6-0 no. 75011 on a Holyhead-Chester semi-fast passing the stone lions which guard the entrance to the Britannia Bridge (1960)

took over in 1923 it altered this operation to some extent (although the Whitchurch connection lasted until 1965 and the night train still ran via Oswestry) but changed very little else. A few Cambrian engines even outlived the GWR, surviving into British Railways stock, and the line still retains some flavour of its old independence in spite of everything, possibly helped by the fact that it remained one of the last large bastions of 100% steam operation in Britain.

Two other railways reached the Cambrian Coast; the L&NW branch from Caernarvon to Afon Wen in 1867, and the more important GWR branch from Ruabon and Llangollen. This was opened in stages between 1862 and 1868; from Dolgelley to Barmouth the GWR had running powers over the Cambrian. Although at least as scenically attractive as the Cam-

brian main line, it was rather more easily graded. Both these branches closed in 1965.

The last railway in North Wales was an oddity, since it brought the Great Central (and later the London & North Eastern) into the country. Needless to say, Sir Edward Watkin, venturing out of bounds again, was behind it. In 1890 he arranged for the Manchester, Sheffield & Lincolnshire to acquire an interest in the little Wrexham, Mold & Connah's Quay, a steeply-graded local line which had existed harmlessly in the North Wales coalfield for 20 years, and to connect it at Buckley with the Cheshire Lines at Chester, crossing a large swing bridge across the Dee at Hawarden on the way. Gladstone performed the opening ceremony here, and made a speech looking forward to the day (alas, not yet) when he could buy a

The last GWR 4-4-0s were the 'Dukedogs', nominally new engines in 1936, but incorporating parts of much older classes, frames from the 'Bulldogs' and boilers from the 'Dukes'. No. 9016 on a Pwllheli-Machynlleth local near Portmadoc (1954)

The 'Dukedogs' were unhappy on freights; nevertheless, no. 3206 heads one from Machynlleth to Oswestry near Carno (1938)

Snowdonian terminus: 0-6-0T no. 7442 ready to leave Blaenau Festiniog with a train for Bala (1954)

ticket from Hawarden to Paris by way of Marylebone and the Channel Tunnel. In 1896 the North Wales & Liverpool section from Hawarden to Bidston, connecting there with the Wirral Railway for the Mersey ferries at Seacombe, was added, but this was something of an afterthought. Watkin had his eye on the South.

South Wales and the Marches

The South Wales coalfield was one of the most enticing objects on the railway promoter's horizon during the nineteenth century. Long before it was connected by rail with the rest of the country it already had a network of canals and tramroads, some of which used locomotives. The first main line in the area was the South Wales Railway, a broad-gauge affiliate of the Great Western. Apart from serving the coalfield itself, this was intended to continue westwards to Fishguard and Milford Haven, with the Irish traffic in mind.

Brunel's original plan had been to start the line from the Cheltenham & Great Western Union at Standish, crossing the Severn by a bridge and avoiding Gloucester altogether, but this was vetoed by the Admiralty and so the eastern terminal was moved to Gloucester, with a bridge above the limit of ocean navigation. Except between Cardiff and Margam, in the Swansea area, and west of Carmarthen, the line followed the coast fairly closely; but although this meant that most of it was level, there were enough gradients to spoil things, particularly the 1 in 50 on either side of Cockett (north of Swansea). Swansea itself was served by a short branch from Landore.

There were some considerable bridges at Newport, Landore, and Carmarthen, and across the Wye at Chepstow. Here Brunel was faced with a difficult problem since there was a high cliff on one side of the river and a marshy plain on the other; the line had to be carried 100 feet above the water on a single 300-ft span, springing directly from the cliff at one end and meeting an approach viaduct at the other. As at Saltash, the tracks were suspended from a tube, but weaknesses finally became apparent and for many years, until the main span was rebuilt to a conventional design in 1962, trains had to pass at low speed.

The South Wales Railway was opened from Chepstow to Swansea in June 1850, but not connected with the rest of the system through Gloucester until the Wye Bridge was finished in July 1852. It was extended from Landore to Carmarthen later in 1852, and reached Neyland, on Milford Haven, in April 1856, when a steam service was started to Waterford and Cork. Work on the line to Fishguard was abandoned, for financial reasons.

The South Wales Railway faced two disadvantages; its roundabout connection with the rest of the country through Gloucester, and its broad gauge. The second was the heavier cross to bear. Only a few broad-gauge branches were built, the most important being the Vale of Neath line from Neath to Aberdare and Merthyr, so breaks of gauge strangled through mineral traffic (only one daily coal train to London was

scheduled during the 1860s) and also gave an additional spur to competing lines. The GWR, who took over in 1863, met with very little success in persuading the local companies to convert or even to add mixed gauge to their lines, and finally the attempt was given up. In May 1872 the entire length from Neyland to Swindon, with all branches, was altered to standard gauge.

The other disadvantage was not so easy to remove, and several attempts were made to shorten the Severn crossing. The first to succeed was the Bristol & South Wales Union Railway of 1864, which established a ferry between New Passage and Portskewett with branch lines in connection at each end. The South Wales & Great Western Direct scheme of 1865 proposed a new line from Wootton Bassett to Chepstow, with a $2\frac{1}{4}$-mile bridge at Oldbury Sands; this was authorized, but not proceeded with. Instead, the GWR took up the idea of a tunnel, and started exploratory work on it in 1872.

Meanwhile another company actually did something; the Severn Bridge was opened in October

A northbound Sirhowy Valley freight at Nine Mile Point, with 2-8-2T no. 7216 (1953)

1879. This was an odd project, connected with the building of docks at Sharpness, where the Gloucester & Berkeley Ship Canal started. Sharpness was going to become a large port, the proprietors hoped, and the bridge would be needed to link it with the South Wales and also the Severn & Wye Railway, an old-established system serving collieries in the Forest of Dean, which was taken over. To the east, a line ran to the Midland at Berkeley Road. But it all proved fairly useless. Neither docks nor bridge ever had much more than a local importance; the whole concern was soon in financial difficulty and became the joint property of the GWR and the Midland in 1894. The bridge remained until October 1960, when a barge crashed into a pier in a fog and brought it down. The damage was never repaired.

After a number of expensive setbacks due to the extremely difficult ground it passed through, the GWR opened the 4¼-mile Severn Tunnel in 1886; at the same time various improvements were made to the old B&SWU New Passage branch with which the tunnel connected. The distance from London to Cardiff was reduced by 14 miles compared with the old line through Gloucester, but the new line was still rather indirect, as trains had to run through Bristol. The full benefit of the Severn Tunnel was not obtained until the cut-off from Wootton Bassett via Badminton to Patchway was opened in July 1903, reducing the distance to London by another 11 miles. The Badminton line also provided a second route to Bristol, slightly shorter than Brunel's original main line. Between Wootton Bassett and Patchway gradients were extremely good, a steady 1 in 300, although this involved a 2½-mile tunnel at Chipping Sodbury; but west of Patchway things deteriorated. The Bristol connection had 2 miles of 1 in 75 past Horfield, and there was a gruelling 7 miles of almost continuous 1 in 100 up from the bottom of the Severn Tunnel for east-bound trains.

Other improvements in South Wales included the exhumation and completion of the original plans for a railway to Fishguard and a new harbour there in 1906, and the 13-mile Swansea District line from Skewen to Pontardulais and Llanelly, with a 1¼-mile tunnel at Llangyfelach, opened in 1913. This was not a great success, so far as improving the main line was concerned. The object of avoiding congestion around Swansea was achieved, but it was a misguided object, as only a few boat trains benefited. The line has for many years only been used by local freights.

While in West Wales one should perhaps mention a might-have-been; the Manchester & Milford Railway. In spite of its title this company only achieved the 41 rural miles from Pencader (where it connected with the Carmarthen-Cardigan branch) to Aberystwyth, in 1867. But it also proposed, and did a lot of work on, a connection from Strata Florida to Llanidloes, which would have included a viaduct 300 feet high, by far the highest in the country. By means of other running powers and connections it aspired to link Manchester with Brunel's new port on Milford Haven. It never happened, of course; but it would have been a wild and wonderful line.

Now back to the coalfields. Here, apart from foreign lines poking their fingers in, there were three, and later four, large local companies, of which the senior was the Taff Vale. This was a standard-gauge line, engineered by Brunel, and opened from Cardiff to Merthyr in 1841. It was later extended and duplicated in many places, the most important branches being to Aberdare (1846) and up the Rhondda Valley to Treherbert (1856). Next came the Rhymney, which opened its main line between Cardiff and Rhymney in 1858; at first it had to use the TVR between Cardiff and Taff's Well, but after a series of disagreements it built its own line from Caerphilly to Cardiff direct, through a 1¼-mile tunnel at Cefn On, in 1871. Thirdly came the Brecon & Merthyr, opened in stages from 1863 to 1868, which was in two sections; from Bassaleg (on the GWR outside Newport) to Rhymney, much of which was in sight of the Rhymney's line from Cardiff on the other side of the valley; and from Merthyr to Brecon. The two halves were joined by a connection from Pontsticill Junction to Bargoed, but between Deri and Bargoed this actually belonged to the deadly competitor, the Rhymney. The B&M had statutory running powers here since Parliament had decided, accurately enough, that there was no room in the valley for more than one railway at that point.

All these lines were mountainously graded, 1 in 40 being common; the B&M was worst, having two separate summits over 1,300 feet up and 6½ miles of more or less solid 1 in 38 from Torpantau down to Talybont-on-Usk. But the Barry Railway, because it was a latecomer and in order to compete had to limit its gradients, and because it cut across the grain of the country, had some very heavy engineering works instead. This company owed its origin partly to the congestion in Cardiff Docks and the need for a new

(*Above*) A Cardiff-Rhymney local near Ystrad Mynach, hauled by a Swindonized ex-Taff Vale 0-6-2T, no. 379 (1952)

(*Left*) A Brecon-Hereford train near Kinnersley, with Dean Goods 0-6-0 no. 2482 (a class dating from 1883) (1951)

(*Overleaf*) A westbound freight on the Chester & Holyhead line passing Conway Castle, hauled by 'Austerity' 2-8-0 no. 90566 (1960)

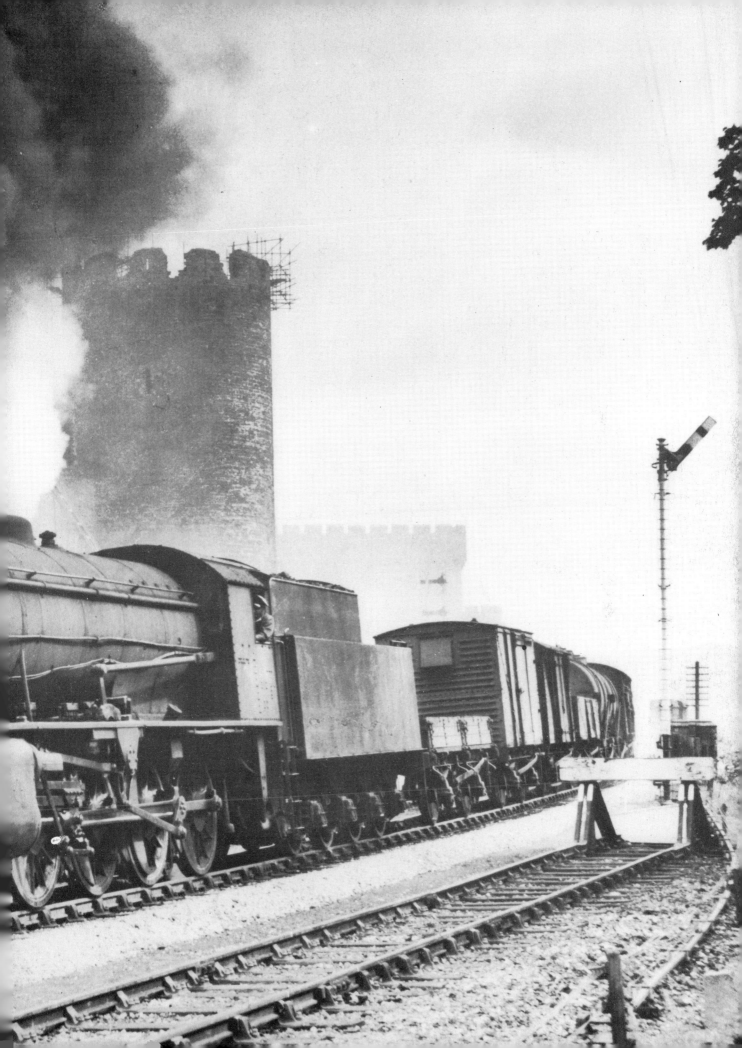

port at Barry, and partly to the desire among coal-owners for more competition between the railways which served them. Its main line was opened in 1889 from Barry to Pontypridd and Trehafod, where it sank its fangs into the Taff Vale; an eastern spur in the direction of Caerphilly followed, putting the bite on the Rhymney in 1901 and the B&M in 1905. Regarded as something of a parasite, the Barry was at one time a goldmine; but with the decline of the coal industry and the ending of railway competition practically all its main line has now been abandoned, a process which started as early as 1926.

All this is far from being exhaustive, even of company titles; there was for instance also the Rhondda & Swansea Bay Railway of 1885, whose main line ran from Treherbert to Swansea through a 2-mile tunnel

A southbound freight at Llanvihangel, summit of the Newport, Abergavenny & Hereford line; 43XX 2-6-0 no. 5378 piloting 28XX 2-8-0 no. 2841 (1952)

under the head of the Rhondda Valley, which also served another part of the coalfield in competition with the Port Talbot and the South Wales Mineral railways. There was also a maze of branches, spurs, and joint lines, some which carried far more traffic than main lines in other parts of the country. But we have enough complication for the moment, and enough to follow the invasion plans of the various foreign lines.

The London & North Western was originally behind the Newport, Abergavenny, & Hereford Railway, opened in January 1854. For the first nine miles from Newport, as far as Coedygric Junction near Pontypool, the NA&H had running powers over the ancient Monmouthshire Railway, newly converted from a tramroad, via Cwmbran; the present main line via Caerleon was not opened until 1874. It also

A 56XX class 0-6-2T on a Neath-Pontypool train, crossing the Crumlin Viaduct (1963)

had an important branch running westwards across the valleys from Pontypool Road, over the 200-ft high Crumlin Viaduct, which reached Quaker's Yard and a series of connections with the B&M, RR, and TVR by 1858. But the NA&H slipped through the L&NW's fingers by becoming part of the West Midland, and so came to the Great Western in 1863.

The NA&H was the first standard-gauge railway to reach South Wales, and until the Worcester-Hereford line was finished in 1861 its only link with the national system was by means of the Shrewsbury & Hereford. This line had been completed by a local company in 1852, and after the L&NW reached Shrewsbury from Crewe in 1858 the S&H considered that it might be able to sell out to them at a good price. This was so; the L&NW leapt at the chance, since the S&H had

statutory running powers over the NA&H and its new owner would therefore have guaranteed access to Newport. But the L&NW, with the trusting innocence of the newly reformed, considered that the GWR might like a half share in the line, and offered it. Thereupon Paddington delivered a low blow; considering that the L&NW ought to be kept out of South Wales at all costs, they refused the offer, and tried to persuade Parliament, when the L&NW bill was in committee, that they should be enabled to obtain exclusive possession of the S&H themselves. But they failed; so the S&H became a joint line in 1862 and the L&NW reached Newport after all. This is the slightly tangled history of what is now the main route from Bristol, the West of England, and South Wales to Lancashire.

The L&NW still had no way of getting to the coalfields proper, since its running powers did not include the branch from Pontypool Road. To fill this gap the Merthyr, Tredegar, & Abergavenny company set out to build a parallel railway, climbing across the heads of the valleys. The L&NW took over during construction, reached Brynmawr in 1862, and by slow stages finally got to Merthyr (using the tracks of the Brecon & Merthyr for the last lap) in 1879. In 1876 the L&NW purchased the Sirhowy Railway, which ran from Nantybwch to Tredegar and Nine Mile Point, with running powers thence over the GWR to Newport; it also reached Cardiff over the Rhymney, and the last section into Merthyr was owned jointly with the B&M. The MT&A was an extraordinarily mountainous and difficult line, starting out from Abergavenny with a colossal climb of 8 miles, mainly at 1 in 38, up the gorge to Brynmawr, and then picking its way across a succession of desolate summits. But it was busy, because it was competitive. After nationalization it lost its purpose, and was closed to freight in 1954 with considerable economies. Complete abandonment followed in January 1958; coming a year before the Midland & Great Northern closure, this was the first major railway abandonment in Britain.

Meanwhile the NA&H branch over the Crumlin viaduct was extended from Quaker's Yard to the terminus of the broad-gauge Vale of Neath line at Aberdare in 1864, and a third rail was then added to the VoN. This was the first standard gauge connection to Swansea and the western part of the coalfield, and was controlled by the GWR; quite apart from its

No. 4083 'Abbotsbury Castle' leaving Port Talbot with a Carmarthen-Paddington express (1948)

value as a through route it generated a certain amount of local traffic also. Nevertheless the bulk of it, including the Crumlin Viaduct, was closed in 1964 as part of the general wave of economies; only certain local spurs remain.

The L&NW was not content with access to Newport, Cardiff, and the valleys; it wanted another line which would bring it to Swansea. The Knighton Railway of 1861, branching off the Shrewsbury & Hereford line at Craven Arms, was therefore taken over and extended to Llandovery by 1868; by means of running powers over the old Llanelly Railway beyond that point L&NW trains then reached Carmarthen, Llanelly, and Swansea (Victoria). Some years later the Llanelly company's assets were carved up by the

L&NW and GWR, parts becoming joint property and parts going to one with running powers to the other. The Craven Arms-Swansea section became known as the Central Wales line, and apart from also being mountainous was quite different in character to the other routes to South Wales, since it was wholly rural and mainly single track. But, like all the others, it was kept busy hauling coal. For many years the L&NW and LMS ran through coaches from London to Swansea via Stafford and Shrewsbury, but this was not quite as absurd as it looks on the map since the main objective was not Swansea but the Central Wales Spas, places like Llandrindod Wells, Llangammarch Wells, and Llanwrtyd Wells, which had some worthwhile tourist traffic. Coal continued to move this way

Newport-Shrewsbury freight at Abergavenny Junction, hauled by ROD 2-8-0 no. 3040 and braked by an L&NWR 0-8-0. The RODs were originally a Great Central design, but some were built for the GWR during the first World War (1955)

in some quantity until 1964, when it was diverted via Newport in anticipation of closure. But permission to abandon the line was refused, and it is now maintained for local traffic only.

The Midland also had its eye on South Wales, and got there eventually by another series of rural single line branches. Having reached Hereford by running powers from Worcester in 1868, it obtained further running powers over the five-year-old Hereford, Hay, & Brecon in 1869, absorbing it in 1886; and having got to Brecon it could tap the eastern part of the coalfield with the co-operation of the Brecon & Merthyr. The western part was reached along the Neath & Brecon, a down-at-heel concern completed in 1867 and worked by the Midland after 1877. To get to

Swansea the Midland purchased the Swansea Vale Railway, which connected with the N&B at Ynysygeinon Junction. Nor was the Midland the last invader; we have already seen how Sir Edward Watkin brought the Manchester, Sheffield & Lincolnshire to Wrexham in 1890. His ambitions did not stop there. The Cambrian also served Brecon by means of its long and rambling Mid-Wales branch from Llanidloes, and an alliance with that company was cemented in 1895 when the 13-mile Wrexham & Ellesmere branch was opened. The moral influence of Marylebone then flowed to Cardiff by way of Chester, Wrexham, Llanidloes, Talyllyn Junction, and the Brecon & Merthyr, Taff Vale, and Barry Railways. It was an influence never detectable in Bradshaw, but it was strong enough for many years to cause a trainload of coal a day to pass to Liverpool via Talyllyn Junction, and it must have doubled the takings on the Mid-Wales branch.

All Brecon's railways have now ceased to exist; the last trains ran at the end of 1962 from Neath, from Hereford, and from Llanidloes. Freight service on the B&M from Merthyr lasted another 18 months, but ended in 1964. The tunnel at Talyllyn Junction, which saw its first train on the old Hay Railway in 1814, is now silent. One cannot complain about the disappearance of three of the four lines, whose remaining traffic was small, but the closure of the line from Merthyr, however difficult it may have been to work with its steep gradients, was a mistake; one of the very few closures to date which have done serious local injury. It is impossible not to feel that the ruin of the Brecon & Merthyr, which has now totally ceased to exist, was due to the fact that even after 1923 and 1948 it continued to be worked as if it was an independent company. The passenger service from Brecon always used to run to Newport, because that was the route by which the B&M would get the largest cut of the fare; the line from Pontsticill down to Merthyr was always treated as a branch. Never mind that the B&M to Newport served no towns not already better served by the Rhymney line; never mind that Merthyr itself was a very worthwhile objective; and never mind that Cardiff was always more important than Newport. A through train from Brecon to Cardiff would have had to cross from the old B&M to the old TVR at Merthyr, and so appalling a break with tradition as this was not only never committed, but apparently never even contemplated. Instead, a grave and proper respect for custom prevailed, and the whole railway was contemptuously junked.

A Machynlleth-Barmouth train running beside the Dovey estuary near Abertafol, headed by BR Standard class 3 2-6-2T no. 8206 (1964)

The 'Granges' of 1936 were a smaller-wheeled version of the 'Halls' of 1924, and so closely related to Churchward's 'Saints' of 1903. Fresh from overhaul, no. 6817 'Gwendwr Grange' heads a Swindon-Gloucester freight at Kemble (1962)

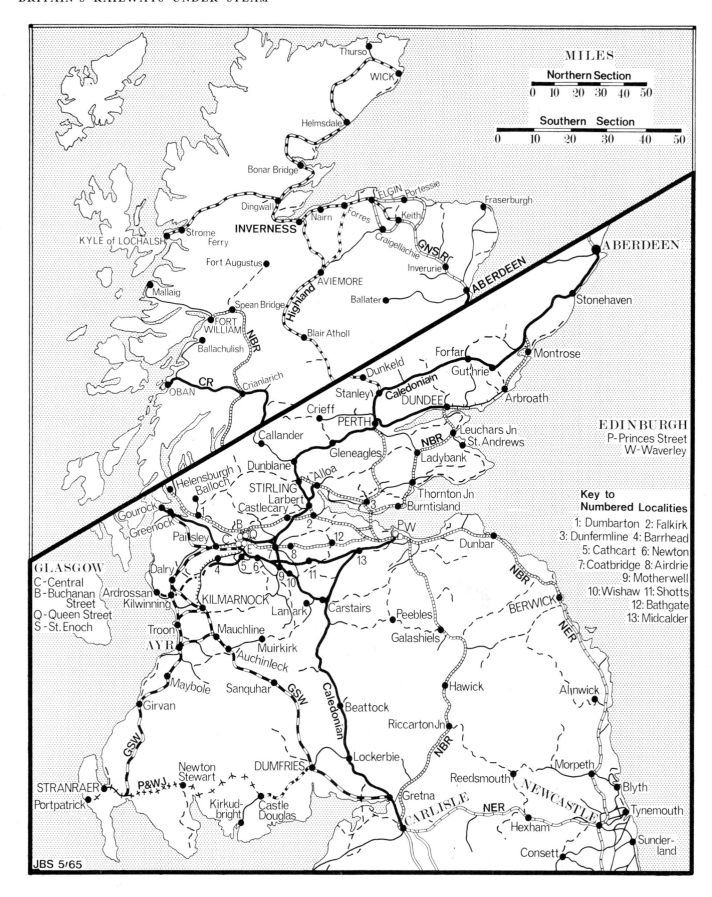

MILES

Northern Section

0 10 20 30 40 50

Southern Section

0 10 20 30 40 50

EDINBURGH
P - Princes Street
W - Waverley

Key to
Numbered Localities
1: Dumbarton 2: Falkirk
3: Dunfermline 4: Barrhead
5: Cathcart 6: Newton
7: Coatbridge 8: Airdrie
9: Motherwell
10: Wishaw 11: Shotts
12: Bathgate 13: Midcalder

GLASGOW
C - Central
B - Buchanan
      Street
Q - Queen Street
S - St. Enoch

Thurso
WICK
Helmsdale
Bonar Bridge
ELGIN Portessie
Fraserburgh
Dingwall Nairn Forres Keith
INVERNESS Craigellachie GNSR
Strome Ferry
KYLE of LOCHALSH
Inverurie ABERDEEN
Fort Augustus
AVIEMORE
Mallaig
Ballater ABERDEEN
Spean Bridge
FORT WILLIAM
Highland Blair Atholl
Stonehaven
NBR
Ballachulish
CR
Crianlarich
OBAN
Dunkeld
Stanley Forfar Montrose
Caledonian Guthrie
Crieff DUNDEE Arbroath
PERTH
Callander
Gleneagles NBR Leuchars Jn
Dunblane Alloa St. Andrews
Helensburgh Ladybank
Balloch
STIRLING Thornton Jn
Gourock Larbert Castlecary Burntisland
Greenock Paisley 1 PW
B 2 Dunbar
C Q 12
Dalry E 7 8
5 6 9 13 NBR
4 10
KILMARNOCK 11 BERWICK
Ardrossan Lanark Carstairs
Kilwinning Peebles NER
Troon Mauchline Galashiels Alnwick
AYR Muirkirk
Auchinleck Hawick
Maybole Sanquhar GSW Beattock
Girvan Caledonian Riccarton Jn Morpeth
NBR Reedsmouth Blyth
STRANRAER P&WJ Newton Lockerbie NEWCASTLE Tynemouth
Portpatrick Stewart DUMFRIES Gretna NER
Kirkud- Castle CARLISLE Hexham Sunderland
bright Douglas Consett

JBS 5/65

6 Scotland

South of Glasgow

Writing in 1890, W.M. Acworth pointed out that although there was generally less traffic to fight for, railway competition in Scotland was much fiercer than in England; Ayr and Inverness were the only important places served by a single company. But competition depended to a much greater extent on statutory running powers, where Parliament had given a railway the legal right to unrestricted use of its rival's tracks. So although there were parallel railways, these were fewer than they might have been, to the benefit of all shareholders. Nevertheless, there were some famous inter-company feuds, perhaps most notably the one between the Caledonian and the Glasgow & South Western, which had its remotest origins in disagreement over the best way to get to Carlisle.

Well before the railway reached Carlisle from the south in December 1846, people contemplated extending it to Glasgow and Edinburgh. Joseph Locke, having laid out the line over Shap, made a preliminary reconnaissance in Scotland during 1836. Two possible routes presented themselves. One could go north-westwards from Carlisle up Nithsdale, over a 650-ft summit, and down to Glasgow via Kilmarnock using a number of already existing or planned railways; or one could strike out over almost completely new ground, northwards up Annandale, across a thousand-foot summit at Beattock, and then down the Clyde Valley to Glasgow, serving Edinburgh by a branch from Carstairs. Locke's first opinion was that rope-worked inclines would be needed at Beattock so he said he did not wish to recommend that route. Indeed, there were a number of sound, practical reasons why the Nithsdale line ought to be preferred. It would serve a more populous area with easier grades and less new construction, and it had the enthusiastic support of the Edinburgh & Glasgow Railway, which would of course have retained all the Edinburgh traffic.

But fortunately there were a number of men who realized the limitations of sound, practical arguments and felt that nothing could outweigh the advantage of a shorter line serving both Edinburgh and Glasgow equally. They persuaded Locke to make a more thorough survey, in which he found it possible to get over Beattock using locomotives only. In 1841 the Parliamentary Commissioners decided in favour of this route, although they rather weakly declared that they did so merely because their terms of reference instructed them to favour only one line between England and Scotland; and in 1845 the Caledonian Railway Company was empowered to build it. The Caledonian scheme was an ambitious one, proposing not only the main line from Carlisle to Glasgow and Edinburgh, but extensions to Perth, Dundee, Aberdeen, Inverness, Ayr and Portpatrick. All these lines were eventually built, but not by the Caledonian.

For the first few miles from Glasgow the CR originally used two older railways, the Glasgow & Garnkirk and the Wishaw & Coltness, both of which it purchased in 1846. The G&G had been opened in 1831 from St Rollox for 8 miles to Gartgill, near Gartsherrie, where it joined a slightly older line, the Monkland & Kirkintilloch, which served part of the Lanarkshire coalfield. The G&G was the first railway in Glasgow; or rather, nearly in Glasgow, for St Rollox was on a hilltop somewhat outside the city, and it remained an inconvenient terminus until the line was diverted down 2 miles of 1 in 79 and 98 to Buchanan Street in 1849. The other company taken over in 1846, the Wishaw & Coltness, had been opened between 1838 and 1842 and ran in a south-easterly direction from the M&K near Coatbridge to Garriongill near Wishaw. The G&G and the W&C sections were subsequently reconnected by a new line, avoiding

On the Portpatrick & Wigtownshire in the wilds of Galloway;
Class Five no. 44996 climbing up to Gatehouse of Fleet with a
Dumfries-Stranraer local (1963)

the need to use the intervening section of the M&K, which had meanwhile fallen into the hands of the North British company.

South of Wishaw the Caledonian was faced with the climb to Beattock, the first part of which was at 1 in 99 up to Craigenhill, north of Carstairs. From there to Elvanfoot it was a steady but easier climb, following the Clyde Valley through the high hills; still impressive and deserted country. For the last couple of miles to Beattock Summit (1,014 ft) the grade increased again to 1 in 99, but the descent of the ravine leading to the south was steeper still, with ten miles of 1 in 75 ruling and 1 in 69 maximum gradient. From Beattock station to Carlisle the country is considerably better going, and 1 in 200 is the steepest grade here. The Carstairs-Edinburgh line, having to climb out of the Clyde Valley, was a rather tougher proposition, with a ruling grade of 1 in 100 on either side of the summit at Cobbinshaw. Just as on the Lancaster & Carlisle,

Locke carried the railway through the hills with a minimum of sharp curves, no tunnels, and a very satisfactory absence of heavy construction work. The first section, from Carlisle to Beattock, was opened in September 1847, and the rest of the line from Beattock to Edinburgh and Glasgow on 15 February 1848, completing a through rail link from London to Scotland.

The original route into Glasgow was not particularly good since it was rather indirect, but it did have the advantage that Buchanan Street station was also used by trains proceeding northwards, and so it was convenient for through passengers. A more direct route from Motherwell into Glasgow over the Clydesdale Junction line via Newton and Rutherglen was available after 1849, but after a short spell of working into South Side terminus trains to and from England returned to their old routine. The Rutherglen line did not come into its own until South Side was re-

Caledonian 4-6-0 no. 943 leaving Carlisle for the north with a fast freight (1921)

placed by the new station at Glasgow Central, just north of the river, in 1879, when the English services were permanently installed there and the few through trains to and from the north, running via Coatbridge, avoided Glasgow altogether. This situation still continues.

The Caledonian's monopoly of the Carlisle traffic was short lived. It was challenged in 1850 by the Glasgow & South Western Railway, formed by the amalgamation of the Glasgow, Kilmarnock & Ayr and the Glasgow, Dumfries & Carlisle companies. The GK&A had been completed from Ayr to Glasgow, 41 level miles via Troon, Dalry, and Paisley in August

1840. The 11-mile branch from Dalry to Kilmarnock followed three years later. The company had some slight bother at first with a canal which tried to compete by running high-speed 'fly' boats carrying passengers, but these soon caused its bankruptcy and for good measure washed away its banks as well. Part of its bed was later used for an alternative exit from Glasgow through Paisley to Elderslie.

The Glasgow, Dumfries & Carlisle was of course nothing but our old friend the Nithsdale route, restored to life after the Parliamentary Commissioners had knocked it on the head. Ayrshire felt that whatever Government might say, it deserved an outlet to

The Muirkirk-Lanark freight at Inches, with ex-Caledonian 3F 0-6-0 no. 57604 (1962)

In the upper Clyde Valley near Abington, ex-Caledonian 3F 0-6-0 no. 57568 heads south with a rather miscellaneous local freight (1961)

the south; the area was after all a prosperous one, with several large towns and a fair coalfield into the bargain. And so the GD&C built the line, starting from Auchinleck (which the GK&A had reached on its way from Kilmarnock to Muirkirk in 1848), and finishing at Gretna, where it joined the Caledonian with running powers for the last 9 miles into Carlisle. It was opened in October 1850, at the same time as the two companies merged. The G&SW was indeed a very much easier proposition than the Caledonian so far as gradients were concerned; the worst length was $4\frac{1}{2}$ miles of 1 in 99 up to Garrochburn, south of Kilmarnock. Elsewhere, apart from a short length of 1 in 150 on the descent to Dumfries, there was nothing worse than 1 in 200. On the other hand, the G&SW was 125 miles long, some 20 miles farther to Carlisle than by way of Beattock, and this put it completely out of court at first so far as through traffic was concerned. It therefore remained a line of local interest only until 1876, when the Midland reached Carlisle and sent its Anglo-Scottish trains northwards via Kilmarnock. In preparation for this the G&SW had shortened itself by ten miles in building the Glasgow, Barrhead & Kilmarnock in 1873. This line, jointly owned with the Caledonian, followed a direct course over the hills, with steep grades; southbound trains had to climb 5 miles of 1 in 69 past Neilston, and northbound ones faced 7 miles of 1 in 75 on leaving Kilmarnock.

Ayr was at first connected with the Carlisle line only by the Kilmarnock to Troon branch, which had replaced in 1847 the 4-ft gauge plateway of 1812, where Scotland's first locomotive had had a brief and unsuccessful career. The more direct link over the hills via Tarbolton to Mauchline was opened in 1870.

From Glasgow to Ayr the old GK&A main line was a level, busy, and profitable railway. Farther south things slowly changed for the worse. Maybole was reached in 1856 and Girvan in 1860, with considerable lengths of 1 in 70 and constant curves; but Girvan is a fair-sized town and several collieries were passed on the way, so this was still a reasonably moneymaking length. Beyond Girvan, where the Girvan & Portpatrick company commenced business in 1877, double track gave way to single, the hills became mountains, and trains started right out up 4 miles of 1 in 54, climbing towards the bleak moorland of the Chirmorie. The G&P proper ended at Challoch Junction, where it met the Portpatrick Railway.

The G&P set out to form part of a route from Scotland to Ireland and it had very little other justification. The G&SW, contemplating the fact that there was already a direct steamer service all the way, did not have much faith in the success of the venture. However, they agreed to work the new line, and did so until 1886; then they gave it up as being unremunerative. So the railway closed, and was put up for auction. Much to everybody's surprise, it was purchased very cheaply by a syndicate of businessmen who felt that the G&SW was bluffing, and would be compelled to buy them out in due course; the chance of a capital gain therefore outweighed the risk of any small loss in working. The line reopened in 1887 as the Ayrshire & Wigtownshire, was run efficiently and economically, and was duly purchased, just as anticipated, by the G&SW in 1892. Shortly afterward the passenger station at Girvan was moved from the original fairly central terminus (still used for freight) to the present building on the outskirts of the town, avoiding the need for through trains to reverse.

The Portpatrick Railway was an older affair. It started from Castle Douglas, reached by a G&SW branch from Dumfries by 1859, and was opened to Stranraer in 1861 and Portpatrick the following year. It ran through some of the wildest and most desolate country in the British Isles, and like the G&P its chief justification was always the connection to Ireland. The original intention had been to run the steamers on the shortest possible crossing, between Portpatrick and Donaghadee, but Portpatrick was soon found to be an unsuitable harbour and the service was transferred to the Stranraer-Larne route, where it remains. In 1885 the PR became the Portpatrick & Wigtownshire Joint, owned equally by the Caledonian, G&SW, L&NW, and Midland companies, and with this more substantial backing ran a very adequate train service. Its earlier years had been rather bucolic. It was one of the last lines to be condemned under the 'Beeching Plan' by the outgoing government in 1964 and was intended to close in 1965, through trains from Stranraer to London being diverted through Ayr and Mauchline.

So much for main lines in the G&SW's sphere of influence; the company had a large slice of south-west Scotland more or less to itself. In both senses; as well as a lack of competition, there was a dearth of customers in much of the district. But nearer Glasgow there was plenty of both. The Glasgow to Paisley section of the main line to Ayr had always been jointly owned; at first the other partner was the Glasgow, Paisley & Greenock, opened along the south bank of the Clyde in 1841, but in 1851 this company sold out to the Caledonian. The two rivals coexisted peacefully enough for some years, but in 1869 the G&SW opened a branch from Elderslie via Kilmacolm to Greenock. This had a heavy climb over the hills, while the Caledonian was level, but it had a better terminus in Greenock and a better pier for the connecting steamers. So it got much of the business. After twenty years of competition, the Caledonian trumped the G&SW by

extending beyond Greenock to Gourock in 1889, a very expensive 3½ miles including the 1¼-mile Greenock Tunnel, the longest in Scotland. After the 1923 grouping the G&SW line languished, and was closed to regular traffic beyond Kilmacolm in 1959.

A rather tenser situation developed between Glasgow and Ardrossan, in connection with steamers in the Clyde estuary. In this case the G&SW was the first arrival, having opened the branch from Kilwinning in 1840, while the Caledonian appeared in 1890 by means of an ambitious new main line via Cathcart and Neilston (High). Both routes were about the same length; each had a rival pier and steamer service at Ardrossan, and things were fast and furious. The Caledonian also hatched a scheme for a rival line from Kilwinning to Ayr, but this got no farther than Irvine. Once again, the steam was taken out of the contest after 1923. The Caledonian line lost its regular passenger services in 1931, but was still used by occasional boat trains and lingered half alive for another quarter of a century, until a new spur connecting its western end to the G&SW put an end ot it.

The two companies could co-operate when they had to, as on the Paisley or Kilmarnock joint lines; or when it suited them, for instance in running a direct service from Ayr to Edinburgh via Muirkirk. But they seemed to prefer fighting. They were both happier after 1879, when each built a new terminus in Glasgow (Central for the CF, St Enoch for the G&SW) and could stop using the old Paisley Joint line terminus at Bridge Street. Perhaps fortunately, they planned more battles than they actually fought. To this day the bare hills around Muirkirk are decorated by the never-completed ruins of a Caledonian Muirkirk Direct scheme; the CR also had a remote, splendid, and profitless branch, the Leadhills & Wanlockhead Light Railway, which served a few mines and until it was abandoned in 1940 reached the highest standard-gauge railway summit (1,498 ft) in Britain. But even in the lonely wilderness up there the G&SW

seriously contemplated building a rival branch, to run up the Mennock ravine from Sanquhar, worked by rack locomotives. One can drive up this valley now (in low gear) and imagine just how much traffic would have been carried.

On the north side of Glasgow, the Caledonian had to face more suburban competition, this time from the North British Railway. Both companies had parallel tracks along the north bank of the Clyde (the NBR's Glasgow, Dumbarton & Helensburgh line of 1855 was the older), and both ran fiercely competitive steamer services. (Since the G&SW did so too, this part of the river was pretty busy.) In Glasgow itself, both the CR and the NBR had parallel underground railways, built during the eighties, which remained steam-worked into the 1960s. Visiting Queen Street or Central Low Level stations during the rush hour, groping down dank and murky catacombs, and seeing trains come roaring at close headways through a choking and impenetrable fog was an unforgettable, if not particularly enjoyable, experience. Glaswegians took it calmly. They are a hardy crowd; Londoners had protested violently at steam working on the Metropolitan and the District, which was certainly no worse, and got rid of it a lifetime earlier. The NB line was eventually electrified in 1960; thereafter the Caledonian's dwindled and was closed in 1964, although no doubt only temporarily, road conditions being what they are.

South of Edinburgh

There were many mineral railways, some of them of great antiquity, in the coalfields of the Central Rift; but the first main line in the area, the Edinburgh & Glasgow, kept clear of them. It was opened in February 1842, and for nearly all the 46 miles via Falkirk it was almost completely level. But at the Glasgow end it dived down at 1 in 45 for $\frac{3}{4}$-mile from Cowlairs to Queen Street terminus. This section was originally worked by a stationary engine, and the rope survived until 1908, although after the first few years it was used only to assist locomotives. The original Edinburgh terminus was at Haymarket; the line was extended $1\frac{1}{2}$ miles eastwards to the present Waverley station in 1846.

Stanier Pacific no. 46226 'Duchess of Norfolk' accelerates away from Carlisle with the afternoon Euston-Perth express (1962)

The E&G remained an independent company until 1865, when it amalgamated with the North British, and it was a successful and aggressive one, building various branches and extensions in the coalfield and elsewhere. The Caledonian rather unwisely provoked a rate war with it in 1849, although its 56-mile road through Carstairs compared very badly with the older line's direct route. The Caledonian's more practical Edinburgh-Glasgow service via Shotts, working over a line shorter but more steeply graded than the E&G, started in 1869. It was worked competitively until

some time after nationalization, when passenger traffic was concentrated on the E&G. The remaining local trains were doubtless saved only by the change of government in 1964. The NB's own alternative route between Edinburgh and Glasgow, via Bathgate and Airdrie, although at 44 miles the shortest of all, never had a good service, possibly for exactly this reason, and was closed to passengers in 1956. Just as in South Wales, most coalfield lines now carry freight only.

The North British Railway's original purpose had been to build from Edinburgh to Berwick, in order to

J37 0-6-0 no. 64585 (one of a class built for the North British from 1914) on a weedkilling train at Dunfermline (1962)

meet the Newcastle & Berwick and so complete the East Coast line to Scotland. Nobody was much upset by the fact that none of this scheme had been sanctified by the Railway Commissioners, who were indeed about to be disbanded; they themselves had tacitly abandoned the idea that there was only room for one railway to Scotland, just as they were giving up the attempt to regulate and rationalize the promotion of new lines. The NBR was opened from Edinburgh to Berwick in June 1846. It had been built in a great hurry, like most railways George Hudson had any-

thing to do with, but it was well graded for the most part. The exceptions were a mile at 1 in 78 up into Waverley station, and 5 miles mainly at 1 in 96 climbing in the southbound direction between Cockburnspath and the Penmanshiel tunnel. There was also a 111-ft high viaduct nearby, at Dunglass, and a famous stretch along the cliffs above the sea on the descent into Berwick.

The North British eventually became the largest railway in Scotland, but it was a slow process. Its other southern main line, the Waverley Route from Edin-

The 12.45 p.m. for Edinburgh leaving Aberdeen behind two North British engines; Reid Atlantic no. 9871 'Thane of Fife', and 4-4-0 no. 9765 (1929)

burgh to Carlisle, was a very long time building; the company had always felt it wise to have a foot in both East and West Coast camps, and with this in view had got as far as Hawick by 1849. But it did not reach Carlisle until 1862, and then only by a single track with a purely local service. Like the G&SW, the NB found no welcome there until the Midland arrived in 1876. Then the line was doubled, and came into its own; despite its mountainous grades, its two separate summits (Falahill, south of Edinburgh, and Whitrope, south of Hawick) reached by miles of 1 in 70 or 75, and a pretty jagged profile even on the easier sections, the Waverley Route was the pride of the NB and remained an important main line until quite recently. But nowadays, its very slight advantage in distance (98 miles, compared with 101 on the Caledonian route via Carstairs) is not thought sufficient to justify its maintenance as an alternative for a rather limited amount of traffic, and it is being run down. The future of the Carlisle-Hawick section, which runs through very scenic but quite unpopulated country, must be regarded as black; and when it goes the rest will once again be of local interest only. This being so, it shows a rather odd lack of foresight to have closed the loop line from Edinburgh to Galashiels via Peebles in 1962. Although 12 miles longer than the main line, it did at least serve some valuable traffic centres on the way.

At the same time as it built the Waverley Route, the NB was also getting to Newcastle independently of the North Eastern. At first this was achieved by the Border Counties branch from Riccarton Junction to Hexham, opened in 1862, and running powers over the Newcastle & Carlisle. But the N&C was almost at once taken over by the NER, which rather spoilt matters. The NB then had to build its Wansbeck Valley branch from Reedsmouth to Morpeth, completed in 1865. At Morpeth it met the little Blyth & Tyne Railway, a prosperous coal-hauler which was then developing the passenger side of its business and had just opened a new extension to Newcastle, where it had its own terminus at Manors. But again unfortunately for the NB, the B&T was bought by the North Eastern in 1874.

So the North British invasion of Newcastle was rather a damp squib. The Border Counties line remained a wholly delightful rural and mountain branch until it was abandoned in 1956. Of the whole undertaking, only a small part of the Wansbeck Valley section remains. As for the Blyth & Tyne, except for the part of it included in the Newcastle-

Tynemouth suburban electrification, the whole of the passenger service in this busy area was axed in 1964, undoubtedly a black year for damaging closures; and the railway is now more or less back where it was over a century ago, hauling coal.

Fife, Perth and Aberdeen

The first main line to Aberdeen was completed in several stages by different companies. The first was the Scottish Central, which ran from a triangular junction with the Caledonian's main line into Buchanan Street at Gartcosh via Stirling and Gleneagles to Perth, and was opened in August 1848. At Perth it met a railway from Dundee which had been opened along the north bank of the Tay a year earlier. It passed under the Edinburgh & Glasgow near Castlecary, with a connection allowing through trains to run from Glasgow (Queen Street) to the north; trains from Edinburgh could do the same by means of another connection near Larbert. The line was fairly cheaply built, and so had several sharp grades, including those down Cumbernauld Glen towards Castlecary (1 in 98), up beyond Stirling past Dunblane (1 in 88) and down from Gleneagles towards Perth (1 in 100); north of Stirling it was clear of the coalfield and ran along the edge of the Highlands.

The Scottish Midland company continued the line from Perth to Forfar in October 1848. There it connected with an older railway, the Arbroath & Forfar, which had been opened in 1839 and which like its neighbour the Dundee & Arbroath had been built to the 5 ft 6 in gauge, nobody having foreseen that a through line from London would be completed inside ten years. Both the broad-gauge lines therefore had to be converted. Finally, there was the Aberdeen Railway, commencing from a junction with the A & F at Guthrie, which reached Aberdeen in April 1850. The traveller walking under the Euston Arch was now further sobered by the reflection that he could (if he had the cash) be transported continuously northwards for nearly 550 miles.

The Scottish Central, Scottish Midland, Arbroath & Forfar, and Aberdeen railways were all acquired by the Caledonian in 1865–6, although the three last named had previously amalgamated to form the Scottish North Eastern company. This arrangement meant that the Caledonian was in control of the area, and that all rail traffic for points north had to pass through Stirling. This continued until another bridge

A Deeside suburban train leaving Aberdeen; ex-GNSR 0-4-4T
no. 6885 and a rake of six-wheeled coaches (1925)

was built over the Forth a few miles downstream at Alloa in 1884. The Caledonian was content enough with the arrangement; and if the North British was not, nobody lost any sleep about that for a long time. However, things changed.

The way north of Edinburgh by land was interrupted by two wide stretches of water, the Forth and Tay estuaries. Between them lay the Fife peninsula, a prosperous land with considerable coalfields on the south side. These were served by their own local railways, linked with the national system by the Stirling & Dunfermline after 1852. This passed in 1858 to the Edinburgh & Glasgow company, who were at Stirling by means of running powers, and so came eventually to the North British. The only trunk line in Fife, although it was at first isolated, was the ambitiously-

named Edinburgh, Perth & Dundee, which ran from Burntisland, on the north side of the Forth opposite Edinburgh, to Tayport opposite Dundee, and had a branch from Ladybank to Perth; it had been opened in 1848. Edinburgh and Dundee were reached by ferries, and in 1850 a train ferry began to work between Burntisland and Granton. It was used only for freight, but it was the first public train ferry in the world. The engineer who designed it was Thomas Bouch. A second train ferry was put on between Tayport and Broughty Ferry in 1851, so there was then at any rate a theoretical challenge to the Caledonian's monopoly beyond Stirling.

Although Fife slowly filled up with railways during the fifties and sixties, nothing was done for a long time about making the Edinburgh, Perth & Dundee really

One of the odder events in early LNER locomotive history was the construction of some engines, Class B12, to Holden's 1911 Great Eastern design for service in Scotland. No. 61536 leaving Maud Junction with a Fraserburgh-Aberdeen train (1948)

live up to its title, even after the North British took over in 1862. But the train ferries were only a stopgap, and finally the bridges were planned in earnest. The Tay was tackled first, and Bouch was given the job. A few yards under two miles in length, and carrying a single line across 86 spans at a maximum height of 88 feet above high water, his bridge was opened in June 1878, together with a new southern approach to it from the EP&D main line at Leuchars. On the night of Sunday 28 December 1879, during a great storm, it collapsed under the northbound mail train, killing all 79 on board.

Of all British railway disasters, this one is now most firmly rooted in legend. The story of the inadequate preparation, poor design, and downright bad workmanship in building the first Tay Bridge, and of the destruction of its builder, has often been told. However, the structure had to be replaced, and the second Tay Bridge was completed in June 1887. Carrying a double track, it was a few yards longer than the old, and thus just over two miles long; the lengthening was to ease the curve approaching the Dundee shore, on which high speeds had seriously weakened the older structure. Elsewhere the new bridge is only a few feet from the remains of the old, most of whose piers still stand just above the waterline. A large number of undamaged girders were salvaged and used again.

Bouch had also planned a vast suspension bridge across the Forth, and work had actually started on it. Very wisely, it was abandoned, and a new design called for; work restarted in 1883. It continued for over six years, and at times employed some 4,500 men.

(*Left*) The Banff-Tillynaught branch train near Golf Club House Halt; Caledonian 0-4-4T no. 55185 (1954)

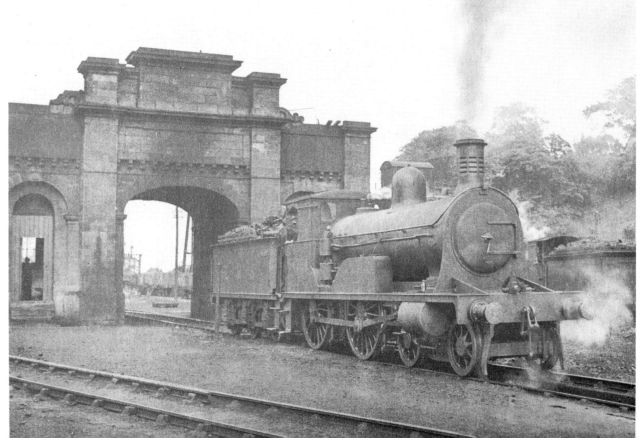

(Left) Ex-Highland Railway 'Small Ben' 4-4-0 no. 14406
'Ben Slioch' piloting Class Five 4-6-0 no. 5460 on an Inverness-
Glasgow train at Forres (1939)

The Highlands

The first railway to Inverness was originally promoted by the Great North of Scotland company, authorized in the Annus Mirabilis of 1846 to build there from Aberdeen. But money could not be found, and things hung fire. The first length of the GNoS, from Kitty-brewster in the northern suburbs of Aberdeen to Huntly, partly along the bed of a canal, was not opened until 1854; the line reached Keith, 53 miles, in October 1856, and there it stopped. From 1856 until 1867 the Aberdeen terminus was on the fishing quays at Waterloo, inconveniently far from the Caledonian station on the other side of the town, and the company's servants are invariably recorded as having taken great delight in despatching trains just as through travellers came panting into view. But in 1867 the GNoS and the Caledonian combined to build a new joint station on its present site in the centre of the city.

With its three cantilever towers 330 feet high, six balanced 680-ft cantilevers, and two intermediate 350-ft spans, the main part of the Forth Bridge is nearly a mile long. The two principal spans are of 1,710 feet, and the tracks are carried 156 feet above sea level. With its approach viaducts, the whole structure is rather more than $1\frac{1}{2}$ miles long, and to this day is one of the most spectacular pieces of engineering in the world. There are plenty of other bridges, including the road one nearby, which are longer and higher, but they do not have the same impact on the imagination. They remind the eye of a spider's web, and effortless suspension across gaps is what we expect from spiders' webs. The Forth Bridge is, in contrast, solid and substantial; and, because the last thing one expects to see in the sky is such enormous quantities of leaping ironwork, far more impressive.

Meanwhile, the inhabitants of Inverness had lost patience with the slow progress of the GNoS, and decided to start building towards Aberdeen themselves. Using the little Inverness & Nairn, which had been opened in 1855, the Inverness & Aberdeen Junction reached Keith via Elgin and Mulben in 1858.

It was opened to traffic in March 1890. But the Forth Bridge scheme included a great deal more than just that. New connections were needed to the Edinburgh & Glasgow line, with high-speed junctions facing each way; while to complete the new main line to Dundee, another connection was needed from Inverkeithing to Burntisland. Finally, a shortened route was built to Perth, using parts of some older branches but with an entirely new section north of Mawcarse, cutting through the Ochil hills at Glenfarg. The distance from Edinburgh to Perth came down from the 69 miles via Stirling to 48.

The 108-mile main line it had set out to build was now complete, but the GNoS was not as joyful about this as it should have been. The loss of its own western end still rankled, and the company cast about for ways to get beyond Keith. It was helped in this by the existence of a cantankerously independent little concern, the Morayshire Railway, which had opened a short isolated line from Elgin to Lossiemouth in 1852, and by 1862 had extended southwards from Elgin to Dandaleith. The GNoS, observing that the upper Spey Valley was full of whisky distilleries, decided it would be worth serving and between 1862 and 1866 completed a rather mountainous and wandering extension from Keith to a point near Broomhill. On the way it had (in 1863) thrown off a spur from Craigellachie to connect with the Morayshire; so there were now two routes from Keith to Elgin. A quarrel therefore started. The I&AJ claimed that all traffic should go by its line, since it was nearly ten miles shorter; the GNoS said no, it should go round via Craigellachie, because there were at least some towns worth serving on the way. The IA&J had the whip hand really, since it could schedule its trains to give a tight connection from Aberdeen at Keith and so get them away from

The North British Railway had now reached its full stature. Its main line had already been extended from Dundee to Aberdeen by the purchase of a half-share in the Dundee & Arbroath in 1880 and the opening of a new link from Arbroath to Kinnaber Junction in May 1883; from Kinnaber to Aberdeen the company had running powers over the Caledonian.

Black Stanier; two views of Class Five 4-6-0 no. 45384 on a Stranraer-Glasgow train (*above*) leaving Girvan and (*below*) crossing Pinmore Viaduct (1964)

Ex-Caledonian Pickersgill 4-4-0 no. 54470, standing by night
outside Dingwall shed (1949)

A Fort William-Mallaig freight near Glenfinnan, with Gresley K2 2-6-0 no. 61784

Elgin long before the GNoS arrived. But there was some justice in the opposite case too, and for many years the public were the butt of the quarrel. It was, and remains, a problem to which there is no tidy answer, and it was compounded in 1886 when the GNoS completed yet a third route from Keith to Elgin, serving the towns along the coast, sixteen miles longer than the Mulben line.

Although it was still trying rather half-heartedly to get to Inverness as late as the 1890s, the GNoS really concentrated on building branches in the area north and west of Aberdeen, and after a long period as a thoroughly disgraceful and reprobate company, blossomed out remarkably after the 1880s and became a model of its kind, well and efficiently worked. Its Deeside branch, from Aberdeen to Ballater, is often held out as one of the best British examples of efficient single line working (not that the competition in this department is very fierce, incidentally; the average Briton still tends to regard a single track as only half a railway, and our insistence on the ceremonial interchange of electric totems at passing loops prompts peals of belly-laughter from Prague to Patagonia). Between 1887 and 1937, when it finally succumbed to the trams, the GNoS worked a remarkable suburban service on its two routes out of Aberdeen, the smallest British city ever to have had such a thing. Distances between stations were to scale; counting the terminals, there were 10 stations in the 6¼ miles from Aberdeen to Dyce, and likewise on the 7½ miles to Culter.

Aberdeen did not control the only approach to Inverness for long. The idea of a direct line over the mountains to Perth had also been put forward in 1846, only to be mocked as one of the more outrageous absurdities of the Railway Mania. Its engineer, Joseph Mitchell, who had been an assistant to Telford when he was building his roads in the Highlands, bided his time, and was finally rewarded when the Inverness & Perth Junction company was incorporated in 1861. The Perth & Dunkeld, a local line with a branch from the Caledonian at Stanley, was taken over, and the railway opened from Dunkeld to Forres during the summer of 1863. By this route it was 144 miles from Inverness to Perth, instead of 198 via Aberdeen. In 1865 the I&PJ and the I&AJ amalgamated to form the Highland Railway.

Mitchell's line over the mountains was built as inexpensively as possible consistent with a ruling grade of 1 in 70, and there were only 3 short tunnels. On the other hand several large viaducts were needed, notably in the Pass of Killiecrankie, and the 105-ft high structure at Dunphail. There were two separate summits; 1,052 ft up on Dava Moor, between Forres and Aviemore, and 1,484 ft at Druimuachdar, between Aviemore and Blair Atholl. This is now the highest point reached by any British railway, except the rack line up Snowdon.

The Highland, like the GNoS, was never a wealthy railway. Even its main lines to Inverness served a very limited population. North of Inverness things were even less promising, and indeed none of these railways were built with any expectation of making any money. Even in the nineteenth century it was realized that some things were worth doing for other reasons, and one of the prime movers in getting these northern lines built was the Duke of Sutherland, who put a lot of his own money into them. Very scenic, cheaply built and steeply graded through difficult country, making long loops inland to avoid the great rivers, none of them can be described as main lines, but they are still as necessary a part of the local economy as they were

The morning Inverness-Kyle of Lochalsh train leaving Dingwall, with Class Five no. 44992 piloted by Pickersgill 4-4-0 no. 54487 for the climb to Raven Rock (1959)

Another Caledonian survival: 'Standard Passenger' 0-4-4T no. 55224 on a Ballachulish-Oban train beside Loch Leven (1961)

when they were built; a fact which was recognized, albeit very belatedly, by the government when in 1964 it refused the application to abandon everything north of Inverness which had been made under the Beeching Plan. Very briefly, let it be recorded that these railways were nearly all built during the space of 12 years. The Inverness & Ross-shire was opened from Inverness to Dingwall in 1862 and Bonar Bridge in 1864; the Sutherland Railway (1868) ran from Bonar Bridge to Golspie, and the Duke of Sutherland's Railway (1871) from Golspie to Helmsdale, while the Sutherland & Caithness was opened in 1874 from Helmsdale to Wick and Thurso. The Dingwall & Skye built the branch westwards as far as Strome Ferry, reached in 1870. By 1884 all these companies had been taken over by the Highland, which in every case had worked them from the start.

Two more railways were built in the Highlands, the second of which caused some alterations to earlier lines. A branch had been built from Dunblane to Callander in 1858, and this was extended westwards by the Callander & Oban company. Work started in 1865, but money was short, traffic was negligible, and the company staggered in and out of bankruptcy, opening the line by stages as the cash came in. The Caledonian took over in 1870, but even so Oban was not reached for another ten years.

In some ways the West Highland was a more ambitious scheme. Backed by the North British, it took shape as the result of proposals to build a railway up the Great Glen to Inverness, which gave the Highland a bad fright. But the NBR decided it was enough just to get to the other end of the Glen; there was no point in spending another fortune just to bankrupt the Highland. So the West Highland Railway was opened from Craigendoran, on the Helensburgh branch, to Fort William in August 1894; it crossed the Callander & Oban at Crianlarich. The West Highland Extension, from Fort William to Mallaig, whose dividends were guaranteed by the government (a thing very rare in British railway history), followed in 1901.

Like all other lines in the Highlands, the WHR was cheap, steep, and scenic; engineering was reduced to a minimum, grades ran to 1 in 50 or 60, and there was a 1,347-ft summit on Rannoch Moor. But although it never came near the Highland Railway's property, it was a menace distantly perceived at Inverness and countermeasures were taken. A direct line from Aviemore to Inverness, saving 26 miles compared with the original route via Forres, had sometimes been suggested, but the Highland didn't like reducing its mileage since this necessarily meant also reducing its revenue. But clearly now it had to be built, and it was opened in 1898. It involved quite heavy construction works, with a 143-ft high viaduct across Culloden Moor, and climbed to a 1,315-ft summit at Slochd with a ruling grade of 1 in 60. The older line via Forres was now rather superfluous, but lived on: it was finally agreed to close it only in 1965.

Another improvement made necessary by the WHR

An ex-North British C15 class 4-4-2T (of 1911); no 67474 on the Arrochar-Craigendoran push-and-pull high above Loch Long, at the southern end of the West Highland line (1959)

was to move the western end of the Skye line from Strome Ferry, where the harbour was unsatisfactory, to the Kyle of Lochalsh, and this ten-mile extension, which needed a lot of expensive rock excavation along the side of Loch Carron, was opened in 1897.

The threat to Inverness which these lines were intended to counter never materialized, so they succeeded. An unusually optimistic local company, the Invergarry & Fort Augustus, jumped in where the angelic (in this context) North British feared to tread, and did actually start to build along the Great Glen from the WHR at Spean Bridge towards Inverness; the line was hurriedly leased by the Highland from its opening in 1903 until it closed in 1911. The NBR later reopened it, but it was a hopeless proposition and finally died in 1946. The whistle of a locomotive sounded only briefly over the waters of Loch Ness, and never seemed to disturb the monster.

BR Class Five 4-6-0 no. 73031 under the coaling tower at
Bristol (Barrow Road) shed, with hoppers for removing ashes
and clinker visible in the foreground (1959)

Part Two
Equipment and Operation

1 Locomotive Design and Practice

Design in 1900: Compound Locomotives

From time to time one hears it said that the steam locomotive has not changed in any important respect since Stephenson's day. This is rather like saying that the saw, because it still has a blade and a handle, has not changed since it was invented by some Neanderthal carpenter. It remains worth noticing that its teeth are made of hardened steel instead of chips of mammoth's tusk.

Perhaps the most striking thing about the British locomotive fleet in 1900 was its enormous variety. To some extent this followed from the (rather unusual) British tradition that each railway company designed and, if it was large enough, built its own engines; forcing the independent manufacturers, incidentally, to concentrate on exports. To some extent also it was made necessary by the fact that locomotives were then relatively inflexible; one intended for passenger work was very little use for freight, and vice versa. But variety was inevitable also because there was no one 'right' answer in steam locomotive engineering. It was all a matter of proportion and judgement, of balancing swings against roundabouts, of making an almost infinite number of choices in a wide field of interdependent alternatives.

But there were wide areas in which there was a consensus of opinion. One of these was in wheel arrangements. Most of the earliest locomotives had been four-wheeled, but soon after long-distance running began these had to be superseded by six-wheeled types, partly because of the need for extra size and power and partly for reasons of safety and improved riding. For the next half-century most British locomotives were built on a rigid six-wheeled frame, with one or sometimes two pairs of driving wheels for passenger service and either two or three for freight. Occasionally, where an engine of particular power was needed, for example Gooch's

famous broad-gauge 4-2-2s of 1848, eight wheels would be used, still held rigidly. Anything larger than this was quite exceptional for many years. But as engines with eight or more wheels became commoner, it was realized that the rigid frame had to go; it was causing far too much trouble on curves. The Americans had faced and solved this problem already by using the bogie, but this was disliked in England; some designers, like Webb on the L&NW, preferred a single radial axle giving a more limited amount of side-play; others, like Stroudley on the LB&SC, clung to the rigid six-wheeler and by maintaining high standards elsewhere got away with it even for express work. But for this kind of duty by the end of the nineteenth century the commonest type was the 4-4-0; it had been introduced to Britain, fittingly enough, by the Stockton & Darlington in 1861 for service over Stainmore. Here and there the single-driver locomotive was still favoured; it had been given a new lease of life in the 1890s by the invention of the steam sander, and some preferred it for high speeds because they feared that power would be absorbed by the coupling rods. Others were already thinking in terms of something larger. For freight work, on the other hand, the 0-6-0 was still almost universal.

There was rather less variety in other departments of design. Large wheels were necessary for fast running; there was a rule of thumb that the absolute limit of an engine's speed in miles per hour was the same as the diameter of its driving wheels in inches. This was the reason for building engines with seven- or eight-foot wheels, which look so ungainly to modern eyes. The key to the situation was unsatisfactory valve performance. Poor valves limited the speed at which steam could be got into and out of the cylinders, and so restricted the rate at which the wheels could be driven round. Just as important, they prevented full use being made of the expansive power of the steam. In practice, the cut-off (the proportion of the stroke during which live steam was admitted to the cylinder) could seldom be reduced below about 30%; as a result, the exhaust steam was still at a fairly high pressure and capable of doing more work.

And so at the turn of the century, the most active field of experiment was in compounding, trying to reduce this wastage. Most designers experimented with compound locomotives to some extent. F.W. Webb, Chief Mechanical Engineer of the L&NW from 1871 to 1904, after a first trial in 1879 on the lines of Anatole Mallet's pioneer work in France, built seven types of compound for passenger work and three more for freight, as well as several varieties of tank engine. The 80 'Experiments', 'Dreadnoughts', and 'Teutonics', introduced between 1883 and 1889, were all 3-cylinder 2-4-0s, similar to or enlargements of his extremely successful simple-expansion 'Precedents' (more often known as 'Jumbos') of 1874. Webb used two rather small high pressure cylinders, outside and driving the rear wheel, and an enormous low pressure one, placed inside and driving the front wheel. Thinking that it would allow the pistons automatically to assume the best relative working position, Webb left the wheels uncoupled, but the lack of synchronization which resulted made smooth working impossible. As often as not, the LP cylinder received more steam on one stroke than the return, which caused violent fore and aft motion through the train at low speeds, and also loss of power, since the HP exhaust was partly choked. In the next two classes, both 3-cylinder 2-4-2s with uncoupled wheels built on similar lines, the 'Greater Britains' of 1891 and the 'John Hicks' of 1894, as in the last of the 'Teutonics', matters were for a while made worse by the fact that in a misguided attempt at simplification Webb removed the independent LP valve gear and substituted a slip eccentric. This sometimes failed to reverse, causing the famous sight of an engine trying to start with its wheels churning round in opposite directions. This helps to explain why the wheel arrangements of these engines is usually quoted as 2-2-2-0 or 2-2-2-2.

In 1897 Webb produced the first of the 'Black Prince' or 'Jubilee' compounds, and in 1901 the slightly larger 'Alfred the Great' class. Both of these were 4-cylinder compound 4-4-0s, with wheels coupled normally, and so they were rather more dependable. His compound freight engines were the 3- and 4-cylinder 0-8-0s of 1893 and 1901 respectively, among the first of this wheel arrangement in Britain.

Some of the 4-cylinder engines, which were found to be front-heavy, were altered to 2-8-0s. There was also a class of 4-cylinder 4-6-0s known as 'Bill Baileys'; these were Webb's last design.

The Webb compounds have had a bad press, and much has been made of their undependability and sluggish performance. Yet most of them could undoubtedly go. Their weakness was rather that with the LP cut-off fixed, as it usually was, at 70%, together with constricted steam passages, the amount of further expansion obtained by compounding was only small, and not worth all the trouble and expense it involved. The compounds showed no advantages over the older simple engines, notably the 'Jumbos', they worked alongside. Webb's successor quickly slaughtered or rebuilt the 3-cylinder engines and the 4-4-0s, although the 'John Hicks' lingered for some years; the 4-cylinder goods engines lasted much longer, many of the 0-8-0s until well into LMS days.

T.W. Worsdell, and his brother W. Worsdell after him, built a large number of 2-cylinder compounds for the North Eastern between 1884 and 1908, for both passenger and freight service. These were much more successful. They had the great advantage of simplicity; the only complication needed was a valve to allow live steam into the low pressure cylinder for the first stroke on starting, while their only drawback was that they could not develop full power in reverse, and so were unsuited for tank engines. But the last and most numerous British compounds were built on the Smith system for the Midland Railway by S.W. Johnson and R.M. Deeley after 1901. This was a 3-cylinder design, but the exact opposite of Webb's, with one high and two low pressure cylinders, all of comparable size. As applied to a series of express passenger 4-4-0s later greatly multiplied by the LMS and not finally extinct until 1961, it was much the most successful compound type in Britain. If, of course, it can properly be described as a compound at all. For there was an automatic valve which fed live steam to the LP cylinders not only on starting but whenever the regulator was much less than fully open; and knowing how rare full-regulator working has always been in Britain (vide all practical works of reference as opposed to most theoretical ones) it seems safer to call them semi-compounds, or perhaps compoundables. It may be doubted anyway how many of their drivers during the last 20 years knew how to put them into compound working, or even what this was.

So compounding on the whole had very little

Two LMS Workhorses Hughes 'Crab' 2-6-0 no. 42800 near Patna with Ayr-Waterside coal empties (1965)

and Stanier 8F 2-8-0 no. 48007, looking tired and grimy, outside Willesden depot (1964)

Webb Compounds
'Dreadnought' class 2-4-0 no. 643 'Raven'. Note the puny outside cylinders, driving onto the rear wheel; the front wheel is driven only by the single monster low-pressure cylinder between the frames (c. 1890)

The most successful and least famous of the Webb compounds were his freight engines. No. 918 is shown in her original form, as an 0-8-0 (c. 1905)

No. 1888 has been given a wheelbarrow-type pony truck to help carry some of the front end weight (c. 1910)

158

success in Britain. The main reason for this was because improvements in valve design and the use of superheated steam made it possible to get almost as much expansion in one cylinder (even though they also improved compound efficiency), and that lack of space prevented sufficiently large LP cylinders. Yet the French built compounds until steam construction ceased, and all but the last and largest had LP cylinders between the frames, where the larger European loading gauge made little difference. Perhaps a clue to the matter lies elsewhere. The compound is a more sophisticated piece of machinery which needs to be understood by its operator. E. C. Poultney, writing on the subject in 1952, remarked that the fixing of the LP cut-off on Webb's later engines was 'a good point because the need for making these adjustments places a responsibility on enginemen they should not have to undertake'. Exactly. The French steam driver, particularly on first-class work, is taught a great deal about locomotive design and function, and consequently knows how to make these adjustments; the Briton, promoted by seniority, is put firmly in his place and told his only job is to make the brute go. If he likes to interest himself in deeper matters, well and good, but he can still reach an honoured retirement without ever finding out what goes on under the bonnet. The analogy, except for a few keen and gifted individuals, is therefore with a Fangio versus an Aunt Edna at the wheel of a Maserati.

So far as ordinary matters of mechanical competence were concerned – the need for big enough bearings, strong enough motion, and so on – practice by 1900 had long been codified and a high level of workmanship and solidity was general, although some individual designers (notably Dugald Drummond) felt it was worth spending a little more on extra solidity, to reduce failures and maintenance difficulties. And it usually was worth while, although perhaps not from the accountant's point of view. One of the causes of the feud between drawing offices and running sheds was that the latter always got the sticky end of any plan to save money. On the road, anything can be forgiven a locomotive that keeps on pulling.

Many designers were also aware of the benefits of standardization, of having as few different classes of engine and as many parts interchangeable between them as possible. But there were still a few lines, beloved of historians, where hardly two engines were alike, and mountains of rarely-used but vital spare parts cluttered the stores. Some companies were more willing than others to spend money on a glossy finish, but that was a trivial matter and with plentiful cheap labour it was rare to see a dirty engine anywhere. The steam locomotive is an unclean animal by nature, but one would never have known this; the shedmaster's motto was 'Ars est celare naturam'. Locomotive builders had been greatly helped in reaching a high standard of safety and reliability by great advances in steel manufacture; broken wheels and axles, which had caused nearly one accident in five during the 1840s, were now rare. Boiler explosions had also once been common, and their reduction was also partly due to the same cause; although hard experience had taught some other lessons, including the evil effects of scale and sludge. These deposits have to be removed quite frequently by washing the boiler out; the use of various chemicals in the feedwater to ensure that they are easily shifted and do not cling to tubes and firebox is fairly recent, becoming general only in the 1930s.

Only slow progress was made in one department now regarded as important; lessening the difficulties and discomforts of the men who had to do the job. Here, as so often, the British workman was his own worst enemy. The Stockton & Darlington 4-4-0s of 1861 were the first in Britain to have really good cabs, for instance, of the type long standard in America; yet the men scorned them. By 1900 something better than the old plain weatherboard was universal, but many engines were still very badly designed from this point of view. Not that anybody complained very much; there were worse things to worry about. To prepare an engine for the road it was still necessary to get in underneath and amongst the inside motion, a dirty, uncomfortable, and dangerous business. Very little was done to make the work less onerous in this respect; there was no motive for it. It would cost money, and any man who objected was welcome to find another job; there were always plenty eager to take his place. Writing in 1877, Michael Reynolds remarked 'it would be an extraordinary railwayman who would never make a slip, never meet with any misfortune through the neglect of others, ... and who retains five fingers on each hand and five toes in each boot, with his ribs intact'. Nowadays this makes one's hair stand on end, yet then it was just an off-hand phrase in the middle of a paragraph, without comment. By 1900 there were the beginnings of a more enlightened attitude.

In their last years large express locomotives have often been given menial tasks that would have been far below their dignity once. Ex-LNER A2 class Pacific no. 60535 'Hornet's Beauty' coming off the Ballochmyle Viaduct with a Glasgow-Carlisle via Kilmarnock parcels train (1964) and (*below*) Stanier 'Duchess' Pacific no. 46255 'City of Hereford' at Greskine, halfway up Beattock, with a Carlisle-Glasgow parcels, shortly before the entire class was summarily executed (1964)

Twentieth Century Design: Boilers

For the first 40 years of the 20th Century, the continual need in passenger service was for locomotives capable of hauling heavier trains. With the introduction of corridor coaches after the 1890s, and later when wooden bodies began to be replaced by steel, train weight per passenger seat increased tremendously. During the 1930s it also became important to design for the extremely high speeds needed to compete with road and air services. And finally, although it had always been important to build engines which were cheap to run, this became the predominating motive. Cheapness had once been mainly a matter of fuel economy, but with the rise in the standard of living and wage rates, particularly after 1945, it became rather more a matter of reducing maintenance in every possible way, even at the cost of some deterioration in fuel economy and performance.

It was Archibald Sturrock, the first Locomotive Superintendent of the Great Northern, who first pointed out that the power of a locomotive depended on its capacity to boil water. This has become a truism, and like most is an over-simplification. It is perfectly possible for an efficient and powerful boiler to be let down by a poorly-designed front end. But while any boiler can meet the maximum demand for steam from any cylinders for a certain length of time (which capacity to meet a gross temporary overload is one of the advantages of the steam locomotive, shared by the electric but not the diesel), the important thing for main line work is how long a large steam output can be maintained. How well the boiler 'steams' is not just a matter of size. A large boiler will be able to meet a maximum demand for a minute or two longer, of course, but the actual generation of steam depends entirely on how much fuel can be effectively burnt and how efficiently its heat can be transferred to the water; in other words, on grate area and the amount and disposition of heating surface. There have been cases of big-boilered engines which looked impressive but whose performance was flabby because they soon ran out of steam (including some of Dugald Drummond's less successful designs on the L&SW); rather

The Old Meldrum branch train at Lenthenty headed by ex-North British Railway J36 class 0-6-0 no. 65282 (1954)

commoner were the comparatively small engines whose best performances were altogether beyond the capacity of their equals in size because they steamed so well (notably, among others, the Ivatt Atlantics on the GNR).

It was one thing to design a boiler that would produce plenty of steam; it was quite another to build one that would do so with a reasonable fuel consumption. By 'thrashing' the engine so that there was an extremely fierce draught through the fire, with gases whirling through the tubes so fast that they made the smoke-box red-hot and a blast so hard that lumps of unburnt coal shot out of the chimney and pattered down onto the carriage roofs (and started lineside fires), a boiler could always be made to produce more power, but at heavy cost. Certain railways, especially the L&NW, made a tradition of this sort of thing, and while coal was cheap there was a respectable case for it. The smaller boiler was cheaper to build, and it was arguable that it was more economical on lighter workings. But it was generally felt to be sounder practice to avoid thrashing, save fuel and reduce the cost of boiler repairs. There were two ways of doing this; one was to reduce the size of the cylinders so that even the maximum steam consumption was well within the capacity of the boiler (this was the secret, again, of the Ivatt Atlantics, and in a slightly different way of Raven's engines on the North Eastern after 1910); the other, more expensive but more rewarding, was to build larger engines.

One important variable has to be taken into account in considering boiler design, and that is the nature of the coal. Most British coal is fairly hard and quick-burning, tends to form clinker, and as a rule gives best results in a shallow fire with air drawn in above as well as through the grate. If the fire gets too thick, or too much fresh coal is put on at a time, combustion is incomplete, thermal efficiency falls, and thick smoke is produced, while the grate gets choked more quickly with clinker and ash. In consequence the effective power of a boiler burning this kind of coal depends to a large extent on the area of the grate. Now a large grate can only be placed between the frames up to a certain point, and it becomes unmanageably long when it is difficult for the fireman to throw coal on the front of the fire. For more powerful engines it is therefore necessary to have a wide firebox, overlapping the frames and supported by trailing wheels.

On the other hand, the South Wales steam coal used by the GWR is soft and burns slowly, but with less ash and clinker; it needs a considerably thicker fire, sometimes heaped up like a haystack, but it tends to stay cleaner, and so it is possible to achieve high power outputs from a much smaller grate when burning this type of fuel. (Compare the 30 and 34 sq ft grates of the GWR 'Castle' and 'King' with the 42 and 50 sq ft of the comparable 'Britannia' and 'A1' Pacifics.) This is the explanation of the fact that the GWR never went in seriously for Atlantics or Pacifics. It was also the reason why GWR locomotives sometimes tended to do badly when deprived of their normal diet. They could perform acceptably on hard coal, sure enough, but only if their crews realized that a different firing technique was needed.

A feature of boiler design which originated (so far as British practice is concerned) on the GWR and later became more or less general was the tapered barrel, having a smaller diameter at the smokebox than the firebox end. It has been claimed that the advantage of this is that it brings a larger volume of water closer to the fire, but this seems rather theoretical. Apart from saving considerable weight, the design has a more practical virtue. When a locomotive reaches the top of a hill and noses over onto the following down grade, or when the brakes are applied, the water in the boiler will run forward, tending to uncover the crown of the firebox; which can be dangerous, as if this gets seriously overheated it will collapse and may explode. With a taper boiler the effects of the water moving forward are less noticeable. It is perhaps only a psychological point, but it does have some effect in countering the unwillingness of some crews to run down the water level to meet a temporary demand for power, as in climbing a hill, and so losing time.

Another way in which the performance of a boiler can be improved is by increasing the steam pressure. This makes it possible to get more power out of cylinders of equal size; in thermodynamic theory it also leads to increased efficiency, but in practice this is not detectable until one comes to pressures only attainable in large stationary plants. In locomotive practice the limits are given by the cost of building and maintaining the boiler (for pressures above 300 lb per sq in more complex types are needed), and the gradual increase of small and unavoidable leakages. At the end of the nineteenth century most locomotives worked at pressures of 150–160 lb per sq in; some advanced designers, including McIntosh on the Caledonian, Ivatt on the Great Northern, and Aspinall on the Lancashire & Yorkshire, were using 175–180 lb per sq in. The first British locomotives to use steam at 200 lb were some Worsdell compounds on the NER, in 1893; Webb and McIntosh followed, and so in 1902 did G.J. Churchward on the GWR, leading the way on to 225 lb two years later (to compare with some imported French compound Atlantics). Pressures above 180 lb were nevertheless rare until the 1920s, when 225 or 250 lb became normal on express passenger types. In the last pre-nationalization designs there was a further advance to 280 lb with the Bulleid Pacifics on the Southern and the GWR 'Counties'.

But the most important improvement in boiler performance was due to superheating, a major breakthrough leading to important advances in other directions. Non-superheated locomotives use 'saturated' steam taken straight from the boiler; naturally this is at the same temperature as the boiling water, and so it contains a lot of finely-divided water droplets. As soon as it starts to expand in a cylinder, it starts to condense round these and power is lost. By 'superheating' the steam, or passing it through elements in contact with hot gases from the fire, its temperature is considerably raised, the water is removed, and it will expand much more before any condensation starts. In practice, and up to the point where cylinder lubrication becomes troublesome, the hotter the steam the better. The first effective superheater, the Schmidt, originated in Germany and was first applied in Britain by Churchward and by Hughes on the L&Y in 1906. The idea spread fast. Earle Marsh on the LB&SC was an early superheater enthusiast, and caused a considerable sensation in 1909 by running an LB&SC '13' class 4-4-2T on through trains from East Croydon over the L&NW to Rugby without a water stop, while the L&NW's saturated tender engines were greedily slurping up water from not one but two sets of troughs on the shorter run from Euston.

In this way the economy previously attainable only by compounding was equalled, at lower cost. Superheater elements do not last very long, since they are made of quite thin tubes and reach a very high temperature, but they are cheap, easily changed, and make a fuel saving of anything from 10% to 25% possible, even at high outputs. The higher temperatures reached in the cylinders raised certain problems. Old hit-and-miss methods of lubrication had to go; heavier grades of oil had to be forced in, preferably by mechanical pumps. The old friction-creating slide valve was out for the same reason.

Twentieth Century Design: Front Ends

The preferred alternative to the flat slide valve was the piston valve, working in a cylindrical valve-chamber. Its main advantage was reduced friction, since it was not forced down onto a large working surface by steam pressure, and so it was no longer necessary to keep the steam ports small in order to limit wear and tear and the amount of power needed to drive the valve. At first, the piston valve was a devil to keep steamtight; the problem of avoiding leakage due to wear between two curved surfaces is of course much more intractable than between two flat ones. A lot of experiment took place before Churchward at Swindon finally adopted an American pattern of expanding piston ring forced into close contact with the valve liner by steam pressure. The area involved was still so small that friction remained unimportant. Later, sprung rings of the simple type used in petrol or diesel motors were adopted.

With generous steam passages now a practical possibility, the way lay open to making an improvement in cylinder performance, and again it was Swindon which led the field. Churchward realized that if the maximum valve lap and length of travel was increased, wider openings to steam would result even with short cut-off working, giving free running and economy at high speeds. Long-lap piston valves therefore became a Swindon standard after the first few years of the twentieth century. Other designers were rather slow to catch on to this point until it was driven home in 1925, when comparative exchange trials took place between Gresley 'A1' Pacifics and GWR 'Castles'. The larger LNER engines, generally considered very successful, were badly shown up. After Gresley had altered their valves to give longer lap on Swindon principles, they were transformed; they could be run at 15% cut-off or even less, and their coal consumption dropped by some 24%. Long lap valves then became universal.

Another improvement followed from the replacement of Stephenson by Walschaerts valve gear. The Stephenson gear was simple and practical, although less compact and rather heavy; it had been standard since the 1840s. But it had one great disadvantage in short cut-off working. Steam has to be admitted to the cylinder before the power stroke starts, partly to build up pressure and partly to help reverse the motion of piston and rod. The extent to which this takes place is known as the 'Lead'. It is a characteristic of Stephen-

The Churchward 'Stars' of 1906; no. 4055 'Princess Sophia' leaving Reading for Paddington with an express from Cheltenham (1949)

son gear that as the cut-off is reduced, the lead is increased, until it ceases to be helpful and becomes a drag. Churchward's first answer to this problem was so to set the valves that the lead was negative in full gear, and this arrangement was applied among others to the 'Saint' class 4-6-os of 1907. In this case it certainly produced a very fast and free-running engine, but there were compensating drawbacks, particularly when it came to finding space also for inside cylinders. On the 'Stars' of 1906 Churchward used Walschaerts gear, which gave a constant lead at all times, and found it preferable. It gradually spread until after some twenty years it was almost universal in British practice. From time to time experiments have been made with poppet valves, somewhat like those used in internal combustion engines, but their theoretical ad-

vantages have not apparently been realized in service. Nevertheless, a fair number (all fitted with cam-driven Caprotti valve gear) are still running.

Another difference between nineteenth and twentieth century practice is the gradual decline of the inside-cylinder layout. There were several reasons why inside cylinders were favoured in the first place; they saved weight, it was easier to provide short and direct steam passages to them, and they were less difficult to balance, since all the stresses and thrusts of revolving and reciprocating weights took place nearer to the centre line of the engine. So they predominated. But with piston valves it became just as easy to arrange good steam passages with outside cylinders, and getting rid of the expensive and potentially dangerous cranked axle was attractive. So was the greater accessibility and ease of maintenance of outside cylinders and gear. Preference therefore swung the other way, and new inside-cylinder designs became rarer and rarer. The last of all, oddly enough, apart from two types of GWR tank, was an engine which otherwise looked as if it belonged to the Martian Space Force; Bulleid's Q1 class 0-6-0 on the Southern, which appeared in 1942.

Balancing still remained a difficult problem, and one whose importance has sometimes been overlooked. For smooth running it is necessary to balance, as nearly as possible, not only the revolving weight of rods, but also the reciprocating weight of connecting rods, pistons, crossheads, and so on. This second task is hardest, since the necessary balance weights are themselves unbalanced in the vertical plane, and produce a 'hammerblow' effect at rail level. On a two-cylinder engine, particularly a smallish one with a long stroke, perfection is impossible. With certain types, notably the GWR 'Halls' and 'Counties', this led from time to time to a fore-and-aft motion being felt in the train at the speed when driving wheel revolutions coincided with the period of oscillation of incorrectly-tensioned drawgear springs. Modern practice has been to balance only about 40% of reciprocating weight on a two-cylinder engine, giving a rougher

ride but doing less damage to track and bridges through hammerblow. There is no recorded instance in recent British locomotive history quite so bad as an American case, where the New Haven Railroad took delivery of some powerful new streamliners in the early 1940s. Complaints were soon made of their rough riding and damage they seemed to be doing to the track, and investigation proved that quite apart from excessive hammerblow, above 60 mph one pair of driving wheels were lifting inches clear of the rails. About the nearest we came to this was soon after the war, when two GWR 28XX 2-8-0s were rebalanced at Swindon to suit the standard rectangular section coupling rods, but which were still fitted with older rods of a lighter I-section. These made several energetic trackwrecking excursions between Banbury and South Wales before they were caught, particularly as GWR men naturally first suspected the nasty foreign 'Austerity' 2-8-0s. Several of these were submitted to spectacular tests at Swindon, slipping on greased rails; but they reached equivalent speeds above 80 mph before the wheels began to lift clear, and so were clearly not guilty.

Since a three-cylinder engine is much easier to balance, and a four-cylinder one almost balances itself, there was a powerful argument for using more

The Churchward 'Saints' of 1907: no. 2932 'Ashton Court' near Tilehurst with an express from Ilfracombe and Bristol (1926)

than two cylinders for high speeds. Another was provided by the restrictions of the British loading gauge (or more accurately, high British station platforms), which prevented a really powerful two-cylinder engine; there wasn't room. So Britain is one of the few countries where 3- or 4-cylinder simple-expansion locomotives were built in large numbers; Germany was perhaps the only other to have so many. Among others, Raven on the NER and Gresley on the GNR went in for the 3-cylinder layout on a considerable scale, which in due course meant that the LNER had many 3- and no 4-cylinder engines, except for a few inherited from the Great Central and some experiments. Churchward, taking the idea from three French compound Atlantics imported for trials in 1903–5, adopted a 4-cylinder layout with divided drive, the inside cylinders jutting out a little in front of the smokebox and driving the leading wheels, the outside ones set farther back and connected to the second pair. This became the standard Swindon arrangement, used on the 'Stars' of 1906, the 'Castles' of 1923, and the 'Kings' of 1927, not to mention Stanier's 'Pacifics' on the LMS. The GWR thus had many 4- but no 3-cylinder engines. The LMS and the Southern had some of each.

The Southern's 4-cylinder engines, the 'Lord Nelsons' of 1926, were unusual. Churchward's layout, like all others except for an experiment on the North Staffordshire, had achieved almost perfect balance by having the two cylinders on each side set at 180° to each other, so that the reciprocating masses cancelled each other out. This meant that the strokes synchronized and the engine gave four exhaust beats per revolution. On the 'Nelsons', however, it was decided to go instead for even torque and a more regular draught on the fire; the cranks were therefore set at 135° and the engines gave eight beats per revolution, which sounded most odd. One engine was left with 180° setting as a control, but the experiment proved little; they were all rather rough and sluggish monsters and the odd one was neither better nor worse. They were undeniably the quietest locomotives in Britain when getting away with a train, especially in their final form, even if their acceleration was not always as rapid as it sounded.

All 3-cylinder engines, plus the 'Nelsons', might in theory be expected to be more sure-footed in starting, because of the more even application of power during each turn of the wheels. Observation of normally impeccable starts on the GWR, compared with volcanic thrashings and strugglings at places like York and Darlington as 3-cylinder Gresley Pacifics endeavoured to get their trains under way proved that this was one of those theories not obeyed by facts. For other things

'Lord Nelson' 4-6-0 no. 858 'Lord Duncan' leaving Dover with an up Continental express (1935)

were more important. Much ink has been spilt over this question, and all kinds of partly true answers have been produced, including in the case mentioned the unequal power development given by worn or ill-maintained Gresley conjugated valve gear (which drove the inside valve by combining the motion of the two outside ones). Much play is also made with the 'factor of adhesion', the ratio between calculated Tractive Effort and the weight on driving wheels; but this is of course only relevant when the engine is moving and working at full throttle. In starting, the question is more nearly how *little* power can be applied, and so (assuming an engine in good mechanical condition) the only important thing is to have a regulator with very fine control at small openings. This was another point which Churchward appreciated, and it explains the sure-footed starts so often commented on with GWR locomotives. During the 1950s the message finally got through nationally, and where possible alterations to other regulators were made. When an engine is in bad order, slipping becomes harder to control for other reasons; shocks due to loose or worn bearings will start it, and worn tyres which do not grip the rail.

The last new development, which was still under way when steam design activity was stopped, was in redraughting. Right up to the 1940s the chimney and blastpipe combination was the one part of a locomotive that had in fact not changed since Stephenson's time, or even earlier. Richard Trevithick knew when he built his first in 1804 that if the exhaust was directed up the chimney a draught was induced through the fire, which increased as the engine worked harder and so enabled the greater demand for steam to be met. The best proportions were worked out by experiment, and matters rested there, while generations of wily drivers and shedmasters knew that an engine's steaming could always be improved, easing their work at the price of a slight rise in back pressure and therefore in fuel consumption, if a ring or 'jimmy' was fixed inside the blastpipe nozzle to reduce its area and sharpen the blast.

For two opposing factors were at work. Exhaust steam passages had to be as large as possible for economy, but the draught had to be great enough to burn even sub-standard coal and give sufficiently free steaming. Until 1902 the theory of the action that took place in the chimney and smokebox was not understood, and since nobody knew how the mechanism worked, it was not possible to improve it. In that year Professor W. F. M. Goss published the results of his researches into the matter at the stationary testing plant he had installed at Purdue University, proving that the pumping action of the exhaust steam took

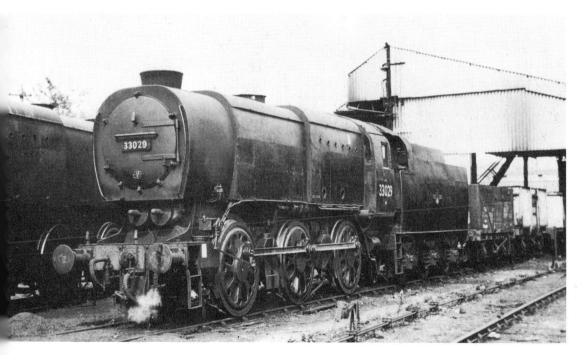

A vision of things to come; the Q1 0-6-0 of 1942 was a very competent locomotive, but as nearly as possible an exception to the rule that utility is beauty. No. 33029 at Guildford (1962)

The 'Patriot' or 'Baby Scot' 4-6-0s were a Fowler design of 1930, nominally a rebuild of the LNWR 'Claughtons'. No. 45550 approaching Shap Summit with a southbound train of empty stock (1962)

place near the surface of the cone it formed on leaving the blastpipe nozzle, and depended on its mingling with and entraining the smokebox gases. The action could therefore be increased by enlarging the cone, while its efficiency (if not its effect) was reduced by shock losses if the blast was sharpened, since the gases moved at more widely differing speeds and mingled less.

Nobody took very much notice of all this. Locomotive men the world over are a rough, practical lot raised in a hard school with no time for abstruse ideas, and British and American ones are only slightly worse than all the others. The thought of an American academic carrying out delicate experiments on a he-man steam engine, in a university laboratory of all places, made them guffaw. It conjured up a vision of some figure like Beachcomber's immortal Dr Strabismus (Whom God Preserve) of Utrecht, the archetypal Absent Minded Professor, who might spend a month on anxious research into such questions as whether a man should wear his braces with the Y to the front or not. Out of curiosity, one or two used Goss's formulas to calculate the best shape of blastpipe and chimney; the result was exactly the same as the best that had been evolved after years of experience. This fitted the Strabismus picture too. So the report was placed in the Round File, and it was twenty years before anything else happened. Oddly enough, this was just the length of time needed for an industrious apprentice finding Goss in the waste-paper basket, and realizing

as his elders had failed to that the moral was that two chimneys are better than one, to attain a position where he could put this into practice. Since two exhaust cones have a greater area than one, the resulting larger area of two blastpipe nozzles gave less back pressure for equal or greater draught. The Kylchap, the first double chimney arrangement to win a wide success, was developed jointly in 1926 by Kylälä of the Finnish Railways and André Chapelon of the Paris-Orleans Railway. It took a long time to win a place in Britain, but it was making some headway on the LNER and SR and in a simplified form developed by the LMS was widely applied after nationalization. Another version was the Lemaître exhaust, as modified by O. V. S. Bulleid on the Southern, which employed a wide single chimney and a blastpipe with five nozzles arranged in a circle. Last and most effective of all was the Giesl Ejector, a cheap and trouble-free precision device combining an oblong chimney and a blastpipe with seven nozzles in line, perfected around 1950 by Dr Giesl-Gieslingen of Vienna. It is now widely used, particularly in Eastern Europe, and reduces fuel consumption by some 10% compared with a double chimney, while also making an increased power output possible. Compared with a conventional front end, it offers as great an improvement as the superheater. However, so far as Britain is concerned, it has come too late. The decision to dieselize, for a calculated economic return of the same order,

9F 2-10-0 no. 92073 on a southbound Great Central freight, taking water at Charwelton troughs (1963)

Class 4 4-6-0 no. 75006 on a crowded Wrexham–Barmouth train at Berwyn, passing a two-mile traffic jam on the parallel road six months before the railway was suppressed (1964)

had already been taken, and ejectors were fitted to two locomotives only, with considerable but unappreciated success. An official explanation was that since British freight locomotives spent so large a proportion of their time standing still or working at low power, it was not worth while spending anything to increase their efficiency. A cogent but revealing argument.

Steam Locomotives in Traffic

We have seen how the 4-4-0 came to be replaced on express passenger work by the 4-4-2, the 4-6-0, and the 4-6-2. However, the type survived longer on a large scale in Britain than anywhere else in the world, remaining in many places the standard engine for secondary passenger duties right up to the late 1950s,

when diesel railcars took over. On the Southern in Kent it still powered heavy expresses until electrification in 1959. The Southern also possessed, in R. E. L. Maunsell's 'Schools' class, 40 engines built from 1930 to 1935, the last and most powerful 4-4-0s in Britain. The GWR after Churchward had relatively few 4-4-0s, instead favouring the 4-6-0, which later became the commonest mixed-traffic type nationally. But although Churchward had played so large a part in the development of the modern British locomotive, Swindon practice, which had been pre-eminent, stagnated after his retirement in 1921. It is hardly an exaggeration to say that no new GWR designs subsequently appeared. The 'Castles' of 1923 were nothing but slightly, and the 'Kings' of 1927 considerably, enlarged 'Stars', while the 'Halls' of 1924 were 'Saints'

(*Left*) LMS 2P 4-4-0 no. 40600 leaving Kittybrewster with the 5.40 pm Aberdeen to Inverurie local (1954)

The Midland Compound 4-4-0s were multiplied considerably by the LMS after grouping; no. 1111 at speed in the Trent Valley (c. 1936)

The largest and most powerful British freight engines (although by no means the all-round equal of the later 9F) were the LMS Garratts, 2-6-0 + 0-6-2s of which 33 were built after 1927. No. 47972 rolls through Manton with coal for London (1953)

with smaller wheels. Hawksworth's 'Counties' of 1945 had some new details, including higher pressure, but were not particularly successful and failed to replace the 'Castles' to the extent intended; in fact some more 'Castles' were built a few years later. For freight, Churchward's 28XX 2-8-0s of 1903 and 43XX 2-6-0s of 1911 were multiplied almost unchanged, further batches being built from 1938 and 1932 respectively; the various 2-6-2 and 2-8-0 tanks were treated similarly, some of the latter being altered to 2-8-2Ts. The only post-1921 GWR engines that did not grow directly out of a Churchward design, in fact, were the 2251 class 0-6-0s of 1930 (based on a design by Dean of 1883, incidentally a much better-liked engine); the 14XX class 0-4-2Ts of 1932 and several varieties of 0-6-0T whose ancestry went back even farther; and

the 56XX class 0-6-2Ts of 1924, which conformed with types generally used on minor lines in South Wales. Swindon was always a law unto itself, and GWR engines all had a close family resemblance; but inbreeding has its disadvantages in the long run. How far Swindon had fallen behind was made clear around 1958, after the performance of the 'Kings' and 'Castles' had been dramatically improved by the imported modifications of double chimney and high superheat, and it was found worth while to alter locomotives that were not expected to continue in service more than another couple of years.

On the LMS the situation was rather different. Of the two main constituent companies, the Midland had traditionally believed in using small engines and double-heading very lavishly, while the L&NW had

Gresley A1 Pacific no. 2561 'Minoru' (later altered to class A3)
climbing from Berwick towards Grantshouse (c. 1937)

traditionally believed in using small engines and thrashing them within an inch of their lives; this was still normal with the various post-Webb 4-4-os, although the 'Prince of Wales' and 'Claughton' 4-6-os had a little bit more in hand. Most LMS expresses were still hauled by 4-4-os in the twenties, although a few 4-2-2s lurked here and there and you could never be sure what might not turn up. Midland Compounds were flooding all over the system, while Derby's Big Goods was a very modest 0-6-0. When Sir William Stanier was brought over from Swindon in 1932, he was highly successful in applying Churchward principles at Crewe, but also went beyond them. Most of his engines were still quite modest in size, but serviceable; the 'Class Five' 4-6-0 of 1934 and the '8F' 2-8-0 of 1935 were multiplied exceedingly. His policy of standardization and sweeping away the immense

variety of different types was also a success. But where heavy passenger engines were concerned, the picture on the LMS was never quite so bright. There were the 'Royal Scot' 3-cylinder 4-6-os of 1927, competent engines further improved by rebuilding after 1943, and the 'Patriots' of 1930 (nominally rebuilt 'Claughtons'), later altered in the same way. But even with these fairly powerful 4-6-os, the LMS was chronically short of really adequate express passenger engines. Stanier's predecessor, Sir Henry Fowler, although responsible for breeding so many Compounds, realized that a bigger machine was needed, and started to build a very promising 4-cylinder compound Pacific. But company policy still favoured inadequate power; when Fowler left his Pacific was suppressed. However, Stanier was allowed to do something. His Pacifics were of two types; the 13 'Princess' class of 1933, and

Ivatt Atlantics
The large-boilered variety (GNR 251 class, of 1902); no. 1444 on the southbound 'West Riding Pullman' near Langley (1933)

The small-boilered variety (GNR 990 class, of 1898); no. 3252 approaching Cambridge with a freight from Hitchin (1936)

the 38 'Duchess' class of 1938. All had four cylinders laid out in the Swindon manner (except for one 'Princess' with turbine drive); certain of the 'Duchesses' were originally streamlined and after 1939 all had double chimneys. Combining as they did the best of Swindon practice with the large boiler and firebox made possible by the 4-6-2 wheel arrangement, these were perhaps the most outstandingly successful British express locomotives ever built, if only by a short margin. But there were never enough of them, due to an over-nice calculation of requirements; and speed and punctuality on what is unquestionably the most important main line in Britain suffered accordingly, especially at busy times, with adverse results on the railways' reputation for dependability in the long run.

The old small-engine policies died hard on the LMS; in fact one doubts if they are dead yet, even under dieselization. Stanier himself produced some 4-6-os for express work, the 'Jubilee' class 3-cylinder 4-6-os, which were numerous enough (191 were built); admirable machines but still too small. The accountants were in charge, and to an accountant the avoidance of scandal or catastrophe in the past is a clinching reason for spending nothing to avoid it in the future.

It was greatly to the credit of the LNER, especially considering the company's relative penury, that matters were different on the East Coast. The Chief Mechanical Engineer at Doncaster since 1911 had been Sir Nigel Gresley, after Churchward undoubtedly the most outstanding figure in British locomotive

In their last few years of service, the performance (and therefore appearance) of the A3s was much improved by the fitting of double chimneys and really effective smoke deflectors of German pattern (1963)

history during the twentieth century. Gresley was the first (except for Churchward's solitary 'Great Bear' of 1908) to build Pacifics, starting in 1922. Later modified with long-lap valves as a result of the 1925 exchange trials, these were finally made standard with the very successful A3 class of 1927. When they were joined, already 79 strong, by the 35 streamlined A4s after 1935 the LNER had a sufficient fleet of express engines. At busy times they could be helped out either by the V2 2-6-2s of 1936, whose capabilities were hardly less, the surviving Ivatt Atlantics, or as they were withdrawn by the postwar A1 and A2 Pacifics.

The A4s deserve special mention. They were designed with the object of running extra-high-speed trains; Gresley had considered whether these should be steam or diesel, like the German 'Flying Hamburger' sets or the Union Pacific 'Cities' and Burlington 'Zephyrs' in the USA. He chose steam because he was confident that it could equal diesel performance (as, in fact, it did on the Milwaukee, and very nearly in Germany), and because diesel trains to these specifications cost more per seat and had rigidly limited accommodation. (The diesels nevertheless arrived, despite these drawbacks, 25 years later in the shape of the Blue Pullman sets.) The A4 was given plenty of power although the intended load was small, since the secret of high-speed running is to go very fast uphill. The streamlining was evolved through wind-tunnel experiments, and gave a worth-while saving at speeds over 80 mph. In the event, the A4 proved not only to be fast (No. 4468 'Mallard' achieved 126 mph on trials in July 1938, the world speed record for steam power),

The rather questionable practice of naming locomotives has sometimes been carried to absurd lengths. Here are two prize LNER examples, from a B1 4-6-0 and an A3 (1955–60)

The Bulleid Pacifics were intended as mixed-traffic engines, but were never so successful in freight service. Unrebuilt 'Battle of Britain' no. 34081 '92 Squadron' climbs to Honiton Tunnel with a Salisbury & Exeter line freight (1963)

Unrebuilt 'Merchant Navy' no. 35003 'Royal Mail' curving under the up Bournemouth line at Worting Junction, Basingstoke, with an express from the West of England (1954)

but also efficient and able to deal with extremely heavy loads. It is a matter of opinion whether they or the LMS 'Duchesses' rate more highly. Four, including 'Mallard', were built with double chimneys, and their performance was always noticeably better. It seems strange that the remainder, and later the A3s, were not altered to conform until the late 1950s. One feels that the reason was that the double chimney was thought unsightly; now we are used to it, of course, the single one simply looks constipated. Which provides a small but classic illustration of the mechanical law which says 'Handsome is as handsome does, and to the devil with aesthetes who argue otherwise'.

The Southern Railway inherited a rather mixed bag of locomotives in 1923, and for the next fifteen years spent all it could afford on electrification. Hence the almost Iberian menagerie of perambulating relics that steamed and jangled around Kent. O.V.S. Bulleid, who had been Gresley's assistant, was appointed CME in 1937, and persuaded the company that something had to be done about it. It was an unfortunate time, of course, for starting any fresh ideas in design; but although his first new type, the 'Merchant Navy' Pacific, was delayed by war conditions until 1941, it

was in many ways revolutionary. Together with the very similar but smaller 'West Country' class of 1945, it included a number of features intended to make daily maintenance easier, notably the chain-driven valve gear enclosed in an oil bath and the easily-cleaned exterior casing. These engines were very successful in service, but at a price; the valve gear was not consistently accurate, and although the excellent boiler easily met the resulting extra demand for steam, fuel (and oil) consumption was rather high. After 1956 all the 'Merchant Navies' and most of the 'West Countries' were therefore rebuilt on more conventional lines.

Bulleid's last design, although it never saw service, was perhaps the most interesting of all. This was the 'Leader', a wholly enclosed locomotive running on two power bogies, with a driving cab at each end; a steam engine, in fact, built to a diesel layout. A prototype was built in 1949, but met technical difficulties with the sleeve valves, and a human difficulty since the fireman had to work in a constricted and overheated cubby-hole: it was scrapped in 1952.

But however wrong he may have been in detail, Bulleid was unquestionably right in principle; there

The only 'Leader' ever to run; no. 36001 on trials near Lewes (1950)

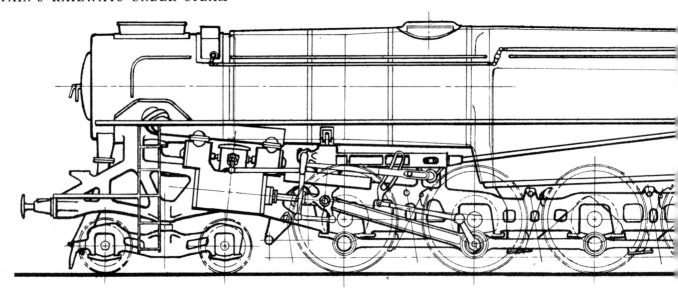

What might have happened next

British steam locomotive development had by no means reached a dead end when it ceased. This drawing shows a scheme, by A. C. Sterndale, for a simple, robust, and conventional medium-power mixed-traffic engine with no features not fully proved in British or foreign experience, which would have been a logical next step forward. Able to handle all long-distance freight work (assuming overall average speeds of 50 mph) and all but the very fastest express passenger services, it would have had better route availability than a 'Britannia' Pacific. Designed to burn low-grade coal of the kind now cheaply produced from mechanized collieries, and unsuitable for existing locomotives, its mechanical stoker would have guaranteed drawbar power outputs of 1,800 hp (maximum) and 1,300 hp (sustained) at 65 mph without effort by the crew. 2,200 hp would be attainable with better quality coal. Turn-round

time would be cut by several factors; roller bearings throughout, large fuel and water capacity, and the big grate would reduce the frequency of visits to shed, while an articulated coupling between engine and tender, with specially designed cab and lookouts, would enable the locomotive to work with equal facility in either direction, reducing terminal delays and avoiding turntables.

Other features of the design are as follows:

Wheel arrangement. Eight coupled wheels are necessary to provide sufficient adhesion (with an 18-ton axleload); 5 ft. 6 in. is the smallest diameter of driving wheel which will allow 70–75 mph to be maintained comfortably. The possible 2-8-2 wheel arrangement is not favoured due to its indifferent tracking at speed, and the fact that weight transfer from coupled to trailing wheels takes place on starting, cutting adhesion. The rear driving wheels have spring controlled sideplay, and the articulated tender provides the

Two Gresley designs that were ahead of their time. (*Right*) P1 class 2-8-2 no. 2394 with a southbound GN line coal train at Langley; (*left*) P2 class 2-8-2 no. 2001 'Cock o' the North' leaving King's Cross. The P1s appeared in 1925, far and away the most powerful freight engines on the LNER, but they were beaten by the lack of continuous brakes; the trains they could pull could not be stopped. The six P2s of 1934 (later streamlined) were intended for expresses between Edinburgh and Aberdeen, and did splendid work; but Gresley's successor ruined them after 1943 by rebuilding them as ungainly and ineffective 4-6-2s

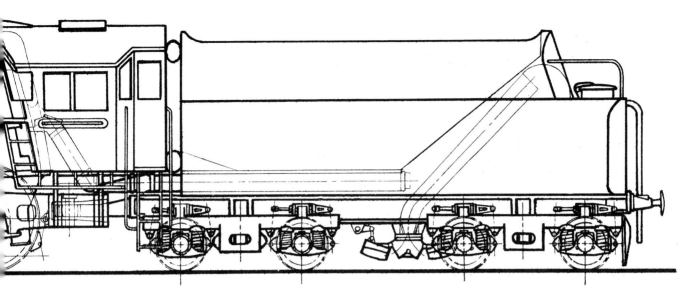

equivalent of bogie control at the rear end for reverse running. Cast steel frames preferably, for robustness.

Cylinders and motion. Two cylinders only, for simplicity; 21 in. by 30 in. Their position is dictated by loading gauge considerations. Poppet valves for ease of maintenance, but driven by Walschaerts gear for the same reasons.

Boiler. A large grate (50 sq. ft.) relative to power output is essential for the fuel intended. The 4-8-0 wheel arrangement rules out a wide firebox, but the mechanical stoker makes a very long one (16 ft.) practical. Moderate pressure (240 lb.). The ratio of heating surface to cross-sectional area of the tubes is increased, due to the superior performance of the Geisl Ejector, which will also aid combustion of low-grade fuel. The same factor allows a superheater which is large (646 sq. ft.) in relation to the total evaporative heating surface (1547 sq. ft.).

Cab and Tender. Fully enclosed cab, with rubber anti-draught seals, to increase crew comfort and cleanliness; air is fed to the firebox through ducts. The tender design has been dictated by the need to allow good visibility when running in reverse. Capacity: 12 tons coal, 5,000 gallons water. Water scoop to work both ways.

Tractive effort: 40,800 lb.

Overall length: 74 ft. 0 in. (including tender).

Weight: engine 93 tons, tender 64 tons, total 157 tons.

The limiting factor on the size of British locomotives was not, as so often stated, the restricted loading gauge, but the grossly inadequate braking and coupling strength of freight rolling stock. Like every necessary improvement, this locomotive of course presupposes universal continuous brakes; without them its capacity, even though it by no means approaches the maximum attainable with steam, would be wasted.

The Orphan; the solitary BR Class 8 Pacific, no. 71000 'Duke of Gloucester' (1960)

must be change and experiment if there is to be progress. This was the weakness of the BR Standard locomotives, designed and built after nationalization. Sound and workmanlike, they incorporated all the best received ideas, but they recorded no important advances. They were not intended to; the object was to build cheap and serviceable motive power. If this was a misguided object, the blame lies elsewhere.

The astonishing thing about the BR standard classes was that there were so many of them. Twelve different types were built, all for road service; if shunters had been needed, there would have been more. This is incomprehensible, when one considers how flexible the steam engine had become. To take a perhaps rather extreme example, the entire traffic (other than railcars) on the Marseilles-Ventimiglia line of the SNCF, express and local passenger, fast freight and shunting,

has for years been worked by just one class of mixed-traffic 2-8-2, covering the entire range of duties for which the twelve standard BR designs were evolved. This said, it must be granted that the engines are competent. The 'Britannia' Pacifics, together with the slightly smaller 'Clans' the only 2-cylinder engines of this type ever used in Britain, were intended to be the equal of large 4-6-0s such as the 'Castles' and 'Patriots'; the heavy 3-cylinder BR Pacific intended to equal the 'Duchess' or 'A4' has been reckoned as a failure, since only one was built and it was a neglected orphan never coaxed through its teething troubles. The various 4-6-0s, 2-6-0s, 2-6-2Ts and 2-6-4Ts all show close resemblance to LMS practice. Particularly difficult to understand, taken in connection with the fact that three types of 2-6-0 and two types of 4-6-0 were built within a very close power range, was the building of a

180

The BR 'Clans' had a mixed reception; only ten were built (in 1952), and allocated to two depots. At one they were popular, at the other they were condemned. No. 72002 'Clan Campbell' storming up to Garrochburn, south of Kilmarnock, with a Largs-Newcastle excursion (1962)

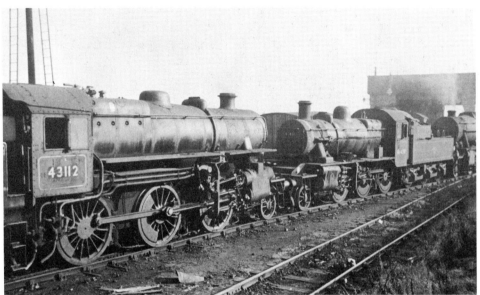

The postwar LMS Ivatt 4MT and 2MT 2-6-0s were continued almost unaltered in the BR Standard series, although another 2-6-0 of intermediate size was added. Here 4MT no. 43112 and 2MT no. 46459 rub noses at Bescot (1963)

A 9F in passenger service; no. 92220 'Evening Star', the last steam engine built for British Railways, on the last 'Pines Express' over the Somerset & Dorset line at Masbury Summit. The 12-coach load had been taken up the 1 in 50 without assistance, as a gesture to show how much more economically the line could have been worked with these engines (1962)

2-6-0 and a 4-6-0 of identical rating. The one really outstanding success among the BR designs has been the 9F 2-10-0. While it is still not large enough to spoil Britain's record of being the only country in the world with bigger engines in passenger than in freight service (its boiler is slightly smaller even than the 'Britannia's), and while its design included no new features (apart from the experimental fitting of a number with the misguided Franco-Crosti boiler), its triumph was that it so exactly filled an ancient crying need. At last there was a freight locomotive with plenty of power and adhesion weight, able to handle the heaviest slow drags with ease and therefore with economy, and able also when needed to run with surprising speed (they have been timed at over 90 mph). They were the last British steam locomotives built, and they do not disgrace any that came before them.

(*Opposite, above*) Engines and engine sheds could be kept clean, but it needed cheap labour to do it. The interior of no. 4 Running Shed, Derby, by night (1910)

(*Opposite, below*) Ex-Great North of Scotland 4-4-0 no. 62268 being coaled from a hand crane at Keith Junction (1953)

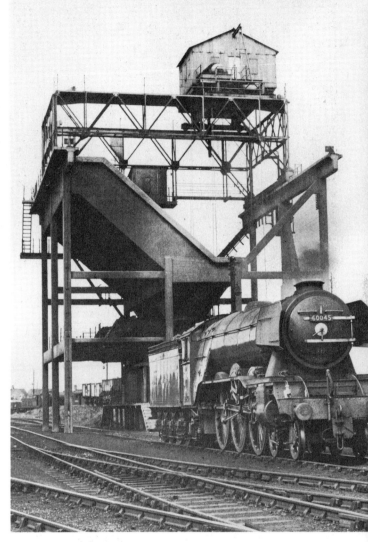

A3 no. 60045 in front of the coaling tower at Darlington (1964)

A cleaner at Old Oak Common removing ashes from the smokebox of a 'King' (1960)

The 'Atlantic Coast Express', until its suppression in 1964 in favour of the GW route to Devon and Cornwall, held a record for the number of through coaches to different destinations. 'Merchant Navy' no. 35029 'Ellerman Lines' pulls out of Salisbury on its way from Waterloo to Plymouth, Ilfracombe, Torrington, Bude, and Padstow (1961)

2 Train Services

The Development of Inter-City Services

From time to time one hears it said that trains were faster, or more frequent, or more comfortable, or more punctual, at some time in the past. One should usually treat these claims with reserve, since time's golden haze stimulates them powerfully. One should particularly mistrust any statement which implies that British railway punctuality was ever of a satisfactory standard, especially on certain notorious main lines. But while statistical proof of these matters one way or the other is not often possible, one can validly compare the services offered in the timetables at different dates.

What follows is a summary of the schedules between the ten largest British cities at intervals over a century. Eleven routes have been selected; eight of them run radially from London, two are cross-country, and one is in Scotland. Southampton, Cardiff, and Aberdeen have been included as well as the ten main cities in order to give some attention to important parts of the country which would otherwise be omitted. In each case every reasonably competitive route between the places concerned is examined; the criterion is that of the average traveller simply interested in getting from A to B.

The summary gives firstly the number of trains scheduled to run in the down direction on a winter weekday, omitting any which because of their slow or inconvenient timings, or for any other reason, were not likely to be of much public interest. Except on Anglo-Scottish journeys, overnight trains are not included. Secondly, the summary gives the time taken by the best train, the average time taken by all the trains mentioned, the overall speed of the best train, and the overall speed of the combined service; both to the nearest mile-per-hour.

No attempt has been made to record the fastest intermediate bookings, since these are of no commercial importance. However interesting it may have been for the railway enthusiast to see how fast a time was made between, say, York and Darlington, the only thing that matters to the public is the length of time between getting on and getting off.

The dates chosen are 1850, 1875, 1900, 1913, 1938, and 1958; in each case the month examined is October. There are some slight variations in a few cases; Anglo-Scottish services are considered for 1876 to include the Midland route, which opened in that year, while London to Cardiff and Birmingham schedules

An unrebuilt 'Royal Scot' 4-6-0, no. 46110 'Grenadier Guardsman', takes more than a tenderful of water from Bushey troughs on a Euston-Birmingham express (1951)

are taken in 1852 for a similar reason. 1958 has been selected because it was the last year in which all the services examined were steam-worked; but since all trains from Euston had by then been decelerated on account of electrification work, 1957 services are taken here.

TABLE 1: LONDON TO BIRMINGHAM

LNWR route: Euston to New Street, 112 miles
GWR route: Paddington to Snow Hill: via Oxford
until 1910, 129 miles; via Bicester after 1910, 110 miles

Date	Route	No. of trains	Best time	Average time	Best speed	Average speed
1852	LNW	6	2.45	3.53	40	29
	GW	4	2.45	3.30	47	37
1875	LNW	9	3.00	3.08	37	36
	GW	4	3.20	3.38	39	35
1900	LNW	11	2.20	2.41	48	42
	GW	5	2.25	2.53	54	44
1913	LNW	11	2.00	2.05	56	53
	GW	7	2.00	2.00	55	55
1938	LNW	8	1.55	2.00	59	56
	GW	7	2.00	2.12	55	50
1957	LNW	7	2.00	2.12	56	51
	GW	9	2.00	2.24	55	47

Remarks

This service was definitely at its peak in 1913, with 18 trains daily and the shortest overall average speeds ever achieved with steam. This was in spite of the fact that the L&NW's average was pulled down by one of its trains starting from Broad Street instead of Euston, and losing 15 minutes in consequence. This was the 5.25 pm 'City to City', which among other attractions carried a typist available to take dictation from travelling businessmen. The L&NWR pioneered non-stop trains (1902) and two-hour trains (1903). In 1938 trains were fewer, and although the fastest time of 1 hr 55 min. was recorded by four departures daily from Euston, the overall inter-city average had declined due to GWR decelerations. In 1957 there was one extra train in total, but speeds were lower still; the 1 hr 55 min. booking had only a very brief post-war revival.

The decline in best speeds on both routes between 1852 (the service quoted is that of the opening month

of the GWR line and so perhaps untypical) and 1875 is interesting, especially when taken in conjunction with the large improvement in the bulk of the L&NW schedules. It would seem as if that company had found that its competitive position was better if based on the total service, rather than on one or two star turns. The GWR trains in 1852 were of course broad gauge.

TABLE 2: LONDON TO MANCHESTER

LNWR route: Euston to London Road, 188 miles via
Crewe; 187 via Stoke
Midland route: St Pancras to Central, 190 miles (192 to
London Rd in 1875)
GNR route: King's Cross to London Road via Sheffield,
203 miles
GCR route: Marylebone to London Road, 206 miles

Date	Route	No. of trains	Best time	Average time	Best speed	Average speed
1850	LNW	5	5.40	7.05	33	26
1875	LNW	7	4.45	4.57	40	38
	Midland	7	4.45	5.01	40	38
	GNR	5	4.50	5.07	42	40
1900	LNW	10	4.10	4.30	43	42
	Midland	9	4.15	4.29	45	42
	GNR	6	4.27	4.49	46	42
	GCR	6	4.45	4.56	43	42
1913	LNW	9	3.30	4.15	54	44
	Midland	8	3.40	4.09	52	46
	GNR	5	4.16	5.14	47	39
	GCR	5	4.12	4.50	49	43
1938	LNW	7	3.15	3.40	58	51
	Midland	6	3.35	3.50	53	50
	GNR	4	4.52	5.11	42	40
	GCR	6	4.05	4.42	50	43
1957	LNW	8	3.35	3.54	52	48
	Midland	7	3.44	4.14	51	45
	GNR	5	3.56	4.54	52	41
	GCR	5	5.04	5.16	41	39

Remarks

Here the best year was undoubtedly 1938, even though trains were not as frequent as in 1913. Once again the post-1945 service was slower, if marginally more often. The Great Central, which had put up a relatively good showing in 1938 (although it never really compared with either the LNW or the Midland) had given up

The Western's fastest; the down 'Bristolian' tears through
Goring at over 70 behind no. 5040 'Stokesay Castle' (1958)

Rebuilt 'West Country' Pacific no. 34022 'Exmoor' leaving Litchfield tunnel, summit of the Waterloo-Southampton line, with a down Bournemouth express (1962)

trying by 1957 and was only a few years from complete suppression. On the other hand, the service from King's Cross, which had seemed near extinction in 1938, showed some revival in 1957; this was because good connections were made at Sheffield and because the Sheffield-Manchester length was by then electrified.

TABLE 3: LONDON TO LEEDS

1850 routes: Euston (L&NW) to Leeds (Midland) via Rugby, 206 miles

King's Cross (GNR) to Leeds (L&Y) via Boston, 205 miles

Midland route: St Pancras to Leeds (City) 198 miles

GNR route: King's Cross to Leeds (Central), 186 miles

Date	Route	No. of trains	Best time	Average time	Best speed	Average speed
1850	Euston	3	5.25	6.47	37	30
	King's X	3	5.40	6.55	36	30
1875	Midland	7	5.00	5.28	40	36
	GNR	6	4.23	4.42	42	40
1900	Midland	8	4.25	4.39	45	43
	GNR	7	3.49	4.03	49	46
1913	Midland	12	3.55	4.25	51	45
	GNR	6	3.42	3.57	50	47
1938	Midland	7	3.48	4.06	52	48
	GNR	9	2.43	3.41	69	50
1958	Midland	7	4.15	4.30	47	44
	GNR	10	3.29	3.56	53	47

Remarks

Here the best year for frequency was 1913, but not by a very large margin over 1958; for speed, on the other hand, 1938 was outstandingly the winner, and 1958 showed a very serious deterioration, partly explained by the imposition of speed restrictions due to colliery subsidences on the Midland line. Part of the reason for the superiority of the 1938 service was the 'West Riding Limited' streamliner, perhaps the most striking of all the LNER speeders, whose life was cut short by the war. The time of 2 hr 43 min. maintained by this train has never since been equalled; the best achieved today by the unusually powerful diesels now employed is 3 hours. But even apart from this, the 1958 services were disappointingly slothful, particularly on the Midland.

Considering that Leeds is on the Midland's main line, and only served by a branch from the East Coast route, it is rather surprising how decisively better the Great Northern's service has always been. Beaten in speed, the Midland tried to compete with frequency, most notably in 1913. Over distances of more than about 100 miles this bait has never worked (a fact still not properly appreciated; we are still assured that more second-rate trains are better than fewer first-rate ones), and it failed again here.

TABLE 4: LONDON TO BRISTOL

One route only, from Paddington (GWR), 118 miles

Date	No. of trains	Best time	Average time	Best speed	Average speed
1850	7	2.35	3.53	46	30
1875	7	2.36	3.20	46	36
1900	12	2.15	2.49	52	42
1913	10	2.00	2.33	59	46
1938	10	1.45	2.22	67	50
1958	13	1.45	2.33	67	46

Remarks

In 1850 this line was wholly broad gauge; mixed gauge was completed throughout in 1873 and thereafter most trains, except the fastest (which continued beyond Exter) were standard gauge.

Whether the 1958 service was better than the 1938 one is a matter of opinion. It was more frequent, but the average speed had declined rather disappointingly. The 'Bristolian' continued as it had before, but it was on a rather lonely eminence.

One train has had to be included in the reckoning from 1913 onwards which did not follow the main line; it ran over the Berks & Hants through Newbury and Devizes, 121 miles. Officially this may not have formed part of the Bristol service, but it must be treated as such because it was advertised as a through train, it filled a large gap in the departures from Paddington (in 1938 it left at 2.45 pm, between the 1.15 and the 4.15), and because it is a matter of record that unsuspecting passengers frequently boarded it without knowing what they were in for. In 1913 it was not so bad, taking 2 hr 47 min.; by 1958 it took 3 hr 18 min., and affects the overall average accordingly (although not nearly enough to explain the decline entirely).

In 1900 there were a considerable number of additional trains calling at Bristol (Stapleton Road) on their way to South Wales through the Severn Tunnel. These have not been included, as although they were widely advertised they were not really run to cater for the Bristol trade; they had previously run via Gloucester and took the Badminton cut-off as soon as that opened.

TABLE 5: LONDON TO CARDIFF

One route only, GWR from Paddington.
  1852–86, via Gloucester, 170 miles
  1886–1903, via Bristol and Severn Tunnel, 156 miles
  from 1903, via Badminton and Severn Tunnel, 145 miles

Date	No. of trains	Best time	Average time	Best speed	Average speed
1852	2	5.30	5.45	31	30
1875	4	4.58	5.24	34	31
1900	8	3.19	4.22	47	36
1913	7	2.50	3.22	51	43
1938	6	2.41	2.50	54	51
1958	9	2.30	2.59	58	48

Remarks

At last we have a service that was arguably better in 1958 than it had ever been before. The slight decline in overall average speed since 1938, in spite of the fact that the 'Pembroke Coast Express' had the fastest-ever booking, was perhaps outweighed by the 50% increase in frequency. On the other hand, considering the very easy nature of the road (the only gradient worth mentioning being the climb in the up direction out of the Severn Tunnel) the running cannot at any time be called good, and did not equal the standard achieved elsewhere on the GWR. The line was broad-gauge until 1872.

TABLE 6: LONDON TO SOUTHAMPTON

One route only, L&SWR from Waterloo to Southampton (Terminus) or (Central), originally 'West End'; 79 miles

Date	No. of trains	Best time	Average time	Best speed	Average speed
1850	6	2.15	2.55	35	27
1875	7	2.09	2.29	37	32
1900	11	1.46	2.22	45	33
1913	10	1.40	1.59	47	40
1938	13	1.27	1.45	54	45
1958	13	1.21	1.40	59	47

Remarks

This is another of the few services to show a steady, if very slow, pattern of improvement over the years. But it cannot really be called good. It is rather surprising that better advantage was not taken of the Bulleid Pacifics after 1945, machines which very greatly outclassed anything used previously, and whose capacity for high-speed running has been amply demonstrated. This seems unenterprising of the operating department.

TABLE 7: BRISTOL TO SHEFFIELD

One route only: Midland Railway via Birmingham and Derby, 177 miles

Date	No. of trains	Best time	Average time	Best speed	Average speed
1850	3	7.30	8.55	24	20
1875	4	5.56	6.17	30	28
1900	7	4.10	4.39	43	38
1913	9	3.55	4.23	45	40
1938	7	3.50	4.12	46	43
1958	6	4.07	4.28	43	40

(*Right*) The last steam-hauled luxury train in Britain; the all-Pullman 'Bournemouth Belle' westbound near Woking behind a rebuilt 'West Country', no. 34029 'Lundy' (1963)

Remarks

In many cases listed above there was no through train, and it was necessary to change at Derby, where connections were generally very good.

This is by no means a difficult, or an obscure, cross-country journey, since it makes direct use of the Midland's important Derby-Bristol main line. Nevertheless, it is disappointing that there was so marked a decline between 1913 and 1958 in frequency, and after 1938 in speed. Cross-country journeys have tended to deteriorate more than most radial services, because they are out of the limelight and only a management more energetic than the one which ruled will take the trouble to search them out and put them right. Trains slowed by blanket decelerations in wartime therefore tended to get overlooked and their sluggishness became accepted as a law of nature. It would not be difficult to find examples worse than this one, as we shall see.

TABLE 8: LIVERPOOL TO NEWCASTLE

Between these two cities there exist a complication of routes, not all of which have been used at the same time. They are as follows:

L&NWR: (i) via Manchester, Stalybridge and Leeds (or Holbeck) L&NWR, thence via Harrogate and Darlington NER; 180 miles

(ii) as above, but via Stockton instead of Darlington; 184 miles

(iii) via Manchester, Stalybridge and Leeds L&NWR, thence via York and Darlington NER; 194 miles

L&YR: (i) via Rochdale and Leeds (or Holbeck) L&YR, thence via Harrogate and Darlington NER; 182 miles

(ii) as above, but via Stockton instead of Darlington; 186 miles

(iii) via Rochdale and Normanton L&YR, thence via York and Darlington NER; 187 miles

Carlisle: via Preston to Carlisle L&NWR, thence NER direct; 179 miles

Since these permutations were of no interest to the through traveller, they have not been shown separately in these summaries, and the distances quoted are those of the shortest in each group. No through trains have ever been scheduled via Carlisle; they have run on both the other groups of routes since the 1870s.

Date	Route	No. of trains	Best time	Average time	Best speed	Average speed
1850	L&NWR	3	8.00	8.45	23	21
	Carlisle	2	9.35	10.07	18	17
1875	L&NWR	3	6.35	7.53	27	23
	L&YR	1	6.20	6.20	29	29
	Carlisle	2	7.10	7.40	25	23
1900	L&NWR	8	4.40	5.26	39	33
	L&YR	6	5.02	5.38	36	32
	Carlisle	4	5.04	5.35	36	32
1913	L&NWR	9	4.25	5.22	41	33
	L&YR	6	4.32	5.20	43	34
	Carlisle	5	5.10	5.47	35	31
1938	L&NWR	5	4.13	4.53	43	37
	L&YR	3	4.29	4.42	41	39
	Carlisle	5	4.35	5.07	39	35
1958	L&NWR	3	4.41	4.49	39	38
	L&YR	2	5.05	5.26	36	33
	Carlisle	5	5.43	6.15	31	27

Remarks

Two things stand out from this summary; perhaps the most surprising is the poor showing of the shortest route, via Carlisle. This is invariably because of bad connections; the service on the Newcastle & Carlisle never seems to have been organized with the slightest regard to trains arriving from the south, and in a very large number of cases throughout the period a connection has been missed by a matter of three or four minutes only.

The other outstanding feature is the appalling decline in the quality of the service between 1938 and 1958. More recently this has been remedied by recast and accelerated schedules on the L&NW route, not by any means before time. It was wholly disgraceful that 13 years after the war (that splendid Universal Excuse) not one train between these two important commercial centres averaged even as little as 40 mph.

TABLE 9: LONDON TO GLASGOW

West Coast route: Euston to Glasgow (Central), 401 miles (403 to Glasgow (Buchanan Street) until 1879)
Midland route: St Pancras to Glasgow (St Enoch), 426 miles
East Coast route: King's Cross to Glasgow (Queen Street), via Edinburgh; 440 miles

Date	Route	No. of trains	Best time	Average time	Best speed	Average speed
1850	West	2	12.55	14.25	31	28
1876	West	5	10.22	10.52	39	37
	Midland	3	10.45	11.02	40	38
	East	4	10.20	11.06	43	40
1900	West	5	8.00	9.09	50	44
	Midland	4	9.05	9.40	47	44
	East	3	9.20	9.30	47	46
1913	West	5	8.15	8.58	49	45
	Midland	6	8.50	9.25	48	45
	East	4	9.17	10.08	47	43
1938	West	4	6.30	8.10	62	49
	Midland	4	8.38	9.09	50	47
	East	7	7.39	9.17	58	46
1957	West	6	6.40	8.14	60	49
	Midland	3	9.31	9.35	45	45
	East	5	8.08	8.34	55	51

Remarks

Apart from demonstrating the relative decline of the Midland route, these summaries show on the whole a steady improvement. The fastest-ever time of 6½ hours was made by the streamlined 'Coronation Scot'; the post-war version of this train, running on a different and rather more useful schedule, the 'Caledonian', was not quite so fast.

(*Opposite, above*) The northbound 'Royal Scot' leaving Rugby; 'Duchess' Pacific no. 46241 'City of Edinburgh' accelerates 14 coaches away from the station, past a 7F 0-8-0 on a southbound freight (1957)

(*Right*) The northbound 'Silver Jubilee', King's Cross to Newcastle, near Potters Bar behind A4 no. 2512 'Silver Fox' (complete with chromium fox on the side of the boiler). With a train of special streamlined luxury stock, this train, together with its companion the 'Coronation', was arguably the most handsome ever to operate in Britain; although possibly the appearance of the A4s was improved when the fairing over the wheels vanished during the war (1937)

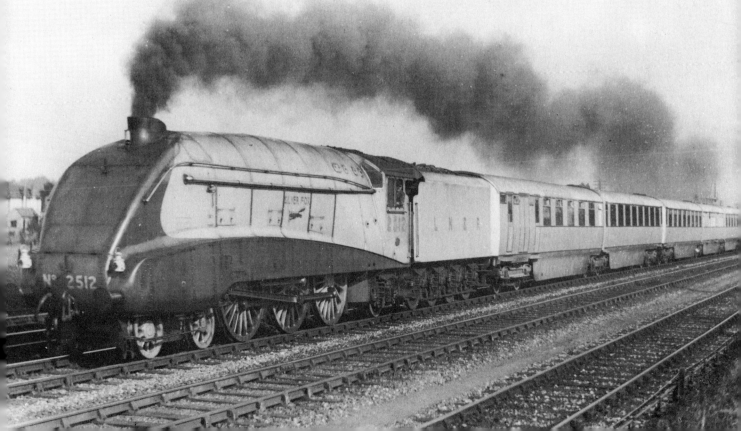

TABLE 10: LONDON TO EDINBURGH

East Coast route: King's Cross to Edinburgh (Waverley)
393 miles (412 miles, via Boston, in 1850)

Midland route: St Pancras to Edinburgh (Waverley),
409 miles

West Coast route: Euston to Edinburgh (Princes St),
400 miles

Date	Route	No. of trains	Best time	Average time	Best speed	Average speed
1850	East	2	11.55	14.37	35	28
	West	2	12.30	14.10	32	28
1876	East	5	9.00	10.39	44	37
	Midland	3	10.20	10.40	40	38
	West	6	10.10	10.42	39	38
1900	East	6	7.45	8.44	51	45
	Midland	2	9.33	9.42	42	41
	West	4	8.00	8.42	50	46
1913	East	7	7.50	8.20	50	47
	Midland	5	8.35	9.01	46	45
	West	4	8.15	8.42	48	46
1938	East	10	6.00	8.02	65	49
	Midland	3	8.40	9.09	47	45
	West	3	7.25	8.01	54	50
1957	East	11	6.45	7.38	58	52
	Midland	2	9.37	10.14	43	40
	West	2	7.40	7.55	53	51

Remarks

With one exception, this summary shows a similar picture to the London-Glasgow service. The difference is a reflection of the fact that the East Coast service to Scotland became decisively better than the West during the 1930s, partly due to the streamlined and extra-fare 'Coronation', and partly to the considerable improvement in frequency. After 1945 this superiority was maintained, although the 'Elizabethan' was not such a good train by any means; still, it had no extra fare, and more accommodation.

TABLE 11: GLASGOW TO ABERDEEN

One route only: 153 miles (Caledonian Railway)

Date	No. of trains	Best time	Average time	Best speed	Average speed
1850	2	6.15	6.33	24	23
1875	3	5.05	6.03	30	25
1900	5	4.00	4.22	38	35
1913	5	3.55	4.10	39	37
1938	5	3.30	3.46	44	40
1958	4	3.25	3.29	45	44
1963	4	3.00	3.14	51	47

The postwar incarnation of the 'Coronation', running in summer only to a slower and less useful morning schedule, but with more seating in ordinary coaches and still non-stop between King's Cross and Edinburgh, was the 'Elizabethan'. A4 no. 60027 'Merlin' at speed near Durham with the southbound train (1955)

Remarks

This main line, although it has often had a number of extremely fast intermediate bookings, has never been well served by fast trains. However, the picture is at least one of continuous improvement, which continued in steam even after 1958. Two trains covering the distance in 3 hours were put on in 1961; they were normally worked by Pacifics displaced by dieselization of the East Coast main line. This was the last important acceleration which involved steam traction.

The fastest train previously, during the pre-1914 period, had been allowed only $3\frac{1}{4}$ hours for the journey. But since it left Glasgow at 4.20 am it was of no use to ordinary travellers, and so cannot be counted.

TABLE 12: THE OVERALL PICTURE

Average figures ought always to be treated with caution, and averages of averages deserve a double dose. Nevertheless, it seems instructive to compile a brief table summarizing the development of the eleven inter-city services we have been examining, and this now follows. It gives a summary of the average speeds and frequencies at each date. The figures are weighted by distance, so that a 60 mph express from London to Edinburgh, 393 miles, is considered more than twice as virtuous as a 60 mph express from London to Leeds, 186 miles.

Date	No. of trains	Best speed	Average speed
1850	4	32	27
1875	5	38	35
1900	6	46	41
1913	7	48	43
1938	6	53	44
1958	6	52	45

It is hardly a very encouraging picture as far as the post-1914 period is concerned. There was quite a large increase in the speed of the best trains by 1938, partly due to the streamliners; but to what extent this was windowdressing can be judged from the minuscule improvement in the speeds of the services as a whole. And considering the effort that was put into restoration of the system after 1945, even if this was delayed some years, the results as shown here are extremely disappointing. The decline in peak speeds (the actual 1958 average is 51·6 mph, so decimals have nothing to do with it) can be explained to some extent by the suppression of the streamliners, and the slight improvement in the overall speed is worth mentioning. But it seems very little to show for twenty years of progress; or perhaps more accurately, twenty years of change. Or even for the thirteen years since the war ended. Nor was 1938 really so much of an improvement on 1913. One could argue that it was a regression, depending on how seriously one takes the slight decline in frequency. So far as ex-LMS lines were concerned, this was often more than slight.

Admittedly, increases on certain lines are partly cancelled out in this reckoning by thinning out and decelerating services on less well-favoured parallel routes (notably the Great Central and the Midland); and this is of very little importance to the ordinary customer. Bearing this factor in mind, we can say that the figures give the lie, just, to the complaint that train services were better before 1914 than during the 1950s; but that an acquittal by so narrow a margin is tantamount to a conviction.

Those with a weakness for statistics can work out for themselves the extent to which matters have been improved by electrification and dieselization since 1958. It is often a very considerable improvement, but not always. The completion of the Euston-Lancashire electrification in 1966 should make a big difference.

Star Turns

Right from the start there was a demand for specially fast trains, which was met even by the Liverpool & Manchester. Expresses are as old as main lines, and however much accountants used to point out (recently they have changed their tune) that on a financial basis they formed only a small part of the business, a railway has always been judged very largely by what kind of a show it made with its best trains, its star turns.

This depended on three things, possibly four. Least important, although usually best publicized, was the highest speed reached between intermediate points; the value of this was mainly a matter of public relations. Most important (and hardest to improve) was the average speed between terminals, and next came the number of intermediate stops and the frequency of the service. Long non-stop runs helped to keep the overall speed high and lessened disturbance to travellers who liked to be somnolent; on the other hand, before corridors, lavatories, and dining cars they also had certain drawbacks. These three necessities were introduced separately and by stages; the first diner was a non-corridor affair placed in service between Leeds and King's Cross in 1879, and it was not until the turn of the century that all three co-existed on most trains of importance.

The other limiting factor in non-stop running was of course the endurance of the locomotive. Its most frequent need was for water, but this was fairly easy to meet; it could be picked up on the run by a scoop lowered into a trough between the rails. The first water troughs were installed in 1860 by the L&NWR to allow the 'Irish Mail' (then at least as important a train as any in Anglo-Scottish service) to run non-stop between Chester and Holyhead, 84 miles. Their use spread until the only part of England where they did not exist was in the South, where long distance running was in any case impossible. The L&SW got so far as to fit some tenders with waterscoops, but the troughs were never built; superheating sufficiently reduced the need for them. But the Great Eastern had some, near Ipswich. Watertroughs enabled British Railways to achieve, and with steam traction, the world's record for non-stop running with the 'Flying Scotsman' from 1928 and the post-war 'Elizabethan' between Edinburgh and King's Cross, 393 miles. In this case it was necessary to change engine crews on the way, and so the locomotives concerned were provided with corridor tenders. The West Coast trains, incidentally, were also nominally non-stop, but in fact called at Carlisle to change crews. This performance ceased when steam gave way to diesel after 1962, partly because there was no longer any possibility of crew change in motion, and partly because air competition had changed the situation and there was no longer any economic justification for the long non-stop run.

The most glamorous star turns of all were those operated during the late thirties by three of the four main-line companies. The London & North Eastern led the way with its three streamliners; the 'Coronation' from London to Edinburgh in six hours, the 'Silver Jubilee' from London to Newcastle in four hours, and the 'West Riding Limited' from London to Leeds in just under $2\frac{3}{4}$ hours. They averaged 65, 67, and 69 miles an hour overall respectively, and were by any standards extremely good trains. They also made a lot of money. But by modern ideas their schedules did not really allow them to make the most impact. The 'Coronation', for instance, needed two sets of stock,

since it was an afternoon train in both directions (it left London at 4 pm and Edinburgh at 4.30). Both the others did the out-and-home journey in one day and so needed less equipment, but on the other hand they started so late in the morning that no passenger could usefully make the round trip. The 'Silver Jubilee' did not leave Newcastle till 10 am, and the 'West Riding' set out from Leeds even later, at 11.31. This meant that they arrived at King's Cross at 2 and 2.15 respectively, not much use to the average businessman. Post-war practice has been quite different, with the object not only of allowing as much time as possible for a day's business at destination, but also to get a higher mileage out of the stock.

The LMS had only one streamliner, the 'Coronation Scot'. Unlike the LNER trains, this did not make any addition to the timetable; it merely substituted for the previous 'Midday Scot' on a faster schedule. It also needed two sets of equipment, since it left Euston and Glasgow simultaneously at 1.30 pm. And since it took $6\frac{1}{2}$ hours and averaged only 62 mph, it cannot really be compared with the competition. The LMS ran it simply to avoid loss of face; it did not really put its heart into the high-speed business.

On the whole the GWR did rather better, although its streamliner was not really streamlined at all. The 'Bristolian' consisted of ordinary coaches, although it might well be hauled by the 'King' or the 'Castle' 4-6-0 which had had a few bulbous pieces of sheet metal riveted on as a gesture to the prevailing fashion (small compliment to Gresley, who designed his streamlining after very careful wind-tunnel experiments). Leaving Paddington at 10 am, and taking $1\frac{3}{4}$ hours to Bristol, it averaged 67 mph overall and allowed the Londoner a comfortable afternoon's work at the other end. The Bristolian himself was not quite so well provided for. On the other hand, the less said of the GWR's fastest train, the 'Cheltenham Flyer', the better. This was a lightly-loaded afternoon working leaving Cheltenham at 2.40 pm, which averaged an unexciting 52 mph overall, but which was allowed only 65 minutes for the last 77 miles from Swindon, where it had to average 71. There was no corresponding train in the other direction, and the whole thing was a pretty blatant piece of publicity-cadging. The engine used proudly to carry a headboard saying 'The World's Fastest Train' as it swept down from Swindon; labouring back up the barely detectable gradient this had, of course, to travel wrapped in sacking in the brakevan.

No. 7023 'Penrice Castle' on the Hereford-Paddington 'Cathedrals Express' near Woodley Bridge, Twyford (1962)

For some time after the war the value of these extra-fast trains was much questioned, and it was pointed out that the amount of good they did to the public was not comparable with the special efforts that were needed to run them and to keep freight trains out of their way. In so far as they had had very little effect on the general speed level, there was some truth in this criticism; but the argument that fast trains are intolerable because they disturb the flow of freight is a prime example of putting the cart before the horse.

The fact was that freights were too slow and clogged up the line; the proper answer was to accelerate them and keep them moving. But this brings us back, of course, to the original fount of all evil on British railways, the unbraked wagon. Fortunately, this was realized during the later 1950s, and aided in many cases by dieselization or electrification, a general improvement in running has by stages resulted, even though not all the heights reached a quarter of a century ago are yet equalled.

Building the Esk Viaduct, at Whitby; the contractor's 0-4-0T
posing behind a collection of cranes, caissons, and counterweights
(not forgetting the diver) (1884)

3 Administration

Fares and Charges

Originally most of the best and fastest trains were available to first class passengers only, and very often, particularly in those cases where second class customers were admitted, fares were charged on a special, higher, express train scale. This practice was gradually eroded by competition; the Midland struck a noble blow in 1872 when it decided to carry third class passengers by all trains, and simultaneously abolished second class. It had circularized all companies to inform them of this intention, but only the Great Eastern followed suit. Both found that the change paid handsomely, but the other companies were stuffier. Grinling, writing about the Great Northern in 1903, remarked that the Midland had 'struck a blow at the profitability of the passenger business on the main lines to the North from which they have never since wholly recovered'; while Sir George Findlay, the General Manager of the L&NW, said in 1890 that 'the revenue to be derived from the conveyance of passengers was a diminished and diminishing quantity; this has been brought about chiefly by the lengths to which the companies have gradually proceeded, under the pressure of competition, in making concessions without adequate remuneration.'

Actually, the pressure of competition had very little to do with it, beyond encouraging those who, unlike Sir George, were prepared to abandon old and traditional ways of thought. Back in the 1850s, with inefficient undersized locomotives and iron rails and wheels, high speed running had indeed been expensive in terms of increased fuel consumption and greater wear and tear, so there had been a sound case for the extra charges. But even by the 1870s things had changed. Locomotives could now handle heavier trains economically at high speeds, and the substitution of iron by steel meant that wear and tear was much less

disproportionate. This being so, the Midland's abolition of express fares and restrictions did no more than adjust to the new realities. Carrying third class passengers by all trains, quite apart from the goodwill it created, also saved the company £37,000 a year by allowing the 'Parliamentary' trains (the daily locals carrying passengers at a penny a mile whose running was enjoined by Gladstone's Act of 1844) to be abolished. As for the suppression of second class altogether, the Midland produced the following figures. First-, second-, and third-class four-wheeled coach bodies cost £450, £250, and £270 to build, and earned an average of £530, £430, and £890 a year respectively. Furthermore, without three classes to be provided the marshalling of trains was simplified, and a smaller total stock was needed, which was stated to have saved a capital sum of £500,000. Indeed, the Midland denied that it had any idea of improving its competitive position by abolishing seconds and upgrading thirds; it said it wanted only to economize. But it succeeded in doing both. That Grinling was writing as he did thirty years later only goes to show how tradition-bound railway managements can be.

Nevertheless, the pressure of competition forced others to follow the Midland's example. Express fares vanished in geographical sequence; the GWR, having a large monopoly area, retained them for a long time, and the South Eastern longer still. In fact they survived in a peculiarly indefensible form until very recently on trains between London and Dover or Folkestone run in connection with cross-channel steamers, on which a specially high rate per mile was charged. Since everybody had booked through to stations on the Continent, they seldom noticed any extortion on this side of the channel; and even if they did, they might be led to suppose it was because the distance from London to Dover was much the same as that from Calais to Paris; the time taken was often

Until its closure in 1963, the Hayling Island branch was worked exclusively by the ex-LB&SCR 'Terrier' 0-6-0Ts of 1872. Here no. 32650 crosses the Langstone Bridge with a train from Havant (1962)

rather similar. Supplementary fares had a brief revival on the LNER (but not the LMS) streamliners before 1939. Since then, policy has been against them, very wisely. Sometimes one hears the argument that they ought to be introduced to earn additional revenue, but this would be a serious mistake. Under modern conditions, the high-speed long-distance train is very much cheaper to run than the slow local, because of its superior productivity in both man-power and equipment, and the faster it goes the cheaper it gets. Not to return some of this saving to the customer, in an age of intense competition, is an elementary business error. It would be indefensible to make matters worse by a speed surcharge. The present 'Blue Pullman' trains, which do charge supplementary fares, are an exception to this only so far as they provide something which does not, and ought not to, exist in the ordinary service. It is a matter of opinion how far they do so.

Second-class accommodation lasted longer in some places than others. On the boat trains, indeed, it remained until it was generally abolished all over Europe in 1956, although by then it was usually provided by third-class carriages with 'Second' labels pasted on, turning the knife in the wound already mentioned. On various suburban services, including the ex-GNR ones out of King's Cross, seconds lasted until 1940. Grinling had remarked again in 1903 that the suburban business was 'a traffic which more than

any other demands a threefold classification'. Well, yes; one had the banker, puffing a cigar and reading *The Times*, his clerk in a threadbare white collar, and the uncouth navvy spitting tobacco-juice on the floor. The navvy wouldn't have minded the banker's company, but neither of them would have got on with the clerk; hence he had to be segregated. The final enforced communion, when it came at last to East Finchley, was one of the horrors of war.

It always seems to have been accepted that ordinary passenger fares should be charged at a flat rate per mile, with little if any reduction for long distances; although in earlier times this rule was modified to ensure uniformity of fares by competing routes of different lengths. Unfortunately, in recent years (after a sensible relaxation in 1948) it has been very strictly applied again, so that for instance the traveller from Bournemouth to Manchester on the 'Pines Express', now that it has suited the railways' convenience to divert the train from the direct Somerset & Dorset line to run via Oxford and Shrewsbury, finds himself having to pay extra for being carried out of his way. The honesty of this is clearly questionable. Perhaps we should be thankful that nobody so far has taken the advice of the correspondent who wrote recently to the 'Railway Gazette' saying in all seriousness that valuable revenue was being turned away since the fare from Brighton to Hastings did not include any imposition to cover the side-trip down the Eastbourne branch and back which

Ex-L&SWR Adams B4 class 0-4-0T (of 1892) no. 30094, shunting at Plymouth Friary (1952)

all trains make. But anomalies of the 'Pines Express' kind will continue until the old monopoly practice of charging by actual rail distance is abandoned in favour of the far more logical and competitive system of charging by distance as the crow flies.

One of the principles by which railway freight rates were determined was that of 'charging what the traffic will bear'. Another derived from the fact that (until 1962) the railways were prohibited by law from showing 'undue preference' to one customer compared with another. Both these principles could be very widely interpreted, particularly the first one. Charging what the traffic will bear can be made into something remarkably like blackmail, screwing the last penny out of a helpless customer who has to send freight by rail or perish; it can also be made into something rather enlightened, charging what rate can best be paid bearing the whole community's interests in mind. Sometimes it seems as if the bandit's approach has not been shunned, but the old companies could and did act in very public-spirited ways. Grinling gives a 1905 example of this, when considering the rates charged for carrying coal to London. Some collieries were farther away than others, and would suffer if they had to pay proportionately more for carriage. 'Were the rates to be charged in the hard-and-fast manner advocated by some theorists, many collieries now worked at a profit would be inexorably shut out of their markets, to the advantage of those possessing the better geographical location. This would be to the

serious detriment of the public, since the price of coal would be raised as the supply was restricted. By adjusting their rates on a free commercial basis, without rigid subservience either to the distance covered or to the cost of the individual service rendered, the railway companies are in a position to keep open all available sources of supply.' This quotation shows a juster appreciation of the part transport plays in the economic life of a community than is to be found in the whole of a famous recent report, much praised for its hard-headed commercial realism.

Grouping and Nationalization

In 1914 all the main lines and almost all the minor independent companies were placed under the control of the Railway Executive Committee of the Board of Trade as part of the general adjustment to wartime conditions. Compared with what happened 25 years later, the railways were not much damaged by enemy action, but they emerged in 1918 very much the worse for wear. Heavy wartime traffic had been handled by a reduced staff, engines and rolling stock had been commandeered and sent abroad, and maintenance was badly in arrears. Worse than this, the companies were also in financial trouble. The government had not allowed railway rates and charges to rise comparably with wages and prices; indeed, they had sequestrated some of the money which had been earned by carrying a swollen traffic under such diffi-

Where railwaymen are forced to live in remote places, it is sometimes necessary to run trains to supply them, or to take their wives shopping. A weekly working of the latter kind is the 'Siege', here loading at Beattock Summit behind Fairburn 2-6-4T no. 42214 (1961)

A North Eastern oddity; inside-cylinder Y7 class 0-4-0T (of 1888), sold to the National Coal Board, shunting at Ravensworth Colliery (1954)

culties. As a result of this, the network as a whole was running at a loss of £45,000,000 a year in 1919–20; a figure which, allowing for the change in the value of money, was worse than any losses made more recently. Clearly something had to be done.

There were two possible answers. Either the railways could be taken over by the State, or they could be amalgamated into a smaller number of companies which could perhaps stand on their own feet. But nationalization was still politically taboo, so a regrouping was decided on, and ordained by the Railways Act of 1921.

The question as to which companies should amalga-

mate with which was settled by one criterion. Each group was to have as complete a degree of territorial monopoly as was possible without division of any of its constituents. An independent Scottish group was ruled out because the Scottish railways were, on the whole, in the worst financial state and it seemed unlikely that they would be viable on their own; this being so, the bulk of the country fell pretty neatly into two groups. The East Coast main line formed one obvious nucleus, the West Coast another, and in England there were only two companies on the borderline between them; the Great Central and the Midland. But each of these had closer historical and geographical links with one group than the other, so they went without difficulty into Eastern and Western camps respectively. In Scotland, the Caledonian and the Glasgow & South Western formed an obvious West Coast extension, and the North British as clearly leaned the other way; this left only the Highland and the Great North of Scotland to divide. Here the balance was closer, but since the HR connected with the Caledonian this tipped the scale, and the GNoS was therefore allocated to the Easterners.

Two-thirds of the national mileage was now apportioned between two companies, each quite large enough already. What to do with the rest? The Great Western was the obvious nucleus in one sense, as much the largest company, yet the South East presented a particular problem. The railways here were battered and decrepit, but they handled a different sort of traffic and ran in a different direction; there was no way in which they could logically be combined with a concern which after all left London in quite the opposite direction. So there had to be a Southern group, and to give it a bit of jam it had to include the London and South Western. So the GWR had to be left alone, apart from being forcibly fed with every independent line of any consequence in its territory.

The amalgamations took place during 1922 and 1923, and the four groups which resulted were as follows:

LONDON, MIDLAND, AND SCOTTISH RAILWAY:
7,525 miles; 10,292 locomotives

Principal constituents	Miles	Locos
London & North Western	2,097	3,336
Midland	2,169	3,019
Lancashire & Yorkshire	601	1,650
North Stafford	221	192
Furness	158	136
Caledonian	1,115	1,070
Glasgow & South Western	494	528
Highland	506	173

Minor constituents	Miles	Locos
Maryport & Carlisle	43	33
North London	16	99
Stratford-on-Avon & Midland Junction	67	13
Wirral	14	17
Cleator & Workington Junction	31	6
Knott End	12	4
Leek & Manifold Valley	8	2

LONDON AND NORTH EASTERN RAILWAY
6,714 miles; 7,385 locomotives

Principal constituents	Miles	Locos
North Eastern	1,758	2,001
Great Central	855	1,358
Great Eastern	1,191	1,336
Great Northern	1,051	1,359
North British	1,378	1,074
Great North of Scotland	334	122

Minor constituents	Miles	Locos
Colne Valley & Halstead	19	5
East & West Yorkshire	9	6
Mid Suffolk Light	19	3
Hull & Barnsley	106	181

GREAT WESTERN RAILWAY
3,795 miles; 3,944 locomotives

Principal constituent	Miles	Locos
Great Western Railway	3,005	3,148

Minor constituents	Miles	Locos
Cambrian	295	97
Taff Vale	124	271
Barry	68	148
Midland & South Western Junction	64	29
Rhymney	51	123
Port Talbot	42	44
Neath & Brecon	37	15
Brecon & Merthyr	60	47
Burry Port & Gwendraeth Valley	21	15
Cleobury Mortimer & Ditton Priors	12	2
Llanelly & Mynydd Mawr	13	8
Alexandra	10	38
Cardiff	12	36
Rhondda & Swansea Bay	28	27

(*Opposite, above*) The GWR led the way with auto-trains, where to save time on the turnround the driver had a cab with remote controls on the leading coach. Here a 14XX 0-4-2T is sandwiched between the two halves of a Westbury-Salisbury local near Upton Scudamore (1950)

(*Right*) No. 1444 on a more conventionally arranged auto-train at Swindon (1964)

One odd thing about the Hawkhurst branch was the way it left the main line at Paddock Wood by way of the basement of the signalbox. Ex-SE&C 'C' class 0-6-0 no. 31588 departing (1960)

A minor mishap in Swindon works yard; ex-Burry Port & Gwendraeth Valley 0-6-0T no. 5 (GWR no. 2195) being jacked back onto the rails (1948)

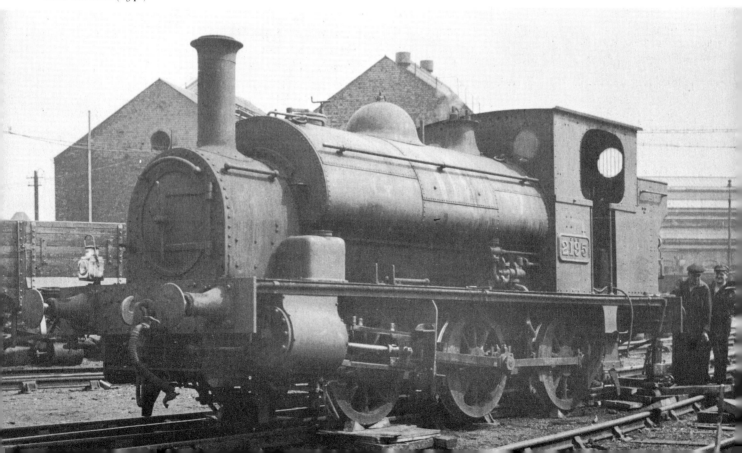

The LNER had quite a fleet of Sentinel steam railcars in the north-east during the 1930s; here one of them climbs to Prospect Hill, Whitby, with the Esk Viaduct in the background (1938)

There were of course many other jointly-owned railways, some quite large, which were not separately operated. Both the M&GN and the S&D local managements were abolished during the 1930s, and their private fleets of rolling stock (their engines were painted mustard and blue respectively, both rather pleasant liveries) were taken over. Only the Cheshire Lines, which had only coaches of its own, retained its autonomy until 1948.

The grouping left out 24 public railways, 12 of them narrow gauge. Most of these had been omitted since they were such dubious economic propositions in themselves that they would hardly have been welcomed. They were as follows:

Company	Miles	Locos
Bishop's Castle	10	2
*Campbeltown & Machrihanish	6	4
Corringham Light	3	2
*Corris	11	4
Derwent Valley	16	—
Easingwold	3	1
East Kent	19	4
*Festiniog	15	9
*Glyn Valley	9	3
Hundred of Manhood & Selsey	8	5
*Isle of Man	46	15
Kent & East Sussex	24	8
Nidd Valley	6	1
North Sunderland	4	1
*Ravenglass & Eskdale	7	5
*Rye & Camber	3	3
*Sand Hutton Light	8	3
Shropshire & Montgomeryshire	26	6
*Snowdon Mountain	5	5
*Southwold	9	4
*Welsh Highland	25	3
*Tal-y-llyn	7	2
Wantage Tramway	3	3
Weston, Clevedon & Portishead	15	5

* = Narrow Gauge

SOUTHERN RAILWAY
2,199 miles; 2,285 locomotives

Principal constituents	Miles	Locos
London & South Western	1,019	912
South Eastern & Chatham	638	729
London, Brighton, & South Coast	457	619

Minor constituents	Miles	Locos
Isle of Wight Central	28	9
Lynton & Barnstaple	19	4
Isle of Wight	15	7
Freshwater, Yarmouth & Newport	12	2
Plymouth, Devonport & South Western Jn	10	3

It will, incidentally, be noticed that the totals given at the head of each Table do not exactly correspond with the sum of the constituent figures. This is because of some double counting of joint lines, and alterations to locomotive stock during the year.

In addition, the following joint lines, which had been managed independently before 1923, remained so because of the decision not to split the assets of any company:

	Miles	Locos	Owners	
Cheshire Lines	143	—	LMS	LNER
Midland & Great Northern	205	101	LMS	LNER
Somerset & Dorset	106	86	LMS	SR

Only seven of these lines still survive in whole or part, with one more in a state of suspended animation. Most of them were fascinating to the enthusiast or antiquarian, since poverty forced them to use vintage equipment; some were as enterprising as their circumstances allowed, notably the standard-gauge group controlled by Colonel H.F. Stephens, who experimented with railbuses. (These lines were the East

Great Central suburban trains. (*Opposite*) A5 class 4-6-2 T no. 9810 leaving Gerrards Cross with a High Wycombe-Marylebone train (1947): (*left*) C13 class 4-4-2 T no. 67416 with the Chesham-Chalfont push & pull, consisting of three coaches which once formed a very early electric unit (1955)

Kent, Selsey, Kent & East Sussex, Shropshire & Montgomeryshire, and Westen, Clevedon & Portishead.)

The 1923 amalgamations succeeded in propping up the system of private railway ownership; but they failed in their larger purpose of restoring prosperity to the industry, and with hindsight we can see it was a mistake not to go all the way and nationalize them in 1923. Those gifted with foresight were saying this at the time. The four companies achieved very little to set beside the record of their predecessors, and the reason for this was financial. From the earliest days, railways had never been allowed full commercial freedom, and the 1921 Act let them levy only Standard Charges with a very few exceptions on such a scale that would make it possible to earn a Standard Revenue equivalent to their profits in 1913. The Railway Rates Tribunal was set up to control this. But because of the generally depressed condition of trade and the growth of road competition, the companies never earned even this restricted profit. So money was always tight. So far as dividend records prove anything (and it must be remembered that the maintenance of a reasonable dividend will almost always be given a higher priority than any but the most vital improvements), the GWR had the best record, never missing an ordinary payment and in only three years (1932, 1933, and 1939) falling below 3%. The LMS performance was less satisfactory, passing ordinary dividends altogether in five years and certain preference dividends in three; the Southern always paid its preferred shareholders,

but not invariably at the promised rate, while its deferred shares paid nothing in six years. Very considerably the worst record was the LNER's; not one of its several series of dated or first or second preference shares was paid regularly or in full, while its 'ordinary preference' shareholders never received anything after 1930. After 1926 its deferred shares were really in the wallpaper category. Both before and after the second war the LNER would certainly have had the gravest difficulty in raising new capital on any reasonable terms, however it emphasized its particularly heavy afflictions during the slump. So even though it may have managed to avoid making a loss, it can hardly be said that private management succeeded in making the enterprise viable.

This rather overcast, indeed thundery, financial situation inhibited the companies from doing very much to modernize. They put a brave face on things, but they played safe. The much-publicized streamliners were a gaudy drop in the bucket, and although a few express freights were put on (again with the LNER in the lead) there was scant progress towards the removal of that unique and permanently crippling millstone of Britain's railways, the unbraked wagon. The extirpation of the beastly thing was admitted privately to be vital, but the task was too enormous; so publicly the need was glossed over.

The Southern had far the best record in improvements, with its ambitious electrification schemes; the LMS deserves mention for its locomotive standardization policy under Stanier, and the GWR for its praise-

Great Northern suburban: Ivatt 4-4-2T no. 1534 leaves New Southgate with a train of four-wheelers for Hatfield. Note the condensing equipment, to ease conditions on the slightly underground section from King's Cross to Moorgate (1923)

worthy installation of Automatic Train Control on all main lines, but little else was done by either. Where electrification was concerned, the situation north of the Thames was generally as described by Herbert Morrison in 1937, and quoted in A.J. Pearson's 'The Railways and the Nation'. The LNER and the GWR realized that electrification offered the best escape from their difficulties, but shrank from sinking their own capital into so large a venture. As Morrison said, 'the railways got into a public assistance frame of mind. I asked them to electrify the main lines and they said, "How much are you going to give us?" I replied, "You are a nice lot. You say that if I want the railways to be run properly, you want me to give you a State subsidy!"'

All four companies put a great deal of effort into their 'Square Deal' campaign during the late thirties. They argued, with much justice, that legal restrictions which had been placed on them in their old monopoly days were an unfair hindrance to their efforts to meet road competition. The old basis of freight charging had been roughly to equate the fee with the value of the service rendered to the consignor, which in turn depended on the value of the article moved. As a result, oysters and winkles, or new and old boots, for example, were carried at different rates, and the 'Classification of Merchandise' book which enshrined these was a publication of such frightful complexity that it deterred traffic in itself. So road transport often got the high-rated job of carrying full cases by slightly undercutting the published rail rate, while the empties were returned more cheaply still at the lowest rate by train. Similar anomalies abounded. Yet the companies got nowhere with their pleas to be allowed to fix their own charges; their critics pointed out, rightly as more recent events have proved, that this would not be enough to cure the trouble, and that nothing except either their total release from all legal and social obligations, or a subsidy, would serve. The Fair Deal's petitions were largely granted by that astonishing

Great Eastern suburban: F5 class 2-4-2T no. 7210 with an Epping train near Theydon Bois, shortly before the Central Line took the service over (1949)

The Stationmaster's Office; Wilton (South) (1964)

exercise in nostalgia, the Transport Act of 1953; as we all know to our cost, the medicine failed to work. It was basically irrelevant.

To its credit, the LNER finally realized it could save itself only by its own efforts, and by 1939 had started work on two large electrification schemes; Liverpool Street to Shenfield and Manchester to Sheffield. But the war stopped these, and much else. Once again the 1914–18 story was repeated, this time on a larger scale and with sometimes serious physical damage from air raids. By 1945 matters were as bad, if not worse, than they had been in 1918; the railways were accurately, if rather unsympathetically, described by the Chancellor of the Exchequer, Hugh Dalton, as 'a pretty shabby bag of assets'. Their generally obsolescent condition in 1939 had not helped, and another major rescue operation was necessary.

This time the choice was between massive subsidy (in one form or another) and outright nationalization, and the latter was chosen. Unfortunately, it became

the centre of a bitter political storm. The idea of railway nationalization had a respectable and lengthy history; Gladstone tried for it near the start of his career, and as long ago as 1908 for example Sir George Gibb, the Chairman of the North Eastern, had expressed cautious approval, pointing out that in order to suit the legislative type of Government in Britain (as opposed to the executive-based regimes abroad), 'a Railway Board with a wide and permanent control should be created, and the possibilities of Parliamentary interference rendered as remote and rare as possible without actually depriving the legislature of its sovereign control'. He was quite wrong, of course; there is bound to be political control of a state-owned industry, and a facade of independence merely means that this will be secret and therefore very likely irresponsible. To say nothing of the fact that Parliament is, or should be, free to 'interfere' wherever and whenever it likes. Nevertheless, his advice was followed in 1947, and the railways passed into national ownership at the end of that year. But only in the teeth of violent and emotional opposition. The four companies actually refused at board level to co-operate in setting up the new organization, an act of irresponsibility which provided a tawdry ending to the generally creditable history of private railway ownership in Britain. (Even so, the 'Railway Gazette' protested indignantly when no director was given a job by the new authority.) Not only was all this bitterness unpleasant in itself, but more importantly and damagingly, it distracted attention for 15 vital years from the real problems of management. Since 1948 the railways have, most unfortunately, been subjected to further reorganizations perhaps more readily explained in terms of political ideology (nostalgic or otherwise) than practical or commercial considerations. It is a melancholy story too well known for further description, which must be brought to an end before much longer.

(*Opposite, above*) The train for Cambridge about to leave Mildenhall, with E4 2-4-0 no. 62785. Once used for hauling expresses on the Great Eastern main line. The E4s in their old age found their way to some of the quietest backwaters of East Anglia (1955)

(*Right*) 0-6-0T no. 1925 spotless after overhaul at Swindon (1947)

No road; J21 0-6-0 no. 65047 halted at the entrance to Kirkby
Stephen with a freight from the Stainmore line (1953)

4 The Vanishing Smoke

The end of steam power inevitably means some lessening in the romance of railways. There are few sights which stir the blood so strongly as a steam locomotive working hard and fast on a heavy train. We all have our memories. I shall never forget, for instance, travelling up across the Peaks in a St Pancras-Manchester express behind a bellowing 'Jubilee', roaring and howling and vomiting smoke as she was whipped on towards the summit, making up time which had been lost somehow back where the going was easy; an unrebuilt 'Merchant' whuffling and slithering its way westwards out of Salisbury, or streaking through Farnborough at 90 on a winter night, sparks shooting up among the stars; an 'A4', whistle chiming low and rods ringing, blasting past harsh and open-throated into the Welwyn tunnels; or a 'King' nosing and rolling through the crossings at Haddenham as she hammered upgrade with the southbound 'Inter-City' at 75. These things can give a glimpse of an overwhelming beauty, power, and terror; beside them, the appreciation of diesels or electrics seems a very arid intellectual exercise. One wants to ask; what if the damn things do cost less to run and pull heavier trains faster? Who cares?

The answer to this one is, of course, the other 98% of us. One cannot let sentiment cloud vision. A convincing case has been made out against steam power on strictly financial grounds; and as money is the most important thing in the world, the steam engine is now dead and damned in the eyes of the vast majority. To some extent the financial case against it has been manufactured; but this does not really affect the issue. What really killed steam in Britain was the growing shortage of good quality coal, and the National Coal Board's definite intimation in writing that the Railways could not rely on a supply of this in the future. Perhaps locomotives capable of burning low-grade coal should have been developed; but there was

A pillar of smoke by day; a West Highland train climbing across Rannoch Moor (1954)

enough of a financial case and enough hope of operational advantages from diesel power to turn the decision the other way.

Certainly steam power never reached the limit of its development in Britain; it went farther in France, the United States, and possibly Germany, but even in those countries much was left undone. Certainly there is room for argument about some economic details, particularly for Britain the wisdom of relying on imported fuels; and certainly one can say that not all promises have been fulfilled by the new power. But none of these things would ever have made any difference to the final result, and the battle is over. The danger now is nostalgia. One can easily delude oneself into thinking that the steam age was a glorious summit of achievement, from which there has been a fall. In fact, it was distinctly patchy.

One scene will stand for many. The Midland's main loco depot for passenger work in the London area was at Kentish Town, three roundhouses lying together inside the curve of the Barking and Southend branch. One shed was partly roofless, following bomb damage never repaired. The engines came in from duty, were coaled and had their fires cleaned, and lay by waiting their next turn. The prevailing south-west wind blew their ashes, coaldust, and smoke over a square mile or so of houses at the foot of Parliament Hill, and for eighty years or more these lay blanketed in silently descending filth. Then came the diesel, and one by one the steam engines vanished. Some lingered for a while, covering awkward parcels workings or transfer trips; a few 'Royal Scots' or 'Jubilees' stood by for specials, or in case a diesel broke down, which happened fairly often at first. Meanwhile, the housewives downwind began to find that for the first time they could keep their houses clean and put bright curtains in the

'Britannia' no. 70014 'Iron Duke' at Stewarts Lane shed (1957)

Kentish Town shed; Fowler 2-6-4T no. 42330 and 2-6-2T no. 40031 (1962)

windows. Finally, the shed closed down altogether, and the cold and rusty hulks of its last allocation were towed away. Standing in the empty roundhouse before the demolition gangs arrived, I talked with a man who had fired steam and was now driving diesel. 'Yes, the big Sulzers are good engines and it's easy to make better time with them,' he said. 'But it's not the same. There was something more satisfying with steam. When you were going down towards Bedford on a 'Scot', doing the ton or something near it, you knew it was all your own work; it was something you had done with your own muscles. But with a diesel it's just like turning on a tap. Anyone can do it.'

So steam power on Britain's main line railways, where once it forced forward the pulse and heartbeat of a growing, wealthy nation, is dead; or all but dead. There has to be this qualification, since it has refused to die completely. People just refused to allow it to disappear. Many have put money, time, and effort behind their wish to see it survive, and several hundred locomotives have been saved from the scrap merchant by private initiative, quite apart from the surprisingly generous list of engines officially retained by British Railways (and now the Department of Education and Science). These preserved engines are kept in many places up and down the country, far too numerous to list here. The task of restoring them to running order has often been enormous, and naturally enough has

Fireman's view from a 57XX 0-6-0T, on the Woodstock branch near Shipton-on-Cherwell (1954)

not yet always been completed; but several dozen engines, including some of the best and biggest, are in a state capable of doing a good day's work. For some years in the late 1960s and early 1970s British Railways prohibited any of them from running on their tracks. This was a rather unreasonable and emotional policy, based on the argument 'we have got rid of all that, and have a new public image to put across.' But in the face of such determination from so many people to the opposite effect, it was a policy quite impossible to sustain. Since 1972 therefore BR have allowed a select dozen or so engines in good condition, passed by their inspectors, to run special trains on certain identified sections of line, where the commercial and administrative effort required to make a success of their opera-

tion can be kept in moderate bounds. And at some such level as this, it seems, main-line steam operation will continue; and apart from reaching very high speeds will, like a living museum, keep the memory of the old days alive and demonstrated for today's young people, as well as the nostalgic pleasure of the older ones. Indeed, the National Railway Museum at York, opened in 1975, has firmly refused to keep all its exhibits chained down, and as a matter of policy maintains several engines in running order, sending them out on BR from time to time.

Quite apart from this, several score more locomotives are in regular commercial service on Britain's private railways. Only eight of the minor lines left out of the 1923 grouping, and listed on p. 207, may survive, but the most astonishing thing about the last twenty years of British railway history has been the growth of entirely new ones; so that what was the remotest of antiquarian backwaters has now shown something of a mushroom growth. The first addition to the list, and as it happens the last wholly new, passenger-carrying non-urban public railway to be built in Britain, was the 13½ mile long, 15-in gauge, Romney Hythe & Dymchurch Railway in Kent, opened in 1927 and at once the last of the 'old' railway companies to be established under the ancient statutes, and the first of the 'new' ones, since its purpose was always entertainment rather than transport. It was a tourist attraction, a thing of interest in itself, not to be justified simply as a means of transport.

In 1951 the Tal-y-llyn, whose life as a transport undertaking had dwindled to an end, was taken over by or rather donated to a non-profit-distributing body whose aim was to restore it and run it in perpetuity as a working museum. During the following quarter-century we have seen something of a tidal wave of similar enterprises, slow at first, but by the end of the 1960s in such a flood that one began to wonder if there was room for so many, since the public's appetite for steam entertainment cannot be unlimited. Most of them occupy a section of abandoned BR branch line, typically about five miles long and in a good scenic area with tourist potential. They use ex-BR coaches, usually hauled by ex-B.R. engines, though some were in industrial service, and a few have been brought in from Europe, and often enough their trains can only be distinguished from the trains which travelled on the same tracks in the 1950s by being much cleaner, and much fuller of passengers. Steam traction is usually the main commercial reason for these railways' existence; the forbidding economics of railway operation in modern conditions are answered not only by the willingness of large numbers of the public to pay premium prices for their tickets, but the ready and motivated support of employees, volunteers, members and shareholders. There are those who say that such devotion to the old-fashioned is self-indulgent and one of the symptoms of Britain's decline; perhaps more of us think that a nation which could not lift a finger to honour its past would have declined indeed.

So, after all, some of Britain's railways are still under steam, and will remain so. The story is not yet, therefore, at an end.

No. 8 'Hurricane', one of the Romney, Hythe & Dymchurch Railway's 15-inch gauge versions of the L.N.E.R. Gresley Pacifics, undergoes inspection at Hythe (1976)

Bibliography

One might think that in view of the flood of historical, descriptive, and technical railway literature that has rolled from the presses in the last few years that no corner of British railway construction or operation had been left unexplored. But there are still a few gaps, some of them yawning ones. There is a large category of historical books about the different pre-1923 companies which in fact concentrates almost exclusively on locomotive data and train running; Messrs O.S. Nock, Cecil J. Allen, and Hamilton Ellis have contributed generously to this list, among many others. But where true company history is concerned, and where an attempt is made to cover the whole field of a railway's activity, the field narrows considerably. In this much smaller category, four works stand out head and shoulders above the others; C.H. Grinling's 'History of the Great Northern Railway, 1845–95' (published in 1903), W.W. Tomlinson's 'The North Eastern Railway' (1915), E.T. MacDermot's 'History of the Great Western Railway' (1927–31, recently revised by C.R. Clinker and republished), and George Dow's 'The Great Central Railway' (1959). The series of small Oakwood Press books on certain lesser companies, by D.S.M. Barrie, R.W. Kidner, and others, also deserves special mention; while covering the entire field readably and reliably is Hamilton Ellis's 2-volume 'British Railway History' (1954–9). The major and most astonishing gap is that no good corporate history of the London & North Western Railway, undoubtedly the most important in Britain, has ever been published.

In addition to the works mentioned above, the author would like to record his indebtedness to the following:

R.W. KIDNER: *The Cambrian Railways* (1954)

H.A. VALLANCE: *The Highland Railway* (1963)

C.J. ALLEN: *The Great Eastern Railway* (1961)

C. HAMILTON ELLIS: *The London, Brighton, & South Coast Railway* (1960)

C. HAMILTON ELLIS: *The London and South Western Railway* (1956)

C. HAMILTON ELLIS: *The Midland Railway* (1953)

C. HAMILTON ELLIS: *The North British Railway* (1959)

W.M. ACWORTH: *The Railways of Scotland* (1890)

R.W. KIDNER: *The London, Chatham & Dover Railway* (1952)

R.W. KIDNER: *The South Eastern and Chatham Railway* (1953)

D.S.M. BARRIE: *The Brecon & Merthyr Railway* (1957)

D.S.M. BARRIE: *The Barry Railway* (1962)

D.S.M. BARRIE: *The Rhymney Railway* (1952)

D.S.M. BARRIE: *The Taff Vale Railway* (1939)

D.S.M. BARRIE and C.R. CLINKER: *The Somerset & Dorset Railway* (1948)

R.P. GRIFFITHS: *The Cheshire Lines Railway* (1947)

W. McGOWAN GRADON: *The Furness Railway* (1949)

G.D. PARKES: *The Hull & Barnsley Railway* (1948)

H.D. WELCH: *The London, Tilbury & Southend Railway* (1963)

J. SIMMONDS: *The Maryport & Carlisle Railway* (1947)

T.B. SANDS: *The Midland & South Western Junction Railway* (1951)

'MANIFOLD': *The North Staffordshire Railway* (1952)

E.C. POULTNEY: *British Express Locomotive Development* (1952)

E.L. AHRONS: *The British Steam Railway Locomotive 1825–1925* (1927)

C.J. ALLEN: *British Pacific Locomotives* (1962)

A.J. PEARSON: *The Railways and the Nation* (1964)

Index of Locomotive Types Illustrated

Arranged under post-1923 owners, in descending order of wheel arrangements.

Index